HUMAN BEHAVIOR IN BUSINESS

HUMAN BEHAVIOR IN BUSINESS

G. Hugh Russell,

Professor of Management, Georgia State University

Kenneth Black, Jr.,

Dean, School of Business Administration, Georgia State University

Prentice-Hall, Inc., Englewood Cliffs, New Jersey

Printed in the United States of America

ISBN: 0-13-444695-X

Library of Congress Catalog Card Number: 72-81309

10 9 8

PRENTICE-HALL INTERNATIONAL, INC., *London*
PRENTICE-HALL OF AUSTRALIA, PTY. LTD., *Sydney*
PRENTICE-HALL OF CANADA, LTD., *Toronto*
PRENTICE-HALL OF INDIA PRIVATE LIMITED, *New Delhi*
PRENTICE-HALL OF JAPAN, INC., *Tokyo*

"The most anguished issue for our age is surely that of the increasingly crucial struggle between man's impulse life and his capacity for intelligent and flexible self-control."

Michael Beldoch

PREFACE

The world of business touches all our lives. We are an economic society revolving about an exchange of human effort, money, goods, and services. What happens at work affects our private lives just as private experiences influence our performance on the job. Of the three factors of any business enterprise—money, materials, and people—it is the people-factor which seems to confuse, confound, and perplex. It is least possible to predict what people will do within an organization. The behavioral sciences of psychology, sociology, and anthropology have produced a wealth of information which could be useful in achieving more success individually and in a group, but much of this information is unavailable to the employee or manager in business.

It would make you angry to discover that information had been withheld which would save you money and stress. If there is a detour ahead on your trip, you would want to know about it. If a product has been found to be unsafe, you want to be informed. If the pollution index in a metropolitan area exceeds safe limits, you would become aroused if you discovered that officials had not made great efforts to inform the public. If behavioral scientists know something which would help us achieve success and avoid heartache, it would seem immoral for them to keep this information to themselves. Yet, unwittingly, this is precisely what is happening. If a behavioral scientist publishes a book or article which is unreadable because it is too technical or too boring, he is accidentally keeping that information from the public.

We have tried to engage you, the reader, in a conversation, as much as this is possible in book form—a conversation which highlights fundamental principles of how people live and work together and yet a conversation which avoids technical terms and pedantic listing of material for the student to memorize. Poets and novelists, through their media, frequently present insights in a powerful and unforgettable fashion precisely because of the informal style of writing. Many of us seem to retain more of what we hear during an interesting speech or oral presentation in a small group than we do in reading a traditional text. In this book, we hope the reader will feel he is engaged in a conversation with specialists in the field of human behavior, a conversation about important values, attitudes, and solutions to human problems.

This is not a scientific reference book. We have listed some outstanding ones in the bibliography. This is not a "how to do it" book. It is too easy to mistake a useful technique suitable for one situation for an overall principle we might apply in our own way. This *is* a book designed to help you start with yourself as a subject of study, examining yourself as an individual, as a member of many groups, and as a partner in the many face-to-face relationships you experience every day. It is a book written this way to help you become more sensitive to your own attitudes, biases, and misconceptions so that you may become more aware of your impact on others and their influence over you.

Success in interpersonal relationships seems to depend more upon basic attitudes we have toward ourselves and others than upon an awareness of techniques which may or may not help us accomplish our goals. *Attitude examination* and *change* are the underlying themes and aims of this volume. Such attitude awareness seems to occur more readily through the indirect use of examples, stories, and allegories than through the attempt to memorize lists of principles or factors.

Chapter 1 starts with the *self,* the reader as he may be when he picks up this volume. Self-awareness needs to be increased to the point where we can recognize some of the major conflicts and decision processes available, as described in Chapter 2. The fact that each of us as individuals is powerfully influenced by many groups is the theme of Chapter 3. Being yourself *is* a goal attainable by all of us. Chapters 4 and 5 examine human communications as a process that depends upon the present situation for its effectiveness and upon the skillful use of language tools to find solutions to human problems.

Chapter 6 has the odd title "If Only" because this seems to be the wishful way many of us begin our efforts to get others to do things. Chapter 7 becomes specific in discussing research findings which help create an awareness of the complexity of human motivation. And finally, in Chapter 8 we see the human being as a faith-seeking, meaning-needing organism who builds his organizations upon some foundation of evaluations called *ethics*. Understanding the facets of human behavior presented in these eight chapters makes it more likely that our human efforts will lead us to relative success rather than failure.

The authors would like to express their appreciation to a number of members of the business community who were kind enough to read the manuscript and give helpful suggestions and comments. These included Dr. James M. Daily of the American College of Life Underwriters; Dr. P. Phillip Sidwell, Director of Advanced Management Programs at Georgia State University; Dr. John M. Briggs of the Home Life Insurance Company; Dr. Paul W. Thayer of the Life Insurance Agency Management Association; Mr. Gene A. Morton of the Life Office Management Association; Mr. Fred G. Kimball, Mr. Arnold F. Beck, and Mr. Edward D. Hesse of the New York Life Insurance Company; and Dr. John A. Farley of the Prudential Insurance Company of America. In addition, the authors would like to express their deep appreciation to Esther E. Russell for her sensitive and tireless editing of various drafts of this manuscript which sharpened the language and made it much more direct, concise, and clear. The authors also feel fortunate to have had the manuscript read by Kenneth Black, III, who provided the insight and perception of a young man. Needless to say, any errors that remain are the full responsibility of the authors.

G. Hugh Russell
Kenneth Black, Jr.

CONTENTS

HUMAN BEHAVIOR IN BUSINESS

1

THE TYRANNY OF
OUR SELF-IMAGE

"You are so self-centered and preoccupied with yourself that you can't see or hear or think of anybody but yourself!" Has anyone ever said that to you? Think back for a moment; see if you can recall how this made you feel. If a friend accused you of being selfish and inconsiderate, you probably were immediately angered and ready to defend yourself by saying, "I am not!" Your friend (?) may have countered with, "Stop being so defensive and listen to what I'm trying to tell you." Did you then say, "I'm not being defensive!"?

Imagine your friend withdrawing slightly and declaring, "Well, you don't have to get so mad about it. I was only trying to help." And didn't you say, "I am not mad! It's just that you don't understand me." If you didn't react this way, you would be an unusual person indeed.

This dialogue illustrates at least two sides of the idea of "self": First, each person has some picture of himself, and second, this may not correspond with the image others have of him. But it also illustrates the strong tendency in all of us to try to preserve the image we have or wish we had in the eyes of others. Implied, even in this brief dialogue, is the concept of the uniqueness of the self. No two selves (or people) are alike; not even so-called identical twins.

Every one of us is a unique person. We are different, and it is this very difference which both delights and frustrates us as we go about our daily business of trying to do things and get other people to do things we want them to do. People are different. This fact has led to clashes, arguments, and wars for centuries.

Individual differences have led to the emergence of the sciences of psychology, sociology, and anthropology. Mankind is self-conscious, and this self-consciousness is reflected in the continuing effort over the years to understand the self. Twenty-four centuries ago Socrates advised us to "know thyself." In this terse and profound message he encouraged a human activity which has continued with increasing intensity until the present age, which could certainly be known as "the age of the self."

THE SIGNIFICANCE OF UNDERSTANDING HUMAN BEHAVIOR

What is the self? What is the nature of man? Why do people do what they do? How can I make friends and influence people? What can I do to improve my marriage? How can I get my children to behave? What makes a customer buy? How can I get my salesmen to make more calls on new prospects? How can I get my employees to be more careful in their work? How can I get my workers not to go out on strike? These questions are being asked every day, and psychologists are called on to help supply some of the answers. Some answers are available, although in some areas we seem far away from understanding people.

If we are to be successful, knowing ourselves and understanding why people behave as they do are two important accomplishments. We all have an interest in human behavior. The salesman, manager, husband, wife, professional person—all of us are interested because we want to *understand, predict,* and *influence* the behavior of other people. We must all adjust to others, and frequently our most important job is to understand others, to know what their motives are, and to be able to predict what they are going to do, especially as it affects ourselves.

The businessman readily understands the need for a thorough grounding in the technical aspects of his business. This he takes for granted. What may not seem too obvious, however, is the need for the same basic level of competence in knowing and understanding human behavior.

By Controlled Observation We
Discover "Laws" of Human Behavior

We want answers to many questions so that we can be "more success-ful." Some useful information we pick up in conversation with friends or the people with whom we work. Some answers are supplied through experience. Some answers come from popular books and magazines which give detailed instruction on "how to do it" for every kind of human activity from selling and managing to achieving "inner peace" and a successful sex life. Unfortunately, much advice we receive from well-meaning friends and acquaintances and much that we read in nonscientific articles repeats the myths and guesses which people in every generation have followed in trying to live and work more successfully. Often this has led instead to failure and frustration.

Speculation about human nature is an old pastime; scientific study of it is new. It has only been since the middle of the nineteenth century that the scientific method of controlled observation has been used to con-tribute to our understanding of the *how* and *why* of human behavior. Such understanding differs in two important ways from the patchwork of guesses and convictions which makes up the belief systems of the non-scientific "man on the street." First, a controlled scientific observation is made by the scientist who usually has learned a disciplined approach in that he sees and reports what happens rather than what he wishes were happening. Second, he observes and reports in a systematic manner and writes down how he did this so that someone else can repeat the observa-tion and independently check the first observation. The more a specific observation is repeated and verified, the more we depend on the reliability of the idea. While a nonscientist may make one observation about a person or place and then proceed to generalize to all similar people or situations, the scientist is cautious about generalizing even after making hundreds of observations.

One of these verified observations of human behavior is that the person who tends to follow a scientific method in his daily interactions with others is more likely to achieve success than one who haphazardly acquires and uses information. The person who can be more honest with himself and others and who responds to a situation as it is rather than as he wishes it were is more likely to make good adjustments both within himself and with other people. The person who is willing to confront himself and others is generally healthier than the person who prefers to avoid, deny, or overlook the reality of his world. Taking a closer look at the scientific method teaches us how one can *maximize* his success and *minimize* his failures. It is assumed that success more often comes when we deal with the real world rather than with a view of the world as we *wish* it to be.

The science of human behavior is organized around principles obtained by following these simple but far-reaching steps:

1. Defining clearly a question or problem so that we know what we are trying to solve.
2. Obtaining all of the relevant facts relating to the problem and suggesting some possible answers (hypotheses) for the problem.
3. Checking each hypothesis by testing to see if it is a solution to the problem. Repeating the experiment to be surer of the results.

If the experiment or observation supports the hypothesis each time it is repeated, we feel confident that the knowledge is reliable. If repeated studies do not support the original idea, then a new tentative solution or hypothesis is established and tested. This process is an ongoing one.

An example of scientific study of motivation will illustrate how we acquire knowledge which is reliable even though it may conflict with "common sense." (We will discuss "common sense" later on.) In an experimental situation the amount of stress is increased and decreased systematically in order to measure and record the reactions of the human subjects. How does stress affect performance? By systematically increasing and decreasing the level of stress (in the form of distracting noise or light), it was discovered that moderate stress actually increased the level of performance of a simple task, but higher levels of stress caused a much lower performance. A teenager who insists that he can study better with the radio on may be right. Listening to music which is repetitive may also help block out other noises in the house which are sporadic and which may have very personal meanings (such as the kitchen noises which raise thoughts of "when do we eat?").

The attempt to study human behavior scientifically, as it actually occurs in life situations, is extremely difficult because so many of the influences upon human behavior cannot be controlled or even measured.

The marketing department of a large metropolitan bank begins its new advertising program hoping that it will lead to new business, additional deposits, greater profits, and a better public image. Scientifically designed questionnaires can be sent to a segment of the population to see whether the new ads have been noticed and new customers have come to the bank. But perhaps the bank employees feel better about their bank because they see renewed efforts to find new markets or because the advertising campaign causes favorable comments about the bank among their friends. Maybe the new ads influence aggressive and intelligent young men and women to apply to that bank for employment, and the improved quality of personnel leads to more effective customer relations. The training department may begin a new series of orientation meetings at the same time so that all employees are better informed about the whole range of bank services. Which of these influences produced the one percent gain in share of market during the following year? To measure the results is often both difficult and expensive, if not impossible. But reliable information about the principles of human behavior as they pertain to the business world is gained when behavioral scientists and business organizations cooperate in isolating the multiple factors which do lead to observed financial results.

Generalizations About Human Behavior May Not Fit the Individual

While the process is slow, we gradually have been building up a structure of generalizations about human behavior which can be of much help in guiding our daily behavior. We make a significant gain in reaching success in our efforts each time we establish new generalizations. We know that we cannot understand human behavior in general by studying only one individual. People are very different; understanding one person and being able to predict his behavior does not necessarily prepare us to understand and predict the behavior of another individual. Also, the generalization which results from scientific study applies to groups of people and not to each specific person. For example, we generally say a person is greatly influenced in his behavior by the standards of the group of which he is a member. It is more accurate to say that *most* people are influenced by the standards of their group. Any one single individual *may or may not* be influenced by group pressure. While generalizations cannot be applied to every individual, the more we become aware of the generalizations which make up the science of human behavior the more we will have things to try in our efforts to succeed.

Consider the following example. The manager of the accounting department in a manufacturing firm tries to reduce errors in calculations and tabulation of account information. He tries threats, bribes, contests to name the most accurate employee, printed slogans on the wall, monthly meetings with each supervisor—and nothing happens. When all else fails, he appoints an advisory committee to study the problem and recommend an error-reduction program. These are frequently good alternatives to try, but they are often insufficient. What the manager may need is an enlarged awareness of the personal, social, cultural, or financial reasons that cause the clerical staff to be so careless. Perhaps they don't really understand the importance of their work, and the consequences of even small errors, or perhaps they are made to feel so insignificant that errors are made unconsciously (consciously, too!) in an effort to "get back" at their insensitive boss. Perhaps the manager is perceived as cold and aloof so that his subordinates do not feel free to come and ask for help or even report work conditions which make concentration difficult. They might work with more interest and conscientiousness if they could rotate from key-punch operations to verifying work and back again during each day. Each employee might work more effectively if he did a whole series of operations with a few accounts instead of only one specific and highly specialized (and boring) clerical activity for all the accounts.

More often than not, the human problems which arise in getting organizational work done through people can be traced to things the manager does of which he is totally unaware. He may not, for example, realize how often he noisily clears his throat; neither would he realize the connection between his throat-clearing and the giggles throughout the office. Only in private conversations between employees would you hear that the office manager "is a joke around here." He might be unaware that he is quick to point out errors or to be critical of the dress standards in the office but slow to praise, recognize, or give credit for good work. Again, he may worry so much about relatively minor problems that he overlooks major opportunities for methods improvements or morale-boosting changes in fringe benefits. The study of all aspects of human behavior is an important resource in working with others.

THE SELF-IMAGE

Scientific study of human behavior in a variety of situations has starkly revealed two characteristics of man: he has the capacity and need *to understand* the truth and meaning of his world and he has the capacity and need *to deceive* himself and ignore the "truth". The first of these characteristics is easy to accept; the latter is often sharply denied. Just as a highly defensive and angry person will defensively and angrily deny that he is defensive and angry, so for most of us the things which are closest to us are often the most difficult to see and understand. Perhaps the closest thing to each of us and the most difficult to see is our *self.* Our *self* is both obvious to us and hidden. Everyone will acknowledge that he has some picture of himself, but few know what that self really is and how it influences his behavior. The extent to which our self-picture influences our behavior is contained in the title of this chapter, "The Tyranny of Our Self-Image." Modern man rebels against tyranny when it is obvious to him, but how can he rebel against something he doesn't see?

Seeing Our Self-Image

This is the problem which confronts us. We are tyrannized by a picture of our self which is only partly conscious. We have a dim idea of what we are, but it remains a dim idea. We are conscious of only part of who we are and even less of how we affect others. Ask anyone who he is and he is likely to respond by telling you his name. The next thing he typically mentions is what he does for a living. While this information tells us something about what our self really is, it is only a beginning. If we were to press someone for more information about himself, he might say, "I am a father, husband, Unitarian, Rotarian, voter, citizen, university graduate, Midwesterner, home owner, Red Cross volunteer," and so on. Each one of these group memberships (for that is what he is listing) helps to define who he is. Some psychologists say that *we are what we say we are.* Others say *we are what we do.* Still others say *we are what we think others expect us to be.* It could be that we are all of these.

We are many things which are difficult or embarrassing to admit. If an individual were to be honest with himself and with us, we would hear him say, "I am prejudiced against blacks (if he were white, or 'against whites' if he were black) and people who go to a different church than I do. I don't like Democrats (or Republicans) or people who wear white socks. I have sexual problems with my wife (or husband) and this makes it hard to resist the advances of that cute girl (or boy) at the office. I think people are irresponsible (except me) and you can't hire good workers any more. My boss doesn't appreciate me and I don't see why I should knock myself out for him. I think the world is in serious trouble and if others would only be more moral, law-abiding, hard-working, honest and God-fearing (belong to my church) I would sleep more easily at night."

Carl Rogers, the psychologist, stresses the importance of the subjective experience of the individual or in other words how the person sees himself. He would say that it is probably more important to know what a person thinks of himself or the situation he is in than to know the objective "reality" of the situation. If a prospect for a sale thinks that he cannot afford the product or service he is offered, the salesman needs to work with *that* perception, even though the prospect actually can afford it. After all, the concept of "affording" something is highly subjective. It depends on what the individual values as being important.

A salesman of vacuum cleaners called on a home during the day expecting to find the woman of the house at home but instead was greeted by the man who was home sick that day. When the salesman began his sales talk, the man said, "I wouldn't buy a vacuum cleaner from your company if it were the only one in the world." The salesman thought of two things to say. He could have said, "But our vacuum cleaner is the best one on the market," or he could say, "Boy, you must have had a bad experience with one of our machines. I'd like to know what happened." A seasoned salesman would probably choose the second statement since that starts with the prospect where he is right now.

The first statement praising and defending the machine is an attempt to deny the perception the man has stated. In the actual example, the man at home did relate a story of very poor service on a cleaner he had purchased the previous year. The details of the story made sense. The salesman understood and communicated to the prospect that he understood. The result was that the old machine which had given trouble was traded in for the new machine and a sale was made. This story may illustrate the point often made by experienced salesmen that people buy a product not always because they understand the merits of the product but because they feel the salesman understands their problems or situation. Doesn't this correspond with the experience you have with the professional people you go to for help? Few people know how to diagnose their own medical condition, but they accept the opinion of their physician if they believe that he understands them.

If a person is afraid, it does little good to try to convince him that there is no reason for his fear. A person who is depressed is not helped by the advice to "cheer up!" Actually, a depressed person feels better if he thinks you understand just how miserable he really is (as he sees himself). While you may not think he should be depressed, your tendency to look at the "objective situation" rather than his perception of himself may well cause him to withdraw even further because he is convinced you do not understand him. And he probably would be right.

We are what we think we are! How obvious this is, but how often we disregard this view because it "doesn't make sense." A person who feels insecure or insignificant will not necessarily be reassured by a success. He may choose to keep the "inferior" image of himself and dismiss the success as an accident or something he really did not earn. It may be easier to see the world in ways which support the image we have of ourselves rather than to cope with a new image.

Building
Our Self-Image

We build this image over a period of years. The picture that we have of ourselves is formed mainly because of the way other people have responded to us in the past. If our parents have not loved us, or if we were without parents, we may grow up with a feeling of low self-regard, a feeling that no one could possibly be interested in us.

We do certain things and avoid doing certain things because of the reactions of people to our actions. Generally, we behave in a way which gives us pleasure or satisfaction and avoid behaving in a way which decreases our satisfaction. We thus establish a kind of equilibrium in our behavior. We behave within certain rather well-established limits. It is our behavior within these limits which we come to think of as "ourselves." This is what people refer to when they speak of our "personality." We behave the way we behave because we think that this is consistent with the picture we have of ourselves and with the picture we want others to have of us.

By the time we are adults, we have achieved a self-picture which is relatively stable and consistent. People who know us can rather easily predict our future behavior, and we ourselves know pretty much what we will or will not do. As we grow older, we are likely to become less adventuresome and less prone to behave in a way which is grossly inconsistent with our self-picture. The common expression, "I just can't see myself doing that," reflects this tendency to restrict our behavior in accordance with our self-picture.

Whatever our self-image happens to be, one thing is clear—we are the most important person in our life. If someone has taken a picture of us in a group and shows us a copy, our gaze centers immediately on the picture of ourselves in the group. We may look casually at the other people in the picture, but when we locate *our image,* our attention is riveted to this spot. This does not mean that we do not have genuine feelings of regard and concern and interest in other people, but it suggests that we spend more time thinking about ourselves, being concerned about ourselves, and protecting and satisfying ourselves than we do any other person. This does not diminish the stature of mankind or any one of us individually, but emphasizes the natural and inevitable self-centeredness of our existence.

Being well-regarded by others is one of our most basic needs. We tend to live in a way which insures that we will continue to be well-regarded. The only way we know to do this is by living up to the picture of ourselves which we believe will most result in pleasing others. Having established this self-image through a process of receiving praise and punishment, none of us is too willing to change the way we behave. We have established an equilibrium in our behavior, and we don't want to "rock the boat." Thus, we develop a strong need to preserve the image we have of ourselves. We need to avoid having our favorable self-picture disturbed. If we happen to stumble and fall while going up some steps, one of the first things we do is look around to see who saw us get into such an embarrassing position. We are concerned about how other people see us. We want to be sure that they get an "accurate" picture of us. What we usually mean by "accurate" is that we hope others see all our good points and overlook our weaknesses.

When someone criticizes us, the favorable picture that we have of ourselves and that we hope the other person has of us is threatened. It is difficult to accept criticism because we would like to view ourselves as being above criticism or reproach. It is difficult because it means that someone else doesn't have quite the same high regard for us that we have.

It hurts to be criticized. We may vigorously deny that we refuse to accept criticism from others, and we may protest that we really want people to tell us what they think of us, but it is still painful to have anyone disturb our self-image. How do you feel if you happen to overhear a locker-room conversation between two of your friends as they are discussing you? If you hear some unflattering things you are likely to feel pretty deflated.

DEFENDING THE SELF-IMAGE

The image we have of ourselves is important! When anyone threatens this self-image, our first reaction usually is to defend it. If we consider ourselves a mature and careful driver but are involved in an accident, our normal reaction is to find ways to blame the other driver. Even if we caused the accident, we are still likely to defend our self-image by saying, "The sun was in my eyes and I couldn't see," or "I was watching the curb to make sure there were no children darting out."

To defend our image is so important to us that we go to rather absurd lengths to avoid seeing ourselves as we really are. Changing our self-image is so painful that we deny reality. It is very difficult for anyone to say to himself. "I am a poor teacher," or "I am doing a very poor job of managing." The teacher is likely to say, "I could certainly do a better job if the parents of these undisciplined children would only instill a little courtesy in them. And in addition to that, if we didn't have to spend so much time filling out these silly reports for the administration we could devote more time to the students." The manager of a profit center may rationalize his failure by believing that "people just don't want to work hard any more." The implication in these examples is that they would do a much better job but other things beyond their control have kept them from reaching higher goals. Of course, it is always possible that uncontrollable factors do keep us from doing our best, but any counselor of people will report that the first tendency is to feel defensive about poor personal performance and find something or someone to blame, rather than find things in ourselves which need changing or improving.

But at the same time, an opposite tendency is frequently seen, and this is just as destructive. Rather than defending the self, some may see every setback or problem as clear evidence of their own lack of worth or talent. The readiness to blame oneself for everything that goes wrong is as unrealistic as never looking inward to see what one can do to be more responsible or more effective in relating to others. A slogan frequently heard during the '30's and '40's was, "There is no such thing as a delinquent child, only delinquent parents." It is hard to imagine any statement more unrealistic or more destructive. Of course, parents influence their children, but they are not the *only* influence. Radio, television, peer groups, teachers, movies, newspapers, and magazines all contribute to the development of the child. For the parents to feel *solely* responsible for the teenager's use of drugs is usually as unrealistic as for them to reject *all* suggestions that they may have contributed to the problem. The extremes of defensiveness and self-rejection are almost never realistic; understanding the standard mechanisms of defense may help us see how they operate in ourselves and others.

Defending Through Aggression

We defend our valuable self-image in many ways. Perhaps one of the most important ways is that of *moving aggressively against the person or thing which threatens to diminish our self-image.* If someone were to tell you, "You are just a mediocre salesman," your reaction might be to say, "Oh, yeah? What makes you think you're so hot?" If we can discredit a person who is making us uncomfortable, we have a better chance of retaining our self-image. The salesman, smarting from criticism from his manager, may say, "It's all right for him to talk. He just sits there in the office and twiddles his thumbs while I'm out doing all the hard work."

Work, whether in the home or in business, can be a source of great satisfaction but also of frustration and even personal humiliation. The department head in a large corporation, the vice president of a bank, the securities dealer, the mother who is a part-time real estate agent, and every other person who interacts with people has to put up with people and things which are sometimes very disagreeable. There are times when we all must do as we are told, even though we hate it; we must put up with small-time dictators, selfish, mean, petty bosses or subordinates, unreasonable, irritating personalities; we do work which goes unappreciated; we try to sell an idea but are laughed at; things go wrong; we're glad it's Friday! Small wonder that a frequent reaction to such irritations and frustrations is aggression!

Aggression is seldom a very constructive reaction to a threatening situation. It frequently encourages an aggressive response. The clerk who is publicly criticized by his boss may yell back, but might be out of a job as a result. The vacuum cleaner salesman who is verbally abused by the man who answers the door may react by telling the man where to go, but he diminishes his chance for a sale. Aggression, as a reaction to attack on our self-image, is certainly understandable, but it rarely leads to a mutually satisfactory solution to the human problem we face.

Defending Through Rationalization

Another way we have of defending ourselves is to find a reason for our behavior which sounds better to us than the real reason. The harried taxpayer fretfully working on his income tax return may find that his raise in salary last year was only a small *real* gain because of the added taxes as well as the rise in the cost of living. Can't we understand his decision to claim charitable contributions not made and business expenses not incurred in order to salvage more of his raise? His conscious thought may be, "Everybody else claims more deductions than they should, so why shouldn't I?" He may be saying, in effect, "I worked hard for that raise, I pay plenty in income taxes anyway, and besides, lots of rich people don't pay any taxes. I'm an honest person, but there comes a time when you have to watch out for yourself." His decision is to cheat. His reason to himself or to his wife is that he's trying to equalize the tax load. The technical term for what he is doing is *rationalization.*

When we resort to rationalization, we usually make a decision emotionally and often for unconscious reasons, but then make up a good-sounding reason why we should have done what we did. The man who succumbed to his strong wish to own a bright-red Mustang might rehearse a story for his wife while he drives home: that he really bought the car for her since she deserves something nice because she has been such a good wife.

Defending Through Regression

Growing up is a series of new adjustments to new problems. As soon as we learn good solutions to present problems, we are often thrust into new problem situations which again require new adjustments. The kind of behavior that was appropriate in high school is no longer appropriate in college. College behavior doesn't always fit the business world. The clerk who becomes a manager finds that he must still make new adjustments to his daily problems. It is inevitable that we sometimes make mistakes and experience failure rather than success. If the failure hurts badly enough, we are likely to retreat. Furthermore, we are likely to retreat in the direction of an earlier kind of adjustment or an earlier behavior pattern which is easier to maintain. This defense mechanism is referred to as *regression*. After a particularly hard day, when our self-image has been bruised, we are likely to think wistfully of the "good old days" when we had fewer worries. Our fantasy may even lead us to action as we stop by the local bar to visit the boys and "tie one on." In this setting, we are surrounded by friends who think well of us and this helps us think well of ourselves.

Regression is not altogether a harmful mechanism, for it does give us time to gather our strength and courage and try again tomorrow. It is when any of these methods of defense becomes a habit or a way of life that we are in danger of losing rather than gaining ground in our climb toward greater maturity.

Defending Through Compensation

If we fail at one thing, we can protect our feelings by excelling in something else. Thus, an employee who is doing only a mediocre job can protect his self-image by excelling in club activities. We can compensate for a shortcoming in one area by excelling in another. The worker, frustrated and chagrined by not being promoted to management, may compensate by working to be elected to office in his lodge. This mechanism of defense is referred to as *compensation*.

Defending Through Repression

To protect our self-image, we may deny the things within ourselves which are not flattering or are disgusting. When it is important that we "forget" something that has happened to us, we refer to this as the mechanism of *repression*. This is nothing more than an attempt to fool ourselves and preserve the self-image of which we are conscious. The "forgetting" that we do is unconscious in that we are not aware that we are pushing the unpleasant idea down into the unconscious. Consciously, we have forgotten; but unconsciously, we still know about it. The unconscious works in much the same way as does the fuse in the wiring system of a house. When the electrical load is greater than the system will stand, the fuse blows and interrupts the flow of electricity. When the load of uncomfortable mental activity becomes too great for us to bear, the conscious thoughts are interrupted by a repression, or a block in our ability to remember.

Defending Through Reaction Formation

One way to make sure that certain ideas stay repressed is to stress the very opposite of what we unconsciously feel. The person who unconsciously hates his children and must deny this to himself in order to preserve his favorable self-image will frequently overreact by consciously displaying a great deal of affection toward them. This helps the parent consciously to believe that he has no hostile or unacceptable feelings toward his children. This defense mechanism is known as *reaction formation.* Shakespeare used this mechanism in his tragedy, *Hamlet,* when he wrote the queen's line, "The lady doth protest too much, methinks." Sometimes a person goes out of his way to protest or deny that he has certain feelings even though no one may have claimed that he did.

We resort to these defense mechanisms in order to protect and safeguard our self-image.[1] They help us to feel better about ourselves on a conscious level, but they have the disadvantage of making it harder for us to really know ourselves and do something about our shortcomings.

While a good deal of our time and energy is spent in defending our self-image, we occasionally do just the opposite: we reject ourselves. Some people do this to an extreme degree in that they ridicule themselves, punish themselves, and may even resort to that ultimate in self-punishment, suicide. However, a person who makes derogatory remarks about himself is not necessarily rejecting himself. If your wife surprises you with the comment, "I don't believe I'm a very good mother," the last thing she wants you to say is, "well, yes, Mary, I believe you are right." Instead of rejecting the image she has of herself, your wife is probably searching for overdue reassurance from you.

It is amazing how much energy we spend preserving the picture we have of ourselves. This desire to maintain a very favorable image of ourselves is perhaps one of the most powerful motivators of behavior. During the depression years, when many men lost their fortunes, their image of themselves was dramatically changed. They had thought of themselves as successful businessmen, when suddenly their fortunes were wiped out.

[1] For a further discussion of defense mechanisms the reader is referred to the following references: Harry Helson and William Bevan (eds.), *Contemporary Approaches to Psychology* (Princeton, New Jersey: D. Van Nostrand Co., 1967), "The Deviant Personality," pp. 512-514; Fillmore H. Sanford and Lawrence S. Wrightsman, Jr., *Psychology: A Scientific Study of Man,* 3rd ed. (Belmont, California: Brooks/Cole Publishing Co., 1970), pp. 561-567.

Some men, rather than face this changed picture of themselves—rather than face the image of failure, humiliation, and defeat—killed themselves.

RESPONDING TO THE IMAGE OTHERS HAVE OF US

Much of our behavior is strongly influenced by our *intense desire to look favorable in the eyes of other people.* This can be both a negative and a positive kind of influence. If someone very important to us has a rather uncomplimentary image of us, we may decide to prove that he is all wrong by outdoing ourselves in achievement. Or we may react in the opposite way, saying to ourselves, "Well, I have the bad reputation; I might as well live up to it."

The parent who thinks his child is not to be trusted and who conveys this feeling to the child probably will encourage rebellion and untrustworthy behavior. The manager who thinks of his employees as being lazy and ungrateful for all the help he has given them may encourage those very attitudes if he conveys that impression to them. Some outstanding managers seem to have the ability to see more in their employees than they see in themselves. This is not a false optimism. The manager simply holds the highest possible image of his people. When *this* impression is conveyed to them, they quite often outdo themselves to live up to that expectation.

The expectations we have help determine how we perceive a person or situation. If we expect a business associate to turn down a suggestion we want to make to him, we are more likely to "see" reactions in his voice or behavior which seem disapproving to us. On the other hand, expecting that he will like our suggestion may alter perceptions so that we overlook his actual lack of interest and assume that he will support our suggestion in a crucial meeting to be held soon. What we *expect* to see frequently determines what we *do* see; even the mature scientist recognizes this tendency in himself and strictly follows the scientific method so that his perceptions are more in accord with reality.

The fear of something happening to our self-picture not only affects how close we can get to other people, but also determines how effective we can be in influencing the behavior of people. Every time the salesman talks to the prospect, he faces the possibility of either failure or success. When he experiences failure or frustration it is possible for some self-doubt to creep into his mind, doubt that he is really as good as he would like to think he is. If you are courting a girl and ask her to marry you, there is always a possibility that she will say no. If we attempt to be friendly toward our next-door neighbor, there is always a possibility that he will tell us to mind our own business. If other people like us and respond favorably to us, we congratulate ourselves on being nice people. But if people respond to us unfavorably or if we are hurt by others, we are likely to feel less sure of ourselves and wonder what kind of person we are.

There is a way to avoid being hurt by other people. There is a way to avoid the incidents in life which threaten to alter or diminish the favorable picture that we have of ourselves. We are not likely to be hurt or to have to change our self-image if we don't let ourselves get too "close" or too "involved" with others. We can hold people at arm's length, emotionally, and avoid being much disturbed if they happen to do something which bothers us. We can avoid damage to our self-image if we keep people from getting to know us too well. Of course, we have to pay a price for this, because in addition to taking less risk of being hurt, there is much less chance of our being loved.

We resort to a good bit of artificial behavior to keep people from getting too close to us or seeing through our defenses. But maintaining this distance from other people is expensive because it also keeps us from being able to "motivate" them to do as we would like them to do. This can become a kind of vicious circle. The fear of damage to our self-image can keep us from getting close to others, and failure to get close to them can result in frustration, which in turn threatens us with the self-image of failure and prompts us to maintain greater emotional distance from people. If, however, we have the *courage to expose* our self-image to possible change and can move toward a challenge, we may find ourselves building a better and sounder self-image, one which simply *needs less defending.*

The self-image can be changed in a positive way so that the individual can "see himself" doing something that he previously thought was impossible. If we think we cannot do something we've never tried before, we probably won't even try it. And if we do try it, our image of failing probably increases the probability we will fail. To think that we can do something does not at all guarantee that we will be able to do it, but it certainly increases the probability of success. Sometimes our self-image can be changed in a positive direction leading to more success because of an "accidental" success. The weekend golfer whose score rarely dips below the one-hundred mark may step up to the first tee one day and drive straight down the fairway well over two hundred and fifty yards. As he grins his way down to his second shot, he may think. "This is my lucky day," and in fact have the lowest score ever at the end of eighteen. Of course, on another day his first tee shot may come to a halt just thirty feet away; quite possibly his score that day will reach an all-time high.

Sometimes our self-image changes in a positive direction because we observe or know of someone else's success. When Roger Bannister first ran the mile in a fraction of a second under the "impossible four-minute barrier" a sports writer said that he had "opened the way" for other milers to do the same thing. The records show that the world's record for the mile run which had been on a plateau for nine years prior to Bannister's feat was broken again less than a month later by John Landy and since then has steadily dropped as dozens of athletes have run the mile in less than four minutes.[2] Undoubtedly, Bannister's successors were better able to "see themselves" running faster than they had thought possible before.

OVERCOMING THE TYRANNY OF THE SELF-IMAGE

In a very real sense we are tyrannized by the view we have of ourselves. Our behavior seems largely controlled by the scope and depth of our self-image. Our defense mechanisms may protect the consistency of the self-image but result in behavior which is essentially self-defeating. When we change our self-image, a wider range of behavior opens up and leads to greater self-fulfillment. But again risk is involved in the attempt to change and enlarge this view of the self. It takes strength and courage to experiment with a new and healthier self-picture.

The very young child is often molded and perhaps oppressed by the reactions of adults important to him. He learns to suppress spontaneous expressions of physical and emotional behavior because he finds these often lead to rejection or disapproval from his parents. He learns that it is not safe to "be himself" if he wants to keep the love or good will of his parents. If this thinking continues into later life, it is easy to see why many adults are convinced that if other people really knew them well they wouldn't like them. An adult may continue to have this child-like view of himself even though it is no longer appropriate. The child is, after all, controlled and confined by his parents; he lacks mature decision-making powers; he cannot "transfer" from his "outfit" (the family) and hence can do little but bow to the weight of his parents' approval or disapproval. Because the child is not yet able to make fine discriminations as to which feelings or behavior are permitted and which will be punished, he is likely

[2] Frank G. Menke, *The Encyclopedia of Sports*, 2nd ed. (New York: A. S. Barnes Co., 1960), p. 1037.

to *overreact* by suppressing most of what he feels spontaneously. He becomes guarded and fearful; he censors what he is about to say so that he will avoid disapproval. Some censorship is necessary to live in a society; over-censorship can create problems for him later as an adult.

Adults can make fine distinctions between situations . . . if they will. They have the potential for avoiding inappropriate overgeneralizations . . . if they choose. If we are laughed at because of a question we asked during an educational seminar, we can make the decision that those who laughed were inappropriate in their behavior and we will be neither embarrassed nor deterred in asking further questions. The "child-thinking adult" may assume that because he was laughed at by others in the group he is therefore stupid (negative self-image) and that they are right in their implied judgment. In a number of ways we can alter our thinking so that the image we have of ourselves can grow and expand to permit behavior which is healthy and satisfying instead of self-defeating.

The person in the seminar may not like the fact that he was laughed at, and would prefer to avoid it, but he can also value learning something. A question is one of the best ways of doing this. Using his ability to weigh values and the importance of things, he decides that it is *appropriate to ask questions* and *inappropriate to laugh* at someone's efforts to gain knowledge. Armed with this perspective, he can say (or think to himself) that those who laughed must have a problem! But the most important consequence of thinking as an adult instead of as a child is that self-improving behavior (asking the question) continues and self-defeating behavior (withdrawing in embarrassment and no longer speaking up) is not permitted.

There are other ways of thinking to help overcome the tyranny of a too narrow self-image. Is there anyone reading this book who has not done something foolish or made some kind of mistake? It is understandable to regret the mistake; it is inappropriate to let *one* mistake become the *total* measure of our worth. Having one accident does not mean that one is a poor driver. Preparing one unpalatable meal does not mean one is a poor cook. How do you suppose the football player felt when he became confused and ran the wrong way to make a touchdown for the other team? Misery would be an appropriate feeling at the time, but if this one incident becomes blown up in the player's mind as evidence that he is the world's worst, then things are out of perspective. One mistake, one indiscretion, one foolish statement does not mean that the person is an indiscrete fool. Tragically, many do feel that one mistake brands the man! From Shakespeare's *Julius Caesar* we read: "The evil that men do lives after them, the good is oft interred with their bones."

We expand our image if at the *time* we make a mistake we remember our past successes. Life is a succession of events; it is the long-range view which is important. In the same way it would be appropriate to remember past mistakes at the time of a great success; this might help minimize delusions of grandeur.

The concept of seeking a larger perspective helps maintain a healthy, growing self-image. The man who fails in the small business he tried to operate need not picture himself as a total failure. Other facets of his life are important, too. He may fail in one business but be a success as a father, husband, friend, or companion. Implicit in this concept is the larger concept of the worth and dignity of any person just because he exists! The ultimate aim of each of these suggested ways of thinking about the self is the ability to like ourselves as the persons we are. Come to think about it, this is the aim of this book!

Learning to like ourselves may, for some, sound like self-adulation or false pride. But Hillel, an early Hebrew sage, said, "If I am not for myself, who will be for me? If I am only for myself, what am I? If not now, when?" And from quite a different source is the similar idea but in the form of a prayer used by those in Alcoholics Anonymous, "God grant me the serenity to accept the things I cannot change, the courage to change those I can, and the wisdom to know the difference."

Self-acceptance is an important aim of the growing individual. It is the very essence of the scientific method discussed earlier: the acceptance of things as they are! It is the beginning for the person who wishes to improve. Self-acceptance does not mean complacency or giving up the desire to change. Self-acceptance is instead the very perspective and the foundation which allows growth. The rational, appropriate, mature human being begins each day by confronting the self he really is, accepting that self for what it is, and, thus freed from the tyranny of having to deceive himself, he takes the next step toward becoming a full and whole human being: *he seeks to expand his value not only to others but, more important, to himself!*

SUMMARY

People are different. We "know" this but often act as if we thought everyone should understand us in the same way when we talk or write to them. We understand the uniqueness of each person when we discover the image or view of himself which so effectively dictates his behavior. We increase our own ability to understand others when we know ourselves more fully. Knowing ourselves includes recognizing when we are more likely to be defensive; it also includes admitting that we often do things to avoid seeing ourselves as we are, which helps overcome the self-defeating tyranny of the self-image.

Much of what people do is aimed at pleasing others and being well-regarded by them. A natural consequence of this strong need to please others is the tendency to cover up our "real" selves and present a "front" to others which we hope they will like. We avoid being hurt by not showing anyone who we really are. This avoidance of open, genuine contact may eliminate some pain but it also inhibits the growth of the individual toward becoming a more loving and loved human being. We can learn to change our behavior and self-image so that we can more often achieve success in life.

QUESTIONS FOR DISCUSSION AND THOUGHT

1. Thinking like a scientist helps us maximize successes and minimize failures. Explain why.
2. "Common sense" is not necessarily a good guide to successful interpersonal relationships. Why not?
3. Reality is how a person perceives it. What are the implications of this statement to the salesman, parent, manager, or husband and wife?
4. We don't like to be rejected by others, but why would we reject ourselves?
5. Defense mechanisms may seem to help avoid conflict but frequently lead to even more conflict. What is an example of this?
6. Defense mechanisms are not always harmful or self-defeating. Explain.
7. What is the conflict between being well-liked, on the one hand, and growing toward greater maturity, on the other?
8. How can the adult overcome fears and self-defeating tendencies which may have originated in childhood experiences?

2

CONFLICT AND DECISION

George looked at his watch for the twentieth time and this time let out an audible expletive. The woman next to him on the DC–9 was startled enough to drop her book. George mumbled, "Sorry," and turned again to his sales report which had to be in the mail that night.

His watch told him that he was going to be at least an hour late arriving at O'Hare, but he might still be able to join his family at the high school where his daughter had the lead in the senior play that night. This was the highlight of her school year and he did not want to miss it. He looked around again to see how soon his tray of food would be brought and with a sigh noticed that the stewardess was serving the row just behind him. Service had been slow because of the rough weather and he was hungry.

The woman next to him had her tray now just as the plane bounced one more time in the storm. The stewardess' voice over the loudspeaker was low and seductive as she announced, "Due to the increasing turbulence in the area we will temporarily suspend service. Please check again to see that your seat belts are securely fastened." For the next fifteen minutes George was acutely aware of every movement and bite of food in the seat next to him.

His dark mood was broken only when the seductive voice again said, in what seemed to be a cheerful tone, "The captain indicates that due to the heavy traffic we will be in a holding pattern temporarily. As soon as we get the clearance to land we will let you know. Please check your seat belts to see that they are securely fastened."

When the plane finally began its approach to the field, George saw that he might get to the play during the intermission. The final scene was the most important one, anyway.

When he got to the baggage area and saw that his suitcase was not there yet, he ran across the parking lot getting thoroughly soaked, still hoping that he would see most of the last scene. He viciously turned the key in the ignition and heard only one low grunt from the starter.

He saw by the pulled-out light switch that he had forgotten to turn out the lights when he had parked the day before. The battery was dead!

Frustration is a daily part of our lives. It can be a small frustration like trying to get the pins out of the new shirt, or a large one like spending four days working on a big sale only to lose out to a competitor. A drawer stuck shut, a knot in a shoe lace, a power failure in the night which results in the alarm not going off on time, a traffic jam, a stock going down in price, a pencil lead breaking during an important phone call—these and many more frustrations help make up our world. The fact that people are different, each one seeking his own satisfactions in his own way, means that every human contact inevitably involves some blocking of a desire. Unless we can go into total seclusion, with an army of servants to care for us, we have to find ways of either overcoming or coping with conflict. The way we do this determines the degree of success or failure we achieve. How we handle frustration and conflict describes our general adjustment to life itself. Frustration, or the inability to obtain satisfaction when we have been motivated to move in a certain direction, leads to a tension or condition of stress which we call *conflict*. The tension we feel when we are torn between two or more equally attractive goals, or when we must choose between two or more painful situations, is another example of conflict.

During a state of conflict, we experience indecision and perhaps vacillation, moving first in one direction and then another, while not knowing exactly what we really want to do. Each of us has his own characteristic way of reacting to conflict. Some of us attempt to resolve the conflict immediately by making a snap decision and moving, even if we are moving in what may be the wrong direction. Others make such a move only after a long period of deliberation during which they suspend practically all activity until they have made a decision to move in one direction or another. Most people fall somewhere between these two extremes.

FRUSTRATION AND AGGRESSION

One of the most common reactions to frustration is aggression. Let someone drive in front of us and block our progress while we are rushing to an appointment and our thin veneer of civilized behavior peels off with a blast on the horn or an angry shout. Volunteering to help in the community fund-raising drive may bring us in contact with an apparently well-to-do prospect who tries to explain that he can't contribute this year because he has large payments to make on his recently acquired boat. While we may feel frustrated because we can't reach our fund quota, our angry retort to the prospect about his personal greed probably won't encourage him to reconsider and write a check. In fact, if we are angry at him and show it, he may talk about us to his friends who then may refuse to see us when we want to call on them for contributions. Showing our anger at the policeman who stops us for driving slowly through the stop sign may change his decision from giving us a warning to giving us a ticket with a fine.

While aggression may be a direct and common reaction to frustration, the reaction itself often leads to additional sources of frustration, especially if it is another person who is the target for the aggression. The other person may hit back! Aggression need not be the inevitable response to frustration. While psychologists have long thought that frustration leads automatically to aggression, recent studies suggest that this is not true in all people or all cultures.[1] If aggression is a learned response, it can be unlearned and other more adaptive responses substituted.

We react to frustration by increasing the amount of energy we bring to bear on the cause of the frustration in order to overcome it. This increased energy can be in the form of senseless rage or it can be in the form of increased interest, ingenuity, and persistence in finding adequate solutions to the problems. This latter use of the increased energy level often results in real progress or invention. It is the healthy and constructive way to rise to a challenge.

When we begin to open a door and find that it is stuck, our automatic response is to push a little harder to try to open it. If that doesn't work we may back off and give it a kick. We may even say things to it. Depending

---

[1] Leonard Berkowitz, "The Frustration–Aggression Hypothesis Revisited," in Leonard Berkowitz (ed.), *Roots of Aggression* (New York: Atherton, 1969).

on our mood, we may continue to pound on the door, we may stand in silent rage, or we may search for another door which opens.

A constructive response to frustration seems to depend on the level of emotional maturity of the individual *and* on his background of knowledge and skill which makes creative problem-solving possible. We can make more constructive use of the frustrations we encounter by becoming more competent in our understanding of human behavior.

The ability to respond to frustration in a more positive and healthy way and to continue efforts to overcome the obstacle is known as *frustration tolerance*. This tolerance is largely gained in our early childhood experiences. One psychologist has suggested that to help a child build frustration tolerance, he should be exposed to mildly frustrating situations, rather than having all his needs gratified.[2]

MATURE ADJUSTMENT:
DEPENDENCE TO INTERDEPENDENCE

The child begins his life by being completely dependent. Almost complete dependence continues for at least the first five or six years. However, we don't have to wait that long to notice efforts on the part of the child to exert his independence. The first efforts to manipulate and explore his surroundings before the child is a year old represent this need to exert himself and learn for himself. The drive to emerge from this total dependence and move toward the relative independence of adulthood is one of the driving forces which underlies the formation of our personality. Some individuals never lose a strong feeling of dependence on their parents. Other individuals appear to be so independent that they may be unable to work cooperatively with other people. Somewhere in between these two extremes most of us find some balance and try to maintain it.

In our efforts to establish ourselves as unique, relatively independent individuals with our own drives and goals, we *emerge as a personality.* This drive to emerge as an independent individual is rewarded by an ever-increasing personal freedom, that is, a greater control over our surroundings so that we achieve more satisfaction and less dissatisfaction. We emerge with a clearer idea of who we are, of what other people expect of us, and what we expect of ourselves. Our family, our school group, our community, and our culture play a tremendous role in shaping and

[2] Leonard Berkowitz, *The Development of Motives and Values in the Child* (New York: Basic Books, 1964).

molding us as individual personalities. Most of the time we are not aware of these influences which so affect our behavior patterns.

Independence

The maturing individual is motivated toward gaining greater and greater control over his environmental limitations. The newborn infant feels a sense of comfort and security when held tightly by his mother, but the older child struggles and resists when he is held. The older child wants to be given more and more responsibility and feels considerably put upon if he is curbed or restrained. The emergence of personality and the growth of values which guide behavior signal a movement toward independence and away from the absolute dependence of the infant. We look forward to the time when we can "stand on our own two feet," "stand up and be counted," and "be out on our own." In the childhood years, this need for independence exists along with a continuing need for dependence on the parents.

In the normal human being, independence as a goal gradually increases in importance as dependence gradually decreases. By the the time we are adults, we do not want to be dictated to. We want to be independent. But at the same time we continue to have some need to be dependent on other people.

Too Independent?

Ordinarily, we think that as a man matures he becomes more independent and less dependent upon others. But is it possible to be *too* independent? The person who resists supervision may be revealing a natural healthy desire for independent action. But he may also be revealing a need to mature still further. What looks like mature independence is often a rather childish rebellion against authority. Rebellion, for the sake of rebelling, may be a reaction formation to which the individual resorts in order to cover up a more basic immature dependency for which he still yearns. Some of the rebellion that is so apparent during the teenage years is often a testing of the limits, or in other words a plea to the parent to assume more control over the children.

The distinction between independence and dominant aggressiveness on the one hand and immature rebellion on the other is important for the credit manager to make in his efforts to select collection agents. A manager may become quite excited when a recruit speaks up and talks back to him during the selection interview. The manager may think such behavior indicates a strong aggressive man who will be able to collect many past-due accounts. But contrary to expectations, the man who asserts himself just for the sake of asserting himself or of arguing or rebelling against an authority figure is likely to be relatively ineffective in the collection interview. He is likely to argue with his prospect, win the argument, and lose any possibility of receiving a past-due amount.

Interdependence

It is doubtful that independence should be considered as the ultimate level of emotional maturity for the adult. Certainly we need to grow away from being dependent on our parents, but if we stop maturing at the point of being "independent," this often means that we are trying to "go it alone," without the healthy and stimulating influence of help and ideas from others. A further phase of maturity for the adult might be to establish himself as an *interdependent* individual. By this we mean an individual who can of course accomplish things on his own, but who also reaches out to others for help. Such an individual would be dependable, but could also be dependent on other people for emotional and intellectual stimulation.

It is characteristic of the individual who has not matured to the point of interdependence that he feels it a weakness to admit ignorance by asking questions or getting directions from others. Interdependence as a goal, and as a level of maturity, describes a way of relating to people by being both dependent on them for ideas, love, and assistance, and at the same time dependable and responsible.

The way the parents of a child respond to his quest for independence, and the way the manager reacts to his employees' dependency and independency needs will determine in a large measure the extent of growth and development which occurs. Too much domination of the child by his parents may force him to grow up as a weak, dependent, passive individual, or as an overly independent or rebellious person. Neither of these extremes represents a high degree of maturity. Likewise, too much control exerted over an employee by his manager can keep him from developing as a person and as an employee.

Inevitably, a business manager is in a superior position to his employees. He controls a number of things which are important to them. He can decide whether they keep their jobs. He can give or refuse to give them materials, secretarial help, etc. The employees must depend on their manager for information, training, supervisory help, etc., and, of course, must depend on him to be fair and honest. Such a situation may encourage some to become emotionally dependent on their manager in the sense that they ask him for help in planning their day's activities, in making minor decisions, in filling out reports, etc. The more emotionally dependent on the manager they become the less likely they are to develop the habit of keeping themselves on a work schedule and the less initiative and creative thinking will be applied to their work.

It is important to some managers that their people be emotionally dependent on them. This is often an unconscious desire, but the effect on the employees is negative just the same. One manager was frank to admit that he wanted his subordinates to "respect me and look up to me." He flatly stated his unwillingness to be bothered by "those prima donnas who try to throw their weight around." What he was revealing, although he was not conscious of it, was that he was essentially afraid of strong, independent people, and was selecting those who would be "yes men." This particular manager not only failed to select people who did an average job, but found it impossible to retain even those men doing a less than average job. The company ultimately removed him from his position because of lack of production.

PERCEPTION: A PERSONALIZED INTERPRETATION

How we look at a situation can make all the difference between a rational, creative decision which may minimize conflict or a blind, self-defeating effort which creates new conflicts. The ability to interpret, or perceive, the words and events which happen to us hour by hour tells the story of human effort which begins at the moment of birth.

"I saw it with my own eyes," said the witness, testifying at the trial of an accused criminal. Rarely do we doubt the reality of what we see or hear. We take for granted that what we see is true. But doubt about this arises when two people "see" two different things while watching the same incident. The eyewitness is of tremendous significance in establishing the "facts" regarding a murder trial. But every once in a while an innocent man is imprisoned because it is later discovered that an eyewitness made a mistake in what he reportedly saw. This makes us suspect that the human being does not always see what is there.

You and I both meet a man in the street. He happens to be a competitor of yours, but I do not know that. To me, he looks like a pleasant fellow, but as we walk on, you remark that he is a "sharpie" who cannot be trusted. Each of us has perceived him in a different way. Our perceptions of him were drastically affected by our own personal experiences. The next time I meet that man, he is very likely to look like a "sharpie" to me. In fact, if I talk to him for a few minutes, I am likely to "find" all kinds of evidence to support the perception of him that I have learned to have. I am likely to "see" mostly those things which are consistent with the mental picture I already have of this person. Unless we are careful we will be *selective* in our *perception* and see only what we want to see.

Sensations and Perceptions

We do *learn* to see. In fact, all sensations we experience must be interpreted by us before they make sense. *We "see" reality through a screen of personal experiences, prejudices, and misconceptions.* Let us examine *how* we go about experiencing sensations and perceptions.

We must first be exposed to an object. From this object certain physical energies act on our sense receptors, that is, our eyes, ears, nose, skin, muscles, etc. From these sense receptors or sensory organs, nerve impulses travel to the brain. Here the nerve impulses are experienced by us as sensations. We are aware that there is some kind of object "out there." It is when we give these sensations a meaning that perception takes place. If we are driving down the street and begin to smell something, we have been made aware of something acting on our senses, that is, we experience a sensation. So far, we don't know what this sensation means. Our friend reports that it smells like a burning brake lining and suggests that the hand brake has not been released. Sure enough, this is what happened. Because we now give some meaning to our sensation, we can refer to this as a perception.

Learning to Perceive. We learn to perceive the world by associating sensation with other information that we have. Let us assume that a person has been born in Florida. As he drives his automobile along a highway while on a winter vacation trip to New York, he approaches an obvious icy patch on the pavement. Because he has had no previous experience with driving on ice, he may regard this as a matter of curiosity and not slow up. A moment later, much to his surprise, he has lost control of his automobile. He begins turning the wheel to the left and to the right, he applies his brakes and finds himself in a ditch. The next time this driver sees a patch of ice, it will have a different meaning to him. He will now see the ice in terms of past experience, and because of his perception of the next icy patch he will alter his behavior as a consequence of the meaning that is given to the sensation.

Errors in Perception. We frequently make errors in perception because of our expectancies, attitudes, and needs. After his harrowing experience on the icy pavement, the southern driver may later see a section of wet pavement that looks shiny and icy to him, and he may react by slowing down unnecessarily. Perhaps we have had the experience of reading a frightening mystery novel late at night and "hearing" someone jimmy open a window of the house. If we work up the courage to investigate, we may find that it was merely a branch of a bush scraping against the window. *We sometimes make errors in perception, then, because of preconceived ideas or expectancies.* We may be expecting to meet a friend at the airport terminal and think we see him in the distance with his back toward us. As we walk up to him and slap him on the back, we may be embarrassed to find that we have slapped a total stranger who bore a slight resemblance to our friend. Our perception has been distorted, then, by an expectation.

The *attitudes*[3] that we have toward an individual or toward a group of individuals can also affect our perception. In a training film produced for management trainees, a group of workmen were seen at work; some of the men were white and some black. The white trainees "saw" that rest periods taken by the black workers indicated "laziness," while identical rest periods taken by the white workers were seen as judiciously spaced rest periods so that their total output would be higher. The manager who feels that the average worker needs to be prodded or coerced to get work done will relentlessly pressure his subordinates to avoid "social" conversations and to "get back to work!" A different manager who thinks that people in general want to do a good job and want to be given more responsible and significant work to do will permit and even encourage discussions between employees as a means of stimulating each other to produce new ideas and effective work methods. Our attitudes determine how we see people and what kind of human-relations approach we take in getting work done through others.

Our *needs* can determine our perception. The explorer lost on the desert without water is very likely to "see" a large lake full of clear, sparkling water just beyond the next rise. The salesman trying hard for a

[3] Attitudes are discussed in detail in Chapter 7. See pp. 293-296.

close may "see" that the prospect is about ready to buy and may press hard for the signature. If the salesman has perceived incorrectly, he may ruin his chances of making the sale because of his poor timing.

Minimizing Errors in Perception. We have defined perception as an interpretation of sensation. In the literal sense our perception is how *we* interpret a sensation and is therefore a perfectly valid experience. How a person perceives an event (if we assume he is telling the truth) is always valid and "true," true in that his report is his individual interpretation of a sensation as he sees it. When we refer to "errors in perception," we mean that our perception is not in accord with "reality." We put the word *reality* in quotes only to indicate that if we use the word to indicate what actually exists, we may be hard put to demonstrate just what does actually exist. Is "reality" absolute or is it only what most of us think it is? Since it takes people to observe and report on the nature of "reality," even if the people are reporting what machines or instruments show, the human element seems always to be involved in definitions of reality. Suffice it to say at this point that the majority of people who "agree" on what reality is are sometimes later found to be in error. Begging the question as we may be doing, we will be referring to "errors of perception" from now on as a difference between one individual perception and the perception of reality generally held by most people. *What can we do to avoid serious errors in perception?* How can we be sure that we are not completely distorting reality? How can we avoid seeing things as we want to see them and learn to see things as they really are? We can best answer this question by looking at the method of observation practiced by scientists in applying the scientific method to their investigations.

First of all, in using the scientific method we are interested in getting as complete information as possible. We are not satisfied with one or two observations, but instead try to get many observations spread over a period of time. We record all relevant information regardless of whether it pleases us or not. We are interested in knowing the truth of the matter, and not in merely supporting our own biases. We can check our own perceptions by *deliberately looking for other possible interpretations* of the facts.

If your boss walks right past your desk without saying a word, it may seem that he is fed up with your work and wishes you would leave. Of course this would be upsetting. But perhaps he is preoccupied with a family problem, or wants not to distract you because you are working on a very important project, or is on his way to the men's room and wonders if his chest pain is due to the Reuben sandwich he had for lunch or is a warning signal for a beginning heart attack. Your wife's silence at the dinner table may convince you that she is still angry at how late you came home last night, even though you were working at the office. But maybe she just doesn't feel well, or received a disturbing letter from her mother that morning, or wonders if your teenager will be injured in the football game tomorrow. One of the major tools we can use in testing various interpretations is communications feedback, one method of which is effective listening. We can encourage others to talk, to express what they are thinking and feeling and tell us what's on their mind. In a later section we shall discuss the importance of real listening and ways to improve our listening ability. It is possible to improve our listening ability by learning to listen more accurately and with less distortion of facts.

Frames of Reference

We have seen that perception is determined partly by the needs, expectancies, and attitudes that we have at any one time. Another determinant of perception is our frame of reference. This is sometimes referred to as a "mental set." What this means is that things are perceived in relationship to the larger or overall setting in which they occur. If we expect an excellent performance from the new branch manager of the bank and he does only a "good" job, we will be disappointed. But if we thought that it would be months before the new manager was able to show any appreciable increase in bank deposits and he instead did a "good" job by increasing deposits immediately, we will be delighted. Assuming the performance is the same in both cases, our reaction to it is relative to our expectation, or frame of reference. The basketball player and the jockey will see their mutual six-foot friend as "average" and "tall" respectively. The office manager may be reasonably satisfied with his secretary's typing speed of thirty words a minute until she is ill and her replacement works steadily at about fifty words a minute. When his own secretary returns she may wonder why her boss is suddenly dissatisfied with her work. Moreover, it is perfectly possible that the office manager may not be consciously aware of why he is dissatisfied. *We perceive characteristics of other people according to our frame of reference, but we may not be aware that we are doing so.*

We form various concepts of classes of subjects such as people, occupations, etc., and we judge new experiences according to these learned concepts. A small farm to a Texan may mean three thousand acres. A suburbanite might describe his one and a half acres as a small farm. These two men have different frames of reference.

Establishing a frame of reference is useful. We judge and evaluate other people on the basis of our past experiences; and unless we have formed some frame of reference, we will find ourselves in utter confusion whenever we have to make new decisions or judgments.

Our frame of reference can change with time. The life underwriter who sold a half million dollars' worth of business last year may have felt quite satisfied, but this year he may feel it is no special achievement. His frame of reference has changed. But our frame of reference is also resistant to change. The various stereotypes that we have are examples of frames of reference which are relatively unchangeable. If we have stereotyped people of a certain nationality as shrewd and clannish, we are very quick to "see" these characteristics in their behavior, whether they exist or not. If we happen to observe kinds of behavior in a person of this nationality which do not fit in with the stereotype, we tend to dismiss this evidence because it has very little meaning to us. The danger here is obvious. Any time that our frame of reference is unyielding to change, we are very likely to be considerably misled by our perceptions and not be "in tune" with reality.

The Vital Significance of Our Perception

The way we form our perception can be a matter of life and death. If we make a left turn in front of an oncoming car because we perceived its being farther away than it really was, then we have made what is perhaps our last mistake. *We cannot know any more about objective reality than that which we allow ourselves to know.* If because of pride, ignorance, prejudice, misconceptions, intense personal needs, or the presence of a strong emotion, we grossly distort the information that comes to our senses, we alone will be the loser. We would not attempt to cross a busy intersection wearing a blindfold. Neither, then, should we attempt to move through life without trying to minimize our distortions of reality. We see other people only through ourselves. *We are prisoners of our own frame of reference.* Our perceptions are formed through learning experiences. We can make our perceptions more accurate or more in line with objective realities only by efforts to test the accuracy, especially through use of the scientific method, and adjust our perceptions accordingly.

We cannot leave the subject of perception without stressing the fact that mental processes can be either conscious or unconscious. We can perceive a stimulus, that is, we can give meaning to a sensation, without even being aware or conscious of having made this perception. We can unconsciously perceive hostility in another person, but when questioned, would conscientiously deny it.

The Role of The Unconscious

We have made repeated references to the existence of what is called the unconscious part of our mind. We have been referring to mental and emotional activities that are somehow beyond the level of our sense of awareness. As we talk about the unconscious, we may get the impression that it is a specific area of the brain, but this is definitely not so. Referring to the unconscious is merely a way of recognizing the existence of mental activity which has force and influence but which is somehow beyond our ability to observe or measure. The concept of the unconscious is strictly an inference. By this we mean that we *assume* that such a mental mechanism as the unconscious exists because of the kinds of behavior observed.

We are aware that there are a number of things about ourselves that we do not reveal consciously to anyone. We may reveal to our closest friends or associates our innermost thoughts, but even to them there are feelings and past experiences that we cannot bring ourselves to reveal. Many times we try to hide our feelings from other people. We pretend to be interested in what someone else is saying even though we may be bored. We may actually feel terrible but will tell an inquiring person that we feel fine. Thus, in many ways, we hide from the rest of the world some of our true feelings and thoughts. In somewhat the same way, we hide certain feelings and thoughts even from ourselves. We say that these thoughts and feelings are unconscious or that we are not aware of them. Of course, we may think we are not revealing a thought or feeling to someone when in fact they do observe our behavior and correctly infer what we tried not to reveal. We may pretend to someone that we are not depressed, but our long face observed during an unguarded moment may give us away.

At any one time during the day, we are conscious or aware of only a very limited number of things which pertain to us and to our past experiences. If we want to, however, we can call forth many memories or feelings which are at the moment unconscious. We have all had the experience of meeting an old friend and being unable to recall his name. At that moment, we are not conscious of his name. In a few moments, however, his name may suddenly occur to us. We can say, then, that when we first met our old friend, his name was somehow "buried" in our unconscious. If someone were to ask us what we were doing exactly one year ago today, most of us would find it difficult to give a very good answer. But if we were reminded of one or two events which happened to us a year ago, this would possibly be enough to stimulate further memories. If we made enough of an effort, we might be able to recall an amazing number of facts which had, until a moment ago, apparently been forgotten.

Many experiences in our past are apparently impossible for us to recall even though we may try hard to do so. Under hypnosis, however, we may find that we are able to recall and verbalize experiences dating back even to the first two or three years of our lives. This gives us a hint as to the vast and almost endless amount of material that must somehow be collected and stored in what we have been referring to as our *unconscious.* The importance of this concept of the unconscious is that our present behavior can be influenced by unconscious feelings and thoughts as much as—if not more so—by thoughts or experiences of which we are conscious.

The example of the iceberg has been used frequently to compare the conscious and the unconscious parts of our psychological being. The part of the iceberg which floats above the surface of the water and which is visible has been compared to our conscious mind, while the submerged part has been related to our unconscious. We might carry this example one step further. The iceberg has achieved a kind of equilibrium as it floats in the water. The weight of the ice above the surface of the water creates a pressure downward while the buoyancy of the submerged ice creates a force upward. In somewhat the same way, there is an opposing force between the conscious and unconscious parts of our mind. Ideas and feelings in the unconscious may be struggling to reach the surface of consciousness only to be forced down again by our need to avoid recognizing their existence.

Most people involved in the world of work have a boss or supervisor who tells them what to do. Even the president of a corporation has his board of directors to whom he must report. In these relationships of being subordinate to someone else, the things we are *told* to do frequently conflict with what we *want* to do. Of course, our frustration at work frequently leads to feelings of aggression, feelings which cannot be expressed to the frustrating boss without leading to further unwanted consequences. What do we do with the occasional angry feelings we have while working? The most prudent thing is to hide, or attempt to hide, angry feelings unless we are on the verge of quitting and find ourselves "telling off" the boss! Not only must we avoid expressing our anger and disgust in words, we must be sure our facial expressions or other actions do not "give us away." For our own comfort and well-being, most of us try to make the best of it and ignore or overlook or even "forget" the things which annoy us. Such angry feelings often become unconscious through the mental mechanism of "repression." The feelings have not gone away; they have simply gone "underground." Unconsciously, these repressed thoughts struggle for expression, but unconsciously we want to adjust and get along as well as possible. The unconscious feeling and conscious desires are thus in conflict: a sort of tug of war.

If, while we are watching an iceberg, we see it suddenly begin to roll and shift in the water, we infer that something has happened to the ice below the surface to cause a change in the center of gravity. In the same way, we infer conscious mental activities by noticing obvious changes in behavior. What might seem like slips of the tongue are often reflections of unconscious desires or impulses.

One of the authors once worked for an irritating boss whose name was Mr. Widney. Mr. Widney was always full of directions and orders concerning every detail of the work. This was frustrating indeed, but any attempt to mention that it was preferable to try new things without having every procedure and movement dictated in detail led only to more voluminous directives. The conscious irritation and anger had to be put aside and were replaced by a kind of lethargy (defense mechanism) such that when asked how the job was by a friend, the reply was "O.K., I guess; it's a job." But one day the worker had to introduce a caller and said, "I'd like you to meet my boss, Mr. Windy." In the embarrassment which followed, the worker recognized anew his smoldering irritation which led to the insulting slip of the tongue; he beat a hasty retreat before things got worse!

We can suspect the influence of some unconscious mental activity when we notice that certain behavior doesn't seem to be appropriate or doesn't seem to follow from something that has just occurred. When we feel depressed or excited for no apparent reason, we may conclude that we are being influenced by unconscious impulses or interests.

One of the interesting things about the functioning of the unconscious is that we can react to another person's unconscious hostility of which we are unaware, and the other person can perceive our hostility without being consciously aware that he has perceived it. When this happens, the two individuals feel strangely uncomfortable with each other, but neither has any idea of what might be causing his discomfort.

Unconscious mental activity can distort our perception and cause uncomfortable gaps in our ability to remember, but *the unconscious is also one of mankind's most valuable and helpful assets.* The unconscious can be of immense help to us in solving problems or in resolving conflicts. Inventors, writers, and other creative individuals often have the experience of attempting to solve a problem consciously and logically, only to meet with frustration and failure. But after a certain period of time, with no apparent conscious effort, the solution or idea that they have been searching for suddenly leaps into awareness. Many of us have had the experience of waking in the morning with the solution to a problem which we did not have when we went to sleep. There is much evidence that our unconscious works for us in many helpful ways.

The human brain has been compared in some ways with our most advanced automatic computing machines. It has been suggested that we actually solve many problems by feeding information to our brain in much the same way that information is fed to a computing machine through tapes. The unconscious then goes to work "with a mind of its own" and grinds out an answer for us.

RESOLVING CONFLICT

A common conflict in business relationships is a reluctance to be assertive. This could take the form of postponing an appraisal interview with a failing subordinate, hesitating to call on a prospective customer, withholding information from the boss which he might not want to hear, or being afraid to speak up for oneself when unfairly criticized. A businessman may find that he is perfectly comfortable being assertive in his work but dreads the idea of making calls on assigned contacts as part of the annual United Appeal fund-raising campaign. Analyzing a situation of reluctance to be assertive will illustrate the interplay of values, attitudes, fears, unconscious barriers, and perceptions leading to self-defeating instead of adaptive behavior.

Bankers, salesmen, contractors, bill collectors, consultants, and many other people must initiate contact with the public. Only by making effective calls can they be assured of success in their field. But a *desire* to make the call can exist simultaneously with a *reluctance* to make the call. The person can want to make a "sale," but he is afraid of being turned down. If he does not make the call, he will not make the sale, but he won't be turned down, either.

Call reluctance invariably centers around the fear of being rejected as an individual. The fear of rejection affects us all, some more than others. As we saw in Chapter 1 we acquire a concept of ourselves especially by noticing how other people react to us. If as a child we are loved by our parents, we tend to regard ourselves as worthy of love. If we are trusted, we are more likely to be trustworthy. It works the other way, too, in that the less respect we have for ourselves, the less respect others will have for us. Most of the conflict that we experience in everyday living centers around this *fear of personal rejection.* What is this fear of rejection? How did it get started? What can be done to overcome it? To answer these questions, and to get a better understanding of frustration and conflict, we need to consider some things that commonly occur in our childhood.

Many parents find that an effective method of disciplining their children is to show love and affection when they are good and take away love when they are bad. The child who has broken his mother's favorite vase may be told, "You are a bad boy. You are clumsy and stupid. Go to your room and stay there until I tell you to come out." The child soon learns that when he fails to perform according to expectations he will be shut away from the love and affection of his parents. Nothing hurts more than to be deprived of the love of an individual, particularly when one is greatly dependent on that person for physical and emotional security. The child learns to behave well, not so much because of the correctness of the behavior itself, but because of the love he will receive after his "good" behavior. This fear of rejection for wrong behavior can be so great as to become generalized to include other adults who resemble the parents in that they are in positions of authority. Such adults might be the schoolteacher, the policeman, the judge, the boss, and even the prospective buyer. The latter is in a position of authority because he can say "Yes" or "No" to the salesman and can deny him something that he very much wants.

Some parents minimize this fear of rejection by responding differently to their children's behavior. They may say to the boy who has just broken a vase, "You have just done a bad thing. Even though I love you, I cannot allow you to do such a thing." Such a parent might even continue to punish the child by denying him some special privilege. When the parent makes a special effort to show the child that he is not a bad child but has done an unacceptable thing, the child can realize that his parents' love for him is not dependent on the specific things he does or does not do. Such a child can feel a sense of worth that would be denied the child of the first parents. This second child, if he grew up to be in a position where he had to initiate calls, could more readily see that his failure to sell to a prospect meant that the prospect was rejecting the *idea* being presented and not the man personally.

In an assertive situation, the individual puts himself in the position of being accepted or rejected. Of course, there is much more to the situation than this, but if he sees it only as a matter of being rejected or accepted personally, he will probably form a habit of call reluctance. It is not easy for us to admit that we are afraid. But fear is with us in some form every day. The manager is not likely to tell his boss that he is afraid to have the appraisal interview with the employee. He may not even recognize this fear. But if fear is the source of conflict between appraising and not appraising, then efforts by the boss to help him organize his time and develop better appraisal forms may not help very much to overcome this conflict.

We can take big steps to overcome such fear if we will recognize it and especially if we have the opportunity to discuss it with a sympathetic listener. Like any conflict, reluctance to be assertive can be overcome if we are willing to move toward the problem, recognize it as a problem, and try out different possible solutions to it. It is when we try to deny that we have fears that we are likely to get ourselves into real trouble.

The *stress of approaching* relative or total strangers day after day, or trying to get work done through unwilling employees, in addition to the *stress of fear of personal rejection,* forces many otherwise well-qualified businessmen to abandon the field of selling or managing. If the person can make the distinction between being turned down personally and having his ideas turned down, the stress of being assertive will be reduced.

Intelligence and Rational Problem-Solving

Individual differences in intellectual capacity and the ability to reason and draw conclusions play a large part in resolving conflict situations.

The businessman deals with a wide variety of individuals. Some may be college professors, some may be laborers, some may be professionals, and a great many may hold routine jobs in large corporations. These individuals are likely to vary a good deal in terms of their intelligence. Some of them will be of superior intelligence, a good many will be average, and some may be below average.

Intellectual capacity is an important facet of human behavior, and it is an especially important factor for the businessman to consider because his success depends at least partly on his employees' or customers' ability to comprehend the various statements that he makes. Most businessmen have learned to give a logical, well-organized presentation of ideas and procedures and are usually well-prepared to answer technical questions if it becomes necessary.

We are becoming increasingly aware, however, that people do not always do things for logical reasons. There may be, instead, *emotional reasons* why people behave as they do. We deal with individuals who vary in their ability to comprehend, who are motivated by emotional as well as intellectual reasons, and who cooperate or fail to cooperate for conscious and also unconscious reasons.

In our society, however, everyone is expected to be logical and to be able to give a reasonable explanation for his actions. Consequently, it will usually be poor psychology for us to point out that a person is acting in an emotional rather than in a logical manner. Many people take this as an insult. Consequently, we must take into account the fact that people often act on the basis of emotions, but we must not indicate that they seem illogical or unreasonable.

Intelligence and Reasoning

Anyone hopes that as he presents material to someone he will be able to do a certain amount of reasoning and come to a conclusion. It might be well, therefore, to consider several questions. How do we think? How do we form conclusions? How does reasoning influence behavior?

We are not born with an ability to be logical or rational in our thinking. The normal human being is born with a brain which has the capacity for learning very complex mental activities, but his thinking and reasoning ability depends largely on maturation and on learning experiences. Thinking is regarded as the most complex of all man's ways of behaving and as the one kind of behavior that, more than anything else, distinguishes man from all other animals. Not all people are born with an equal capacity to learn and think. Intellectual ability seems to be distributed among the general population in much the same way as other characteristics such as height and weight. Look at a group of men standing together and you will notice that most of them are between five feet six and six feet tall. A few are taller than six feet and a few are shorter than five feet six, but the average seems to be around five feet nine. In the same way, a little over 50 per cent of the general population is grouped between the I.Q. scores of 90 and 110, while 83 per cent fall between 80 and 120 I.Q. points. The implication of this is that we will be dealing with people who have varying degrees of ability to comprehend the meaning of what we say. While we must never make the mistake of underestimating a person's intelligence and making this estimate known to him, neither should we assume that he can grasp ideas and facts as readily as we do. An employee or customer who fails to understand the material being presented or the logic behind the argument may refuse to agree, not because he has no need to use the material but because he doesn't understand the proposal and will not admit that he doesn't understand it. Most of us do similar things to "save face."

Our intellectual capacity also changes somewhat during our lifetime. The sixty-year-old man usually will not be as quick and facile in his intellectual abilities as he was as a younger man. At the same time, however, increased knowledge and experience in a particular field may allow him to increase his ability to solve problems in that field. The decline in reasoning and thinking ability with age seems to be mostly a matter of speed of learning. The older person must simply take a little longer to learn and understand something.

One of the best single indicators of a person's general level of intelligence is his vocabulary. The more intelligent the person, the more extensive his vocabulary is likely to be. Of course, educational opportunity also affects the size and complexity of a person's vocabulary. There is a tendency for the more intelligent person to have a better memory. Again, many other factors besides our intellectual capacity influence our ability to remember. We more easily remember the things in which we are interested and find it practically impossible to remember those in which we have little interest.

Thinking and reasoning, of course, depend upon what has been learned previously. Reasoning is distinctly a mental activity which may be thought of as a kind of trial-and-error process. When we are given a problem to consider, certain previous experiences which seem to be related to this problem are remembered. These are tried out mentally and some discarded and some retained. This process continues until a likely solution is arrived at out of our fund of past experiences.

The process of reasoning involves at least five different activities: (1) A problem is recognized; (2) a problem is adequately described; (3) a number of possible solutions are suggested; (4) the possible solutions are examined to see how they might bear on the problem; and (5) observation or actual trial-and-error behavior is begun which leads to the acceptance or rejection of each of the possible solutions.

Reasoning, like every other human activity, is subject to error caused by personal desires, biases, or conscious motives. We occasionally see someone reasoning out the solution to a problem but arriving at a false solution because of unwarranted assumptions that may not have been critically examined. For example, an insurance salesman may propose a plan for a father which is a reasonable and logical way of providing for the education of his children. The logic of the plan may be lost on the prospect who feels that, although his children should be educated, they should work their way through college just as he did. The salesman's assumption that the prospect wants to provide money for his children's education is, therefore, unwarranted.

In order to be effective in our thinking and reasoning activity, we need to be relatively free from rigid assumptions or even false assumptions. If the behavior of the prospect seems unreasonable to the salesman, it may be that he has made assumptions about the prospect's desires or financial needs which are unwarranted. We do some checking on the validity of assumptions through the process of inference. If we see that the prospect is following a certain trend of thought, we may ask ourselves, "What assumptions must he be making in his own mind for him to think that way?" We may then proceed to ask the prospect if he thinks that this or that is true and perhaps thus be able to remove a possible block to the sale that is in his mind.

Because of the possibility that an entire presentation may be based on a faulty assumption made by the speaker or that the listener's understanding of the presentation is based on a faulty assumption, we emphasize once more the importance of improving our communications feedback ability. If we are essentially self-centered and preoccupied with our own presentations and financial needs, we may not be in a position to detect mistakes in our logic or reasoning abilities, or faulty thinking on the part of others.

Conflict and Anxiety

Our reaction to conflict can vary from momentary indecision to a total breakdown or collapse. Underlying all conflict is the vague state of uneasiness, unrest, and even terror that is called *anxiety*.[4] Anxiety and fear are somewhat alike, but anxiety is a vague anticipation of an unknown danger, while fear is a more direct reaction to a specific and identifiable object or situation. Anxiety gives rise to feelings of hopelessness and

[4] For further reading on the functioning of anxiety see Rollo May, *The Meaning of Anxiety* (New York: The Ronald Press Company, 1950).

impotence, while fear most often generates some specific actions to escape from the danger.

Anxiety is distressing and is something we want to avoid. Because of this, anxiety is a powerful motivator of human behavior. When we accidentally or on purpose behave in a way which *reduces* the level of our anxiety, this behavior is *rewarding* to us and is *learned*.

Since anxiety is often unconscious and is vague as to its origin, we may not be able to do much about it. But if we can turn our anxieties into fears, then we can begin to plan ways of overcoming these fears. If we can locate the source of the disturbance, we can move toward it and attempt to cope with it. The person who is unconsciously afraid to be assertive will feel anxiety without knowing why. When he can discover that he is afraid of being personally rejected and can *admit* this to himself, then he will know the source of his discomfort and can make plans to overcome the fear. Someone else can often see what is making us anxious when we ourselves are blind to it. The more mature the individual, the more likely it is that he will go to his manager or friend and ask for help.

To illustrate the difference between fear and anxiety we will examine some common reactions to authority figures such as the policeman, teacher, president of a corporation, governor of a state, etc. Anyone who has driven an automobile for a number of years has probably been stopped by a policeman for a minor traffic violation. Was this event anxiety-arousing to you when it happened? Some of the more obvious signs of anxiety are rapid breathing, rapid heartbeat, a tightness in the stomach, sweaty hands, clearing of the throat, sudden itches which must be scratched, belching, and even sudden feelings of weakness and fatigue. But why would we experience anxiety merely because we are given a traffic ticket and are ordered to appear in court? It is logical that we might be afraid that we will have to pay a fine of twenty-five dollars if found guilty, and who wants to lose twenty-five dollars? If we were to put a dent in the fender while backing into the garage, it might cost twenty-five dollars to repair it (in the '70's this would be a mighty small dent!) but we probably would not feel the same anxiety. What is the difference? Perhaps we feel anxiety in dealing with an authority figure because of childhood events or traumas with our parents.

To many children, being criticized or disciplined by a parent appears as a withdrawal of their love, and to a young child this is disturbing. It is anxiety-arousing. The child frequently feels powerless or helpless in dealing with the parent. The child misbehaves and then worries about how the parent will react. Whatever the punishment meted out, the child must passively accept it, or else rebel and incur greater wrath. But much of this early history drops into the unconscious, only to reappear in a symbolic form some morning while speeding to get to work on time. The policeman who stops you for "misbehaving" is a symbolic and unconscious reminder of the parent. The child in you feels anxiety at the prospect of losing parental love (the policeman, as authority figure, is a substitute parent) but the adult in you may be puzzled at how upset you are merely because the policeman politely wrote out the summons to appear in traffic court. But the policeman is not your parent. All he has done is cause you inconvenience and a probable financial loss. Being able to understand what the policeman represents in your unconscious may not eliminate the anxiety, but it is a helpful step in the right direction.

Inappropriate anxiety in traffic court (the judge is not your parent, either) may cause you to be tongue-tied and to give a poor account of the violation in your own defense. Depending partly on how well you can plead your case, you may pay the fine or simply be given a warning and a suspended sentence. Anxiety can reduce our ability to perform and this in turn can create other problems.

The boss can be an unconscious reminder of an arbitrary parent and the anxiety aroused by the reminder may make you stutter or forget important points while presenting an idea to him. The buyer or customer, similarly, is an authority figure in that he can make a decision to accept or reject the seller's request to buy. Fear can motivate the seller to practice his presentation, to discover the buyer's needs, and to plan the right time and place for the presentation. It is appropriate to be afraid that inadequate preparation will not lead to acceptance and this may lead to greater efforts which lead to success; anxiety tends to be self-defeating and the anxiety about not achieving success may lead to failure.

Either canceling or postponing something in order to reduce or avoid anxiety is a common method of adjusting to problems, but it is not mature or constructive. Facing and coping directly with the anxiety-arousing situation can often be too painful for us to attempt. A useful compromise between these two extremes is the use of humor.

Humor can be an anxiety-reducing mechanism. Man's ability to look ahead and imagine things frequently builds up anxiety within himself. His ability to create humor helps reduce this anxiety and restores a balance. If we can find some humor in our own situation when things look black, we generally feel better. The toastmaster who gets his tongue twisted in introducing the distinguished speaker and who can laugh at his own mistake is probably healthier emotionally than the toastmaster who broods for days after making such a mistake. The nervous salesman with sweaty palms and shaking hands who can chuckle at himself and say, "Boy, you'd think I was walking the last mile," is well on his way toward overcoming his anxiety. Humor helps us see life situations in a different, larger, and less tragic perspective.

A sales manager once used humor to help one of his men overcome severe call reluctance. The manager suggested to the man that as he entered the office of a particular prospect, he should picture how the man might look if he were sitting behind his desk without his pants on. The image concocted by the salesman was naturally very funny. When he did enter a prospect's office and remembered his manager's suggestion, he approached the prospect in a smiling, light-hearted mood. Interestingly enough, he was no longer uneasy.

The suggestion by the manager actually did two things to help the salesman find some relief from his anxiety. First, it introduced humor into an otherwise anxiety-arousing situation. Second, but perhaps more important, it focused his attention not on himself but on the prospect, where of course it should have been. While we may question this manager's particular suggestion, the end result of using some form of humor was successful in overcoming call reluctance.

THE DELICATE EQUILIBRIUM AND ITS CONTROL

From infancy to adulthood we engage in countless learning experiences, meet with countless frustrations, and are faced with countless conflicts which must somehow be resolved if we are to move forward. Generally, we try to move in the direction of receiving pleasure and away from receiving pain or punishment. We are often in conflict because we need things which are themselves in conflict or opposed to each other. We are often in conflict because various people who are important to us want us to live in ways which conflict with each other. As we become uncomfortable for any reason, we are aroused to activity which we hope will make us more comfortable. Human growth and development, then, may be thought of as a never-ending cycle of establishing an equilibrium, having the equilibrium disturbed, and finding it necessary to establish a new equilibrium. *We are balanced somewhere between doing what we want to do and what other people want us to do.*

If we are to get along reasonably well with people who are important to us, it is necessary that we strike a balance between doing what we want to do and doing what they want us to. We can do this by compromising, and emphasize the points on which we agree with another person and minimize the points on which we disagree.

In spite of our best effort to maintain an acceptable equilibrium or balance between the many forces which bear upon us, we often find that we are not maintaining a satisfactory equilibrium. We are "off balance." Statistics show that approximately one of ten persons will at some time be hospitalized for severe mental illness. This means that their balance will be disturbed sufficiently so that they cannot take care of themselves in our society. One out of four families will at some time or another have a member in a mental hospital. It is estimated that at least fifty percent of the patients visiting a general medical practitioner are suffering from mental or emotional illness or from a physical illness closely associated with a mental illness.

When our delicate equilibrium is disturbed and we find it difficult or impossible to maintain a healthy balance in life, something has happened to our control mechanism. As we have seen, this equilibrium becomes disturbed if certain vital areas of our psychological life are repressed or unconscious. If our perception of the world is grossly distorted, we will be receiving faulty information and will fall into the trap of nonlogical thinking. Maintaining our equilibrium depends to a large extent upon our ability *to observe our own behavior scientifically, to understand the causes and consequences* of our own behavior, and *to readjust our behavior* on the basis of new information. Acquiring a deeper understanding of human behavior and its endless possiblities and variations will help us maintain a more effective equilibrium throughout life.

SUMMARY

We experience conflict and frustration daily. Living in a crowded, complex society there is little we can do to avoid conflict, but we can determine to react to it constructively rather than destructively. Intelligent efforts to solve the conflict can replace blind aggression against the source of conflict. Frustration tolerance is one measure of the mature personality. The most mature individual can allow himself to depend on others when necessary and is dependable when others seek his help. But this interdependence may lead to more conflict than the person would experience if he chose to be independent or a "loner." It is not avoiding conflict but how we look at it which determines the degree of success we experience.

We learn to see our world in a unique way. Individuals differ in their perceptions, attitudes, frames of reference, and methods of solving problems. Sometimes we are aware of the attitudes which shape our behavior but often we are not. Becoming aware of the unconscious forces which influence us takes practice and helps resolve conflicts. While individuals seem to differ in their basic intelligence, the ability to reason and solve problems can be improved greatly. Being able to handle the anxiety which often accompanies conflict opens the way to more effective conflict resolution.

QUESTIONS FOR DISCUSSION AND THOUGHT

1. Is aggression ever a constructive reaction to frustration? Explain.
2. Why is independence as a characteristic not the same as full emotional maturity?
3. How should we analyze the situation when we hear a person giving an "eyewitness" account of something?
4. What is meant by the expression, "Needs determine perception"? What are the implications of this idea for the businessman, parent, or child?
5. If we are not aware of what goes on in our unconscious, how can we do anything about unconscious distortion of our perceptions? Give an example of steps we can take to discover unconscious influences on our own behavior.
6. What prevents us from using intelligence and reasoning to solve conflict?
7. What is the similarity between the processes of reasoning and the scientific method described in Chapter 1?
8. Give an example from your own experience to illustrate the anxiety-reducing effects of humor.

3

SOCIALIZATION AND PERSONAL FREEDOM

The greatest gift God's bounty has created,
The gift that most conforms to His own good,
That He himself of all most precious holds,
Is freedom of the will, wherewith are blest
All creatures that possess intelligence;
But they, and only they, are so endowed.[1]

If the will of every man were free, that is, if every man could act as he chose, the whole of history would be a tissue of disconnected accidents.[2]

In 1789, the year of our Constitution, men desperate to avoid the tyrannies of pre-Revolutionary foreign control signed their names to a document unparalleled in the world. But this blueprint for a nation was already a compromise with freedom; the Articles of Confederation ratified by the colonies in 1783 had provided for a national government too weak to deal effectively with other nations, provide for its own funding, or cope with the problems between the states, The Constitution of 1789 provided for a much stronger national government. The ten amendments guaranteeing individual freedom seemed to make possible the dream of "life, liberty, and the pursuit of happiness" which was uppermost in the minds

---

[1] Dante Alighieri, *The Divine Comedy,* trans. Lawrence Grant White (New York: Pantheon Books, 1948), Paradiso, Canto 5, line 19, p 136.
[2] Lev Nikolaevich Tolstoy, *War and Peace* Epilogue, Part II, Chapter 8.

of people in the eighteenth century. How far has that freedom eroded as we approach the end of the twentieth century?

How free are we? Sociologists, students of society, claim that social control is necessary if a society is to exist at all. Social control ". . . refers to the various means used by a society to bring its recalcitrant members back into line."[3] Customs, manners, systems of morality, ridicule and gossip, laws, taxes, police action, martial law, covert or overt racial or sex or religious discrimination, licensing boards, trade unions, threat of ostracism, unwritten rules for admission to clubs, lodges, fraternal organizations, opinions of friends and relatives, level of income and social class, place of birth and place of residence . . . in view of these forms of social control of the thoughts and behavior of the individual, how can anyone continue to believe in the myth of full personal freedom?

We observed in Chapter 1 that man is both a *seeker of truth* and a *deceiver of self.* Montaigne, who created the literary form known as the *essay,* wrote in the sixteenth century, "I speak truth, not so much as I would, but as much as I dare; and I dare a little more, as I grow older."[4] If we consider Montaigne a wise man, then he is reporting that with increasing wisdom comes added willingness to face the truth. Admittedly out of context, it appears in John 9:32, ". . . and you will know the truth, and the truth will make you free." Does it not seem logical that freedom for the individual comes with the acceptance of truth, as far as it can be known, and that loss of freedom accompanies any effort to deceive?

The individual is born into a family from a particular socioeconomic stratum within a subculture, within a city in a state of a nation in a hemisphere of a globe (seen for the first time in its entirety in color photographs from an Apollo space flight) on which mankind must coexist or die. Individual behavior is influenced by an enormously intricate network of social and cultural forces which are largely invisible and subtle and therefore powerful and pervasive. Freedom would seem to come to those enlightened persons who most clearly recognize the manifold pressures which shape and limit personal freedom. In this paradoxical statement is the main impetus for scientific exploration in both the physical and the social sciences.

To the average American, freedom of action and choice is important.

---

[3] Peter L. Berger, *Invitation to Sociology: A Humanistic Perspective* (Garden City, New York: Doubleday Company, Inc., 1963), p. 68.
[4] Michel DeMontaigne, *Of Profit and Honesty,* Book III, Chapter 1.

Perhaps there is little conscious thought given to this concept of personal freedom on a day-to-day basis, but let the individual perceive that his freedom is abridged either by another individual or by the government, and his outcry is loud and clear. The first amendment to the U.S. Constitution guarantees freedom of speech. The man in the street feels free to express his opinion: except *politically* when with his boss who voted for a different candidate; except *recreationally* with his wife who doesn't understand his interest in football; except in *buying* when the persuasive salesman insists that double-breasted suits are "in", except *humorously* with a mixed group where the latest dirty story has to remain untold; except . . . The point is that we are influenced in thousands of ways of which we are minimally or not at all aware. We think we exercise free choice when we purchase a product widely advertised, not realizing that subtle forces pounded into us after countless repetitions on radio and TV have relentlessly "programmed" us frequently to respond like Pavlov's dog which was conditioned to salivate to the ringing of a bell.

THE INDIVIDUAL LOST IN THE CROWD?

"All men are created equal." This is one of the beliefs that we hold to most strongly in our American culture. What we mean by this is that men are equal in the sense of being valuable in and of themselves and in their right to equal opportunity. While in practice we do not always behave as if we believed this, especially in regard to minority groups, generally this is part of the philosophy of life held by most Americans. In all other ways, however, we are quite different from each other.

We differ in terms of our various positions within the different groups of which we are members. The position we occupy in a group can be thought of as our *status* in that group. We know that as we were graduated from high school, we enjoyed a high status as members of the senior class. But as we moved on to college we found ourselves at the bottom of the ladder again in the status of freshmen. As we go on through life and become members of various groups, we find that our status in the group varies depending on our abilities, our length of time in the group, and perhaps our "social background." We occupy a high status in some of our groups and a low status in others. The position we occupy in any group is of vital importance to us and helps determine our individual behavior.

One of the obvious facts about our society is that we are divided into various groups depending on our income, actions, beliefs, attitudes, values, and occupations. One way of discussing the various layers in our society is by use of the concept "social classes." Generally we can divide our society into upper, middle, and lower classes. This classification can be further extended to an upper-upper class, a lower-upper class, an upper-middle class and a lower-middle class, and an upper-lower and a lower-lower class.

Each of these classes has somewhat different value systems, different interests, and different goals. In general, the so-called upper classes in America are individuals of greater than ordinary wealth. The occupations of people within this class include bankers, corporation executives, attorneys, physicians, engineers, and business proprietors. In the upper class, family background and family tradition are of great importance. Upper-class family members are usually long-time residents in their communities.

Occupation is an important element in determining our social status and may be one of the best single measures for determining our rank in the community. In the mind of the public, all familiar occupations in the United States carry with them definite prestige values. In an opinion poll to determine just what these values were, a Supreme Court Justice, a physician, and a state governor were ranked at the top in terms of prestige, and the shoe-shiner, street sweeper, and garbage collector ranked at the bottom.

One of our most prized freedoms, although we may take it for granted, is that of occupational choice. Assuming that we can obtain the necessary training and education, any of the more than forty thousand jobs listed in the *Dictionary of Occupational Titles* is open to us. But is it? Sociological studies show a continuing tendency for sons to hold jobs in occupational categories very similar to those of their fathers.[5] It appears that the socioeconomic class of the family into which one is born strongly conditions one to follow in his father's footsteps. The family, friends, the neighborhood, and the school so influence the child that his "free choice" of occupation is sharply limited to a relatively narrow range of jobs. Of course, there is some class mobility in that a son of a laboring-class family may enter one of the professions, but the small percentage of such children doing this tends to confirm the observation of intergenerational recapitulation: "Like father, like son."

Intelligence levels of high school seniors influence the hopes these students have of entering jobs having high social status; those of higher intelligence aspire to higher status levels of occupations. But when stu-

[5] Reported in E. K. Wilson, *Sociology: Rules, Roles and Relationships* (Homewood, Ill.: The Dorsey Press, 1966), pp. 190–194.

dents of similar intelligence but differing in the socioeconomic class of their families are compared, the research findings show that the hope of entering occupational categories varies directly with the class background.[6] The image the child has of himself is shaped during the highly formative years he spends in his family group. The child of a professional family is exposed to different people as family friends, different literature in the home, different recreational experiences, and to a whole way of life different from that of a child born into a lower-class family where the father works at an unskilled or semi-skilled job. The child would probably "see himself" doing work similar to that of which he was aware and could not see himself doing a type of work unfamiliar to him. Occupational guidance experts may succeed in "freeing" a child of high native ability, but lower-class expectations, by helping him to become aware of a wider range of occupations. This alone will probably not be sufficient to counteract the subtle and pervasive social conditioning of the child's early background, but it could be a start.

Perhaps mobility is the real key to human freedom and security. Awareness leads to mobility and mobility leads to freedom. The freedom we speak of here is similar to the concept of "true freedoms of man: To do all of which he is capable . . . to realize his full potential within his society . . . to speak what is in his mind . . . to go his own way without interference from other men."[7] There is no way we can be completely beyond the influence of our social conditioning, but awareness of these cultural constraints and increased awareness of the intricacies of human behavior are ways of achieving human freedom and security which are available to all of us who are ready to learn.

To an overwhelming extent our buying habits, voting patterns, religious preferences, sexual habits, occupational choices, and life styles reflect the traditions and expectations of the group culture into which we were born. It is true that each of us develops a *unique* and *identifiable* way of behaving that is called our personality. We develop into a person unlike any other. We are individuals. And we wish to be treated as individuals by our friends, relatives, work colleagues, and those trade or professional people with whom we deal. We do not stand alone as individuals, however, but instead are buffeted by a sea of social forces and pressures which are only partly visible. In one sense we are free to come and go as we please,

---

[6] *Ibid.*, pp. 210–212.
[7] Davis W. Gregg, "Freedom and Security," 1970 CLU Forum Report.

but in a larger sense we are blocked by visible and invisible barriers. These forces and barriers are *social* forces and *social* barriers.

MAN, THE SOCIAL ANIMAL

Man is a social animal. He lives, works, and creates as a member of a group. He is made more free from the restrictions of his environment because of the help he gives and gets in groups. But, at the same time, he is hemmed in and held prisoner by his group memberships. Man is an animal that can care more about the good will of his group than about his life. He may actually commit suicide because he perceives that he has "lost face" in the eyes of a group important to him. He is stimulated to great heights of creativity by the approval or love of others, but outside influence can also demand slavish conformity.

We are obviously influenced by the person next to us on the bus, by our neighbor, by our family and friends. But our social environment also includes many people we never or seldom see, such as the mayor of our town, the manager of the radio or TV station, the local censor of the movies, etc. There are literally thousands of people who affect the way we live, although many of them do so indirectly.

An even broader and more far-reaching influence on the way we behave is known as our *culture.* The influence of our culture is powerful precisely because it is a subtle, often unseen, force which is hard to pin down. Because our culture plays such an important part in every human relationship, it becomes an important subject of study for the person who wants to be more effective in motivating himself and in achieving effective interpersonal relationships.

The Concept of Culture

What is culture? The word *culture* has acquired different meanings and is consequently a confusing word. Culture is popularly thought of as a special training or refining of the mind or manners and the acquiring of certain tastes. Used in this sense, we might say of an individual that he is "cultured." Another meaning of the word has to do with *a way of life for a group of people.* Culture in this sense includes *the behavior patterns which are learned, the attitudes which are transmitted from one person to another and which were created by man.* It is in the latter sense that culture will be discussed here.

Culture is a collection of ideas. Culture is the pattern of ideas and habits in men's minds which gives them the solution to many of their problems. Culture is that part of a person's surroundings, or environment, which is socially created. Culture is made up of all the achievements of all the people who have ever lived within a certain area to the extent that these achievements have been remembered or recorded or somehow communicated to people who are now living.

One tiny facet of our culture is the idea of "ladies first." In another culture, the woman walks behind her husband. Other facets of our culture are underground sewers and chlorinated water, football, the hot dog and ice-cream cone, the Sunday drive, the new model car every year, soap operas, free elections, large hospitals and mental institutions, the concept of life insurance, taxes, and an almost endless list of other things. Like a jewel with an almost infinite number of facets or surfaces, our culture is a compound or collection of material things, ideas about material things, and ideas about ideas.

The Significance of Culture

The influence of culture is of tremendous importance in motivating men to act socially. Culture is all around us and moves us in obvious and mysterious ways. Culture is as ever-present as the air we breathe. We cannot actually see the wind blow. We can only see the effect of the force of the wind. When the wind blows hard, we automatically lean in the direction of the wind to maintain our balance. We grab our hats or hold down our skirts, and we do these things almost without realizing it. In the same way, our culture exerts pressures upon us and we almost automatically move in response to these pressures. If we could somehow develop a conscious, objective view of cultural pressures, we could be more aware of their influence. The study of culture allows us to do that very thing. It is impossible to have a complete understanding of one's own culture; too much of it is unconscious. But the more we can learn about the seen and unseen things which influence us individually and as group members, the more we can predict and control not only our own behavior, but that of other people as well.

Culture Can Be Thought Of as a Balance Wheel

Culture allows a large group of individuals to exist with a minimum amount of disruptive variation. We can expect, for example, that as we drive down the street, most of the other drivers will stop for red lights and stop signs, and, in the American culture, will drive on the right-hand side of the street. The fact that cultural patterns exist allows us to do a much better job of predicting human behavior. Individuals who come from a common cultural background are likely to have similar responses to the problems and situations they face. Culture provides many ready-made solutions to the problems that each of us face. This is a tremendous advantage since it elminates much trial-and-error experimentation that we would otherwise have to go through in order to find our own individual solution to problems of daily living. Culture, then, makes our society more *consistent,* more *predictable,* and more *economical* in the sense of conserving human time and energy.

The All-American Culture

There is not much in our American way of life that is exclusively "American." Much of what we do and much of what we are have been borrowed from other cultures and other times, The following description helps us understand this process of cultures contributing to one another, sometimes referred to as *cultural diffusion:*

Our solid American citizen awakens in a bed built on a pattern which originated in the Near East, but which was modified in Northern Europe before it was transmitted to America. He throws back the covers made from cotton, domesticated in India, or linen domesticated in the Near East, or wool from sheep, also domesticated in the Near East, or silk, the use of which was discovered in China. All of these materials have been spun and woven by processes invented in the Near East. He slips into his moccasins, invented by the Indians of the Eastern woodlands, and goes to the bathroom, whose fixtures are a mixture of European and American inventions, both of recent date. He takes off his pajamas, a garment invented in India, and washes with soap invented by the ancient Gauls. He then shaves, a masochistic rite which seems to have been derived from either Sumer or ancient Egypt.

Returning to the bedroom, he removes his clothes from a chair of southern European type and proceeds to dress. He puts on garments whose form originally derived from the skin clothing of the nomads of the Asiatic steppes, puts on shoes made from skins tanned by a process invented in ancient Egypt, and cut to a pattern derived from the classical civilization of the Mediterranean, and ties around his neck a strip of bright-colored cloth which is a vestigial survival of the shoulder shawls worn by the seventeenth century Croatians. Before going out for breakfast, he glances through the window, made of glass invented in Egypt, and if it is raining, puts on overshoes made of rubber discovered by the Central American Indians and takes an umbrella, invented in southeastern Asia. Upon his head he puts a hat made of felt, a material invented in the Asiatic steppes.

On his way to breakfast he stops to buy a paper, paying for it with coins, an ancient Lydian invention. At the restaurant a whole new series of borrowed elements confronts him. His plate is made of a form of pottery invented in China. His knife is of steel, an alloy first made in southern India, his fork a medieval Italian invention, and his spoon a derivative of a Roman original. He begins breakfast with an orange, from the eastern Mediterranean, a cantaloupe from Persia, or perhaps a piece of African watermelon. With this he has coffee, an Abyssinian plant, with cream and sugar. Both the domestication of cows and the idea of milking them originated in the Near East, while sugar was first made in India. After his fruit and first coffee, he goes on to waffles, cakes made by a Scandinavian technique from wheat domesticated in Asia Minor. Over these he pours maple syrup, invented by the Indians of the Eastern woodlands. As a side dish he may have the eggs of a species of bird domesticated in Indo-China, or thin strips of the flesh of an animal domesticated in Eastern Asia which have been salted and smoked by a process developed in northern Europe.

When our friend has finished eating, he settles back to smoke, an American Indian habit, consuming a plant domesticated in Brazil in either a pipe, derived from the Indians of Virginia, or a cigarette, derived from Mexico. If he is hardy enough, he may even attempt a cigar, transmitted to us from the Antilles by way of Spain. While smoking he reads the news of the day, imprinted in characters invented in Germany. As he absorbs the accounts of foreign troubles, he will, if he is a good conservative citizen, thank a Hebrew deity in an Indo-European language that he is 100 per cent American.[8]

When we listen to a politician tell us that, if he is elected, he will do everything in his power to maintain "the American way of life," just what

[8] From Ralph Linton, *The Study of Man* (New York: D. Appleton-Century Company, Inc., 1936). Reprinted by permission of Appleton-Century-Crofts, Inc.

does he mean? He is talking essentially about our total culture. Because the phrase includes so much, it has relatively little meaning. One of the most outstanding characteristics of our nation is the amazing diversity of its people. America constitutes not one culture, but many. Rather than talk about "the American way of life," it is more accurate to speak of the American *ways* of life. As a nation, we are tied together by a common language and a common form of government. But regional differences in customs, values, opinions, and attitudes vary so much that we can understand the American way of life only by studying its variability. Within any one region there are likely to be a number of races and nationality groups. These various subgroups have their own characteristic ways of thinking and acting. We can think of these groups as cultures within a culture, and we refer to them as subcultures.

From the beginning, America has been heterogeneous in its composition. Immigrant groups making up the American population have originated in various European and Asian countries, such as Germany, Sweden, Italy, Russia, Greece, England, China, Japan, etc., and each of these groups brought with them unique cultural practices. With the passage of time, there has been a certain mixture among these subcultures. Some regions of the United States still contain predominantly German or Swedish, Italian or Chinese groups which can be recognized as distinct subcultures with their own customs, mannerisms, vocabulary, values, and goals. "Chinatown" is an example of a small subculture within the larger culture of San Francisco within the still larger culture of California.

Each individual is a *product* of the total American culture (or foreign national culture, if foreign-born) plus several smaller cultures. Each of the cultural influences has shaped his way of thinking, his way of responding to events, his beliefs, attitudes, prejudices, preferences, and perceptions. The businessman reared in an upper-class home in Utah, who has grown up in the Mormon Church, who was an Eagle Scout and is currently the president of a leading civic club in Los Angeles, will not hear the same things said by his financial adviser as will the person who was a member of a street gang, educated in a trade school for "exceptional" children, who manages a ladies' ready-to-wear shop and is now the vice president of the same civic club in Los Angeles.

These two men are different personalities partly because of their different cultural backgrounds. They may be wearing almost identical suits, support the same candidate for mayor, and both appear on a list of prospects obtained by the adviser from the same client. But their different cultural backgrounds have given them a different slant on life, and a different way of reacting to motivational appeals. The person who has an awareness of cultural variations within our own overall culture and who realizes the impact of these variations on his own effectiveness as a motivator will have an edge over his colleague who does not.

Ethnocentrism as a Cultural Value

It is difficult to conceive of what a one hundred percent American would be like. Within the broad American culture are hundreds of subcultures which, because they are specific and local, have a more direct influence on the behavior of the person growing up in that situation. Inevitably, when groups differ, or when people from different subcultures come into contact, conflict arises. One characteristic of people within a certain cultural group is that they usually feel superior to those from other groups. This emotional attitude that one's own race, nation, city, religion, political affiliation, or culture is superior to all others is called *ethnocentrism.* An ethnic group, then, possesses characteristics, values, attitudes, and behavior patterns in common.

Ethnocentrism appears to be characteristic of all cultures in all parts of the world. This attitude is a measure of the loyalty necessary for the self-identification and persistence of the groups. Group members resist, both consciously and unconsciously, any threat to the stability of the group. This need to resist influence from the outside may be in the form of attack on outside groups, isolation from different groups, or pressure applied to inside members to avoid criticism of the group itself. An example of this is the appearance of bumper stickers with the slogan, "America—love it or leave it." While our form of government guarantees the individual's right to be openly critical of that government itself, overzealous (ethnocentric) citizens may take it upon themselves to decide that anyone who does not fully support all domestic and foreign policies should therefore live elsewhere.

Ethnocentrism can have the function, then, of maintaining the security of the group, and at the same time enforcing a rigid conformity which retards or prevents needed changes and improvements. One difficulty in being highly ethnocentric is that it is not an objective point of view. The person who feels that his particular likes and affiliations are superior to those of his colleagues may keep himself from a full appreciation of his colleagues. He would have difficulty understanding and cooperating with them. When we consider our own culture to be the best and fail to learn from other cultures and subcultures, much can be lost.

What does the concept of ethnocentrism say to the individual who lives in the world of business and depends on his effectiveness in working with people to provide a livelihood for his family? The self-centeredness of ethnocentrism not only diminishes objectivity in seeing and understanding others, but also becomes a real barrier to communication. It furthermore interferes with the coordination of efforts of those with whom we work. Ethnocentrism spawns prejudice, suspicion, antagonism, hatred, ill will, and blindness to the ideas and the multiple contributions made by people of varying backgrounds. The financial consultant, whether he be in life insurance, mutual funds, securities, real estate, or a trust officer, attorney, etc., finds that his clientele consists of people from every type of ethnic group, some of which he likes and others he dislikes. These likes and dislikes are probably the result of early social conditioning, but the sentiments remain to bias the perception. These likes and dislikes are bound to influence the results of coordinative efforts, in spite of the conscious wishes of the participants.

If our early cultural conditioning leads to preconceived notions of superiority and inferiority, the probability increases that we will engage in behavioral patterns which are essentially self-defeating. The individual who defeats himself through prejudiced perceptions of those on whom his success depends and who is unaware of the self-defeating nature of his perceptions, is doomed to repeat a pattern of diminished accomplishment and lessened satisfaction. The person who becomes aware of how *his perceptions are determined by his culture,* and who *practices the art of scientific thinking* rather than falling victim to the scourge of "tribal superstition," achieves a partial or full measure of human freedom. This is dependent upon his mastery of confrontation with reality. When we confront what is there, we stand a chance of becoming a real, authentic, genuine, self-determining, free individual.[9]

SPECIFIC GROUP INFLUENCE

We are what we are largely because of what we have learned from our culture. We acquire our culture through the influence of various groups of

[9] See Rollo May, *Love and Will* (New York: W. W. Norton and Company, Inc., 1969).

which we are a member. It is through a group that a child learns to behave in certain ways. It is through a group that a child becomes civilized and able eventually to *contribute* to later group activity as well as to *receive* knowledge from the group. When someone asks you, "Who are you?" you are likely, after giving your name, to identify yourself as being a member of a group. Depending on the occasion, your answer may be, "I am an American citizen, I am a banker, a Democrat," etc. Upon reflection we realize that we are members of not just one or two or three groups, but as many as forty or fifty different kinds of groups.

We can be a member of these kinds of groups: a generation, a community, a religion, an ethnic group, a country, a family, a neighborhood, a region, a social class, a nation, a state, a county, a ward, a political party, a club, an industrial or work group, or a pressure group. Occasionally, we are members of groups which might be called *informal groups,* such as passengers on a commuters' train, shoppers in a department store, patrons of a theater, or a crowd watching a football game.

A person's behavior is likely to change a great deal, depending on the groups of which he *sees himself* a member. A man may behave differently at his lodge meeting than he does when he puts on his uniform and marches in a public parade. We accept boisterous behavior in an individual during a parade or party, but in the office we are annoyed by such behavior. Knowing something about a man's specific group memberships allows us to know quite a bit about the man himself. Such knowledge *increases our ability to "motivate" and influence his behavior.*

We deceive ourselves if we think that we can stand apart from our society or group memberships. From infancy we are molded by the customs and beliefs of our family group. As we enter any kind of school system, we are again members of a group which has far-reaching influence on our behavior patterns. At any time in our life, unless we are on an island completely by ourselves, we are pressured and molded by the influence of groups. Group pressure can cause us to change our opinions. A group may control rewards and punishments and thereby exert a powerful influence on us. A group forces us to conform. The individual who thinks he is taking independent action in defying the norms of a particular group is usually only rigidly conforming to another group which supports his "rebellion." The college student who participates in a campus rebellion against the "establishment" administration may be rigidly conforming to another group which means more to him: a student activist movement. Conformity is conformity wherever we find it.

The Group Defined

A group may be defined as consisting of two or more people between or among whom there is a pattern of social interaction. A group is recognized as such because of a particular type of selective behavior. A group may be formal or informal. The formal group usually has rules and regulations which are written down and understood, and it is characterized by a good deal of organization and structure. The informal group, such as friendships, cliques, etc., is less well-organized and the rules of behavior are implicit rather than explicit.

The Importance of Understanding Groups

In our business or professional work, we usually deal with individuals, but these individuals are members of various groups. Knowing something about groups and how they function is, therefore, important (1) because of the influence of the group on the individual, and (2) because of the influence of the group on the way our society functions. Society consists of groups whose makeup is determined in part by the individuals in the groups. A neighborhood group which is organized in the sense of holding a certain view regarding community matters can exert great influence and pressure on city government. In the same way, pressure groups influence the members of our legislatures who in turn pass laws which affect us.

As we have seen, man has biological needs, needs for physical protection from the elements, and a *strong drive to belong to a group.* He feels more secure within a group and he also needs to feel that he is personally important and significant to the groups of which he is a member. When an individual joins a group, he brings to it his unique contributions, abilities, experiences, etc. It is usually advantageous for the group to include him as a member just as it is advantageous for him to be a member.

While he gives much to the group, he also must give up some of his own desires in order to be a satisfactory member of it. He cannot always do what he wants to do, but must sacrifice some personal desires to enjoy the benefits of his membership in the group. At the same time, it is important for the group to recognize the individuality of its members. This adjustment of the individual to his group and the adjustment of the group to the individual is referred to as a *fusion process.* In a later section on conformity and creativity we will see some of the intensely important ramifications of the conflict between the individual and his group.

The Family Group—Transmitters of Culture

One of the important groups of our society is the family. One's culture is acquired or learned at first largely from his parents. Much of what the parent teaches the child about his culture is taught consciously. We make a conscious effort to teach our children "good" eating habits, toilet training, ways of dressing, and the like. Yet we are unaware of much of what we teach our children about our culture. Our culture moves us to behave in certain ways without our being conscious of it. We pass these behavior patterns on to our children, likewise being unaware that we are teaching them.

A child is taught what he is permitted to do or forbidden to do by the kind of reaction his parents show to his actions. For behavior of which the parents approve, the child receives rewards in terms of smiles or even gifts. But if he does things which he should not do, he quickly discovers that his parents are disturbed and react to him with displeasure. Families are not alike in terms of their basic attitudes or structures. To some heads of a household, their families are their most important possessions, while to other husbands and fathers there may be little concern about their families' existence or their continuance as family groups. In some families, the husband and father is the dominant figure, whereas in others the mother assumes this role. These are some of the many things a salesman must consider if he plans a sales approach to the family.

The Changing Function of the American Family

The family as an institution is undergoing marked changes in its functions.[10] Patterns of family life have been changing gradually, corresponding with the shift in this country from an agricultural to an industrialized nation. In the early years, the family was much more of an economic group than it is now. The husband and father frequently worked in the home or near it and quite often the entire family participated in his "business." This type of family unit is still found in certain parts of the country, especially in rural communities.

[10] For a thought-provoking critique of the modern American family, see David Cooper, *The Death of the Family* (New York: Pantheon Books, 1971).

Increased urbanization along with the techniques of mass production not only has increased available material goods and services but has changed standards of living and the way family members relate to each other. As the various functions of the family change, the role of the children in the family also changes. In the predominantly rural culture of the nineteenth century, children were an economic aid to their parents. This was true partly because it was difficult to hire adult help. Children could be put to work at no cost. In modern urban culture, children are probably as much an economic liability as anything. More and more education is required to train them for a more complex economic system. There is less tendency for children to be employed by their parents or to help their parents in their old age. Perhaps the greatest satisfaction that parents have today is the affection they receive from their children, instead of any economic return.

While it is a culturally accepted assumption that parents are vitally interested in their children's future education and welfare, actually many parents may be reluctant to sacrifice for the comfort of their children tomorrow. This attitude would perhaps not be admitted to a stranger but may be a factor in whether or not an education-fund savings account is started, life insurance is purchased, a school bond issue is voted for, etc.

The function of the family is also changing in its role as an educational institution. Less responsibility is being assumed by the family for the teaching of the children. There appears also to be a tendency for the parents to give public school systems and churches the responsibility for teaching the child basic values and religion as well as formal education.[11]

Generally speaking, the home and family have become less and less the place for recreation. Members of the family find their recreation with more organized "institutions" such as motion pictures, radio and television programs, state parks, clubs and other associations.

Partly as a result of its changing function in its economic, educational, and recreational life, the family has lost a large part of its control over its members. Whereas the father was the principal authority figure for children for many years, modern children receive much of their discipline from other men and women outside the home, especially during the school years.

[11] Research findings and insights into the changing parent–child relationship are reported in Urie Bronfenbrenner, "The Split-level American Family," *Saturday Review,* October 7, 1967, pp. 60–66.

The Changing Roles of Mothers and Fathers

The role of the man in the family is also undergoing changes. At the turn of the twentieth century, the father was most often the unquestioned head of the household and the source of authority. Legally the wife had little status. The man made all decisions regarding money and property, and his wife was considered to have almost no legal rights. The man owned and controlled his wife's property, and also controlled anything she earned after marriage. While the legal status of the American wife and mother in a few of our states is no different now, generally speaking it has changed considerably.

More women are receiving higher education and training for business activities. Such women frequently see their role of homemaker as drudgery and they view it with resentment. There is an increasing tendency for women to participate in various activities outside their home and family. The women's liberation movement represents a pent-up desire of many women to acquire more control over their lives and satisfactions. That this movement is threatening to many males illustrates the relative and shaky basis of the social concepts of "masculinity" and "femininity."

In many ways, the wife and mother of the family unit is less and less dependent upon the family for many of her satisfactions. She is less dependent on her mate for security. Women not only have more choice in the kind of men they pick for husbands but are freer to follow a career or occupational pursuit of their choice. This increased independence in woman's role as a wife and mother has brought with it some confusion in her own mind as to what her role should be. One of the most frequent conflicts existing within the American wife and mother is the degree to which she should be either homemaker or career woman. These conflicts and uncertainties tend to weaken the structure of the family group.

Women are becoming more important in decision-making, especially with regard to decisions on making purchases for the family. More and more, the family structure is such that the husband and wife share the responsibility for making decisions.

STATUS AND ROLE

Status refers to a position that we hold in a group. An individual's relative status in a group has sometimes been compared to the "pecking order" among chickens. In the barnyard the chickens peck each other according to some rather rigid rules. At the top of the order is one chicken that pecks but is not pecked by any other chicken; at the other end of the scale is a chicken that is pecked but in turn does not peck any other chicken. Likewise, people see themselves as being above some and more powerful, but below and inferior to others.

> All the world's a stage,
> And all the men and women merely players.
> They have their exits and their entrances:
> And one man in his time plays many parts.[12]

Most of us are members of a great many different groups, and since we have a rather distinct status within each group we consequently play many roles. We may play the role of the strong, dominant, aggressive business-man during the daytime, but change to the role of the meek, respectful husband as we come home to our wife in the evening. We may play the role of the dashing, sophisticated, brilliant conversationalist while chatting with a pretty girl at a cocktail party, but later play the role of the gruff, inarticulate male when called upon for our opinions at a P.T.A. meeting.

To be a member of any social group we must behave to some extent as the members of the group expect us to. If we fail to play the role as it is outlined, we may be expelled from the group. If an individual steps out of his role, if he behaves in ways that are not expected of him, we feel that he has somehow made a mistake, "gotten out of hand," and needs to be "brought back into line."

The more important our group is to us the more rigidly we are likely to persist in playing the role expected of us. But the role we play is more than just a series of activities. Our role includes an appropriate emotional response. A funeral director may make all the necessary arrangements to insure a decent and dignified burial, but if he hums and smiles while doing this because business is good, those who observe him are likely to feel that he is not properly "playing his role." The mother who takes excellent care of her children but who does not show the expected emotions of warmth and love gives others the impression that she is not properly playing her role as a mother.

When we talk about the role we play in life, we are referring to a pattern of behavior that is appropriate or expected in a given situation. In using this term *role*, we are not using it in the same sense as the role an

[12] William Shakespeare, *As You Like It,* Act II, Scene 7.

actor plays, because most of the time we are not particularly aware we are playing a role. We only become conscious of our expected role or that of someone else when the role is not played as it should be.

When we enter a new group, we frequently are unaware of exactly what our role should be. The members themselves may not be consciously aware of the expected role we should play. There is usually agreement, however, when the expected role is not followed. As with conformity in general, deviating from the expected role draws increased attention to ourselves and generates some activity on the part of the group to force us back into the expected role. Many of our social standards and our role expectations are unwritten rules, but deviation from these rules is recognized and often punished just as swiftly—if not more so—as our well-known and clearly stated civil laws.

We learn what to do in a given situation, we learn to play a certain role, largely by watching other people. We see *learning by imitation* most clearly in children. Every father knows how his son tries hard to imitate him in behavior, in posture, and even in dress by clomping around in his father's shoes. When we join a new club, we alert ourselves to the particular customs and manners of the members so that we can "fit in."

To borrow Emerson's metaphor about groups and their leaders, we might say that the organization is the "lengthened shadow" of the man who heads it. This is, on the one hand, a description of the group and the way it is structured, and, on the other hand, an important principle of motivation. The careful, cautious sales manager who emphasizes service to the customer is likely to "teach" this role to his men. The manager who likes to "do things in a big way" will be indirectly teaching quite a different role to his men. An example of behavior is set by the manager and copied by the salesman, usually without awareness on the part of either.

Role Conflict

We all play many roles, and some of these roles are in direct opposition to each other. This does not normally cause difficulty because we can separate our several roles, either in time or in distance. We sometimes read in the newspapers how it is possible for a man to play the role of the dutiful husband to two different wives as long as the wives are in different cities. A problem arises when the distance between the two wives is reduced or eliminated!

The role a man plays at the company's conventions varies according to whether or not his wife accompanies him. If his wife is along, he may play the role which seems appropriate to her but strange to his colleagues who are familiar with his role-playing activities during previous conventions when his wife was not with him.

We play one role as the father of our children and quite a different role when we take them to visit our own parents. A visit to the grandparents is often strained, precisely because we feel compelled to play two conflicting roles. We may experience conflict with the roles we must play in another important area. The manager may be well aware of the role he must play in order to contribute to the profits of his company. If, however, he is in doubt as to the quality of his company or if he feels that its products or services are inferior to others, he will feel a certain amount of personal conflict. Under such circumstances, he may find it difficult to carry out, at the same time, the expected role of a manager and the expected role of an honest, decent individual of integrity.

Sex Roles

We are pleasantly aware that there are differences between male and female. The biological differences are important, but of equal importance are the differences in the way society expects men and women to act.[13] Much of masculinity and femininity is learned, and these learned reactions are roles. Depending upon our sex, we learn how we are expected to behave from our earliest family experiences. Boys and girls are expected to behave differently, as this nursery rhyme tells us:

> Sugar and spice and all things nice,
> That's what little girls are made of.
> Snips and snails and puppy dog tails,
> That's what little boys are made of.

In our culture, boys are taught to be aggressive, adventuresome, and bold, while girls are taught to be refined, clean, careful, and passive. We know that males and females are not born with traits, but learn them. We know this from studying a number of other cultures and finding in some an almost exact reversal of what we consider to be the normal male and female roles. In our culture, men tend to have greater prestige than women. Men are

[13] For an interesting sociological analysis, see the following books: W. M. Ruitenbeek, *The Male Myth* (New York: Dell Publishing Company, Inc., 1967), and M. Brenton, *American Male* (New York: Fawcett World Library, 1967).

considered more practical. In business positions, men and women doing the same work are rarely paid the same salary, with men enjoying the advantage. Civil rights legislation should gradually change this in the '70's.

Men generally have much more freedom of action than women, who are expected to be more conforming. In sexual behavior, a double standard exists whereby a woman is more severely punished for violating the sex taboos than a man. This, too, seems to be changing as women are demonstrating a desire for equality in sexual expression in the decade of the '70's.

Our concept of what is properly masculine and feminine changes with time. Today, it is not unusual to see a husband pushing a cart in the supermarket, holding a baby in one hand and doing the grocery shopping with the other. Such behavior a few years ago would have been ridiculed. Today, a woman has much greater freedom to choose her occupation. This freedom often creates a serious conflict in her between the values of motherhood and homemaking and the values of a career and service outside the family.

Achieving a sense of adequacy as a male or a female becomes a motivator of tremendous importance in our culture. A woman may feel that she has not fully achieved her sex membership until she has been able to conceive and give birth to another human being. Adequacy as a sexual partner has been emphasized in this culture almost to the point of an obsession. Men seem to need to prove their masculinity more than women do their femininity. Understanding the male stereotype in the American culture helps explain the subtle discrimination against hiring female executives by men in positions of influence.

An "adequate" male in the American culture is defined in accordance to a common stereotype.[14] Part of this stereotype is the idea that the man demonstrates his masculinity in being superior to women, taking care of them, being more logical, intelligent, and objective than women, etc. If a woman is able to take care of herself, is able to think logically and objectively, and succeeds in a position of management, this can be threatening to a man suffering from feelings of inadequacy. Since most top executive positions in American industry are filled by men, the female applicant for an executive position may be turned down not because of lack of executive ability but because the very concept of a female execu-

---

[14] *Stereotype:* "... 2. A conventional, formulaic, and usually oversimplified conception, opinion or belief," *The American Heritage Dictionary* (New York: American Heritage Publishing Company, Inc., 1970).

tive is threatening to the male currently in a position of authority. If "masculinity" is defined by a male executive partly in terms of seeing women as illogical, passive, dependent, disorganized, and helpless, his own sense of masculinity will be threatened by acknowledging the existence of a logical, active, self-sufficient, organized, and capable woman. Rather than risk a sense of personal threat, the male executive escapes the problem by asserting that "women should not be in business management—their place is in the home."[15]

The Dilemma of Social Control

It is important that society exercise some measure of social control over its individuals. However, this pressure on the individual to conform to the group's standards of behavior may discourage the individual initiative, innovation, and creativity which are often the basis of real advancement in our civilization. As a society becomes larger and more complicated, more exacting methods of social control are required. There may therefore be a tendency for group thinking to be emphasized and praised more extensively than individual thinking. Society must exercise enough control to maintain a relative stability. But society must not go so far as to curb the deviations from present standards of behavior which may lead to contributions toward a more effective and stable society.

CONFORMITY AND CREATIVITY

Social control or authority is necessary to prevent a society from disintegrating. But every invention, every innovation, every improvement is a rebellion against existing knowledge and authority. This presents mankind with a dilemma. Each one of us is faced with the same dilemma.[16]

A successful person pays a price for his success just as surely as he does when he purchases any material thing. He gives up much of his personal

---

[15] A very readable and scholarly book giving a penetrating analysis of "women's place" is Elizabeth Janeway's *Man's World, Woman's Place: A Study in Social Mythology* (New York: William Morrow and Company, Inc., 1971).

[16] For a provocative discussion on the dilemma we experience in reacting to pressures to conform, read Robert Lindner, *Must You Conform?* (New York: Holt, Rinehart and Winston, Inc., 1956). For a discussion of different kinds of conformity in our changing way of life, see David Riesman, *et al., The Lonely Crowd* (New Haven, Connecticut: Yale University Press, 1950).

freedom to do the many things he enjoys in order to do the things he must do. He may pay the price of having a greatly diminished family life, the price of giving up active participation in sports or other activities, and the price of having to attend to many irksome details. In somewhat the same way, we all pay a price for being part of our contemporary civilization. We pay a price for being a recognized member of our society. We pay a price to gain the advantage of group effort. We pay a price to grow up and mature as useful citizens.

We Compromise

We must conform generally to the dictates of our society and yet we want to develop our individualism. We want to realize our greatest potential in our own unique way which may be a departure from strictly traditional ways of doing things. We need to find a healthy balance between the pressure to develop our individuality and the pressure to become "socialized" or, in other words, become part of our social group. This balance is not easy to achieve. We find ourselves exposed to pressures which force us to behave "the way it's always been done" but at the same time urge us to "stand on your own two feet."

We Give Up Freedom

In the American culture, we prize individuality highly. Freedom of the individual is one of the basic concepts of our democratic form of government. Americans praise and reward individual thinking and effort. But too much individualism brings not reward or acclaim, but punishment, chastisement, and even enforced separation from society. If we believe that each individual reaches greater heights of accomplishment primarily by developing and accentuating the talents and capabilities he has, then the development and nurture of human potentialities becomes one of our greatest goals as a nation. We must give up some freedom to become members of a complex society, but we must not give up the freedom to be creative.

The Value of Conformity

Reduction of Anxiety. Conformity for the child and for the adult is a way of obtaining relief from anxiety. Most of us feel comfortable when we are in harmony with the things around us. A new situation, an unknown situation, a changing situation forces us to learn new solutions and new ways of behaving. In learning anything new, there is usually a period when we feel uncertain, confused, and unsettled. It may be more comfortable to conform to an existing pattern of behavior, even if it is not as effective as a newer or revised pattern might be, in order not to undergo the anxiety of new learning and adaptation. Conformity does aid the individual in avoiding or minimizing some of his anxiety.

Economy of Energy. Conformity to existing cultural patterns means a great economy of energy and thought for the individual. Previous generations have worked out good solutions to recurring problems. By conforming to existing patterns of behavior, the individual can solve these recurring problems almost automatically. In establishing a new club, we automatically follow the rules of parliamentary procedure that have been carefully worked out beforehand. This avoids confusion, misunderstanding, and loss of time that would occur if we were to attempt to work out our own way of organizing club meetings. We do not have to "invent the wheel" each time we want to use one.

The Dangers of Conformity

Encourages Mediocrity. Every organization requires conformity of its members, whether it be a business, school, church, club, or family. There are certain rules and regulations it must follow for successful coordination of the individual efforts of its members. But this same need for conformity can also create a subtle pressure which results in an average or mediocre performance. "There's no reason for it; it's company policy!" is a frequently heard plaint of the harassed manager when someone questions why things should be done just so. A policy or network of policies is necessary as an ongoing guide for a business organization; but the very existence of a policy suggests that someone formulated a guide for behavior which was felt to be appropriate at one time but is probably less appropriate for the changing organization in our changing society at some later point in time. Urging conformity to outdated policies in a dynamic, changing, evolving organization is one way of insuring that the organization loses opportunities for innovation, creativity, newness, and excitement. Blind conformity, indeed, does predispose an organization toward mediocrity!

The manager who is disturbed by business procedures which deviate from company policy may unwittingly select new employees who have little need to explore, be curious, or search for new and more effective ways of dealing with daily problems. The young, eager, potentially creative and productive employee who somehow escapes the screening process unconsciously (or perhaps consciously) designed to reject the inventive but trouble-making employee may work at first with a zeal impossible to "buy" with money; we should not be surprised to find him later a "statistic" in a personnel report regarding employee turnover.

The manager can give lip service to the desirability of developing creativity in his subordinates, but at the same time actively discourage innovation or departures from the norm by his behavior or by unexpressed, nonverbal, negative attitudes toward their behavior. To one manager, for example, it was important that he have "one big happy family." He stressed in many subtle ways the importance of the various people "getting along well with each other." His office resembled a social club more than a business office. At the same time, he wondered why it was that his office's production had been on a plateau for so long. This manager demanded conformity to norms of social behavior at the expense of encouraging stimulating new ideas.

Causes Loss of Ideas. We are in danger of losing ideas because of the pressures to conform. The classic story of the persecution of Galileo illustrates this point. Only a little over three hundred years ago, Galileo dared to question some of the assumptions and the logic of his time formulated by Aristotle which had remained relatively unchanged for centuries. But Galileo was a pioneer—he dared to question existing authority. He felt that even though particular "facts" had been handed down from generation to generation as being the truth, they could still be questioned. He felt that they should be investigated by systematic and controlled observation. He challenged existing belief by stating that the earth was not the center of the universe, and that the earth itself moved. These ideas were so upsetting that church officials forced him to swear publicly that he had made a mistake. Because of the pressure of conformity, one of the greatest thinkers of all time was confined to his home and discouraged from further deviance in thinking.

We can also see the effects of conformity on the members of a top management group in a company. Because an executive wants to be promoted, he may decide to take the "safe and sure route" and plan his work so that he avoids "mistakes" rather than plan to maximize his creative contribution to the business. The cost of ideas which may be lost because the president or board of directors will not tolerate mistakes or "deviant" thinking must be enormous! In our public schools the "good" or "well-adjusted" child is often the one who follows directions and avoids asking strange or unusual questions. The bright or creative child is often punished because he misbehaves by wanting to try new things or read new and different books. This kind of influence discourages a bright child from using more of his natural creative ability. What countless ideas or inventions must have been lost because of this early pressure on an impressionable mind to conform rather than to create!

How Conformity Works

Conformity Reduces Variation. The pressure of conformity tends to reduce the variation in behavior of individuals in a group. When individuals are apart from a group, they express more diverse opinions and judgments. The group exerts a restraining or a conservative force on the behavior of members of that group. Often when a company is managed by committee rather than by individuals, the company tends to be more conservative and more cautious in its policies.

Conformity Reduces Extremes. The pressure of conformity tends to eliminate extreme variation. As the individual behaves in a way that is further and further away from the group norm, the pressure for him to return to the group increases. Minor deviations from the group pattern may be tolerated, but as the deviations become more extreme the group will take action and may even take the life of the deviant. The degree to which the group will permit nonconformity depends on the kind of social situation in question, the status or standing of the individual in the group, and the actual behavior involved. College students are often permitted to perpetrate minor crimes against individuals or groups which would be severely censured or punished if done away from the university. Occupying administrative offices and "kidnapping" the president are examples. But as the 1970's progress, society is losing tolerance for these college "pranks" and is reacting with greater use of force and legal sanctions.

Influence of the Group. The size of the group of which one is a member has a bearing on the force of conformity which is applied to him. The larger the group, the more deviant the behavior can be and still remain accepted by the group. In a small town there is usually far less variation or deviation from the group pattern than would be found in a large metropolitan center. A Greenwich Village can exist in New York City, but would not be tolerated in a small town.

The pressure of conformity on the individual is related to the degree of attachment that the individual has for the group. When the attachment is loose, the pressure of conformity may produce some overt changes in behavior, but less change or even no change in inner convictions. When the individual greatly values his membership in the group and is afraid of being ostracized, the group is likely to have a more permanent effect on his inner convictions. Personal convictions influenced or changed by the pressure of such a valued group are likely to remain changed. Conformity and behavior which are enforced by a larger group or a group less important to the individual are very likely to lose their hold once the influence of the group is removed.

New Agencies of Conformity. While the family is probably the most important pressure-enforcing conformity in the individual's early life, it does not retain this power to influence behavior in general. In earlier phases of our developing American culture, the family, the community, and the church were the main agencies of social control. Now these have been replaced by new agencies of conformity or social control, such as business and governmental groups. While it is less true in smaller communities, a man's economic group probably exerts greater pressure on him than does his family or his church. If a business has a closed-shop agreement, a man cannot even get a job unless he agrees to join the union. The union may even exert pressure on the individual member to support certain political candidates. At the management level, executives often find that their business exerts a pressure of conformity which extends even to the choice of marriage mates. An executive may understand, if he has not been directly told, that if he expects to rise high in management, he must be sure that his wife becomes active and socially prominent in civic affairs.

Creativity

It is likely that the person who is mature, flexible and creative can do a much better job of solving people-problems than one who is afraid, rigid, overconforming, and uninspiring.[17] The executive who is prepared to understand and accept the individuality of his people, and who has the courage to consider new and different ways of providing proper training and supervision, is likely to have a more efficient work force than one who mechanically follows the book. It is important that we learn how to use more of our creative ability. We must learn not to conform to tradition slavishly, but *to conform intelligently* and *to deviate from conformity intelligently* when it is appropriate.

Creativity has much to do with persuasion. In any effort to negotiate or to reach an agreement with an individual, failure is most often caused by rigidity on the part of one or both individuals involved. The more flexible and creative one can become, the more effective a persuader of people he will probably be. The businessman who adopts *one* method of management or selling may achieve a high degree of success because he works hard at this method. But what about the literally hundreds of individuals who are "turned off" by this one approach? Is it not possible that using a more flexible, a more creative approach will allow him to do an even better job? People are different!

The Nature of Creativity. Creativity is the capacity to innovate, invent, or place elements together in new ways. Some inidividuals are more creative than others. But all of us possess a certain degree of creativity and have the ability to make better use of our creativity. *Creativity is probably not so much an inherited trait as a product of life experiences.* The creative person has been a subject of great interest throughout the ages. It is the creative individuals who are frequently discredited by their contemporary groups, but who provide us with the significant advances in technology and in social institutions. What is it that gives rise to creativity? What stimulates creativity?

There are at least two basic theories as to the nature of creativity and why it emerges. The two theories seem to be rather directly opposed to each other. One theory of creativity is that it emerges only when a person has solved his basic problems of biological survival and security in his social group. It supposes that only when the individual has achieved

---

[17] For the reader who wants to pursue scientific studies of the factors influencing creative problem-solving, see N. R. F. Maier, *Problem Solving and Creativity* (Belmont, California: Brooks/Cole Publishing Company, 1970).

security—when he is fed, clothed, safe from harm, and loved by others—can he be free to innovate and create.

A second major theory regarding the emergence of creativity is that creativity is itself a response to major dissatisfaction in important desires. In support of this theory it has been suggested that the world's greatest creative leaders come from unhappy or unsatisfactory environmental conditions. Highly creative people often come from broken homes. Furthermore, it can be seen in the history of creative people that there has been perhaps more than the usual amount of freedom in their early lives. This may have come from the loss of parents when they were young or perhaps because of a real absence of parental coercion. When the child does not have firm direction from adults, it apparently becomes more necessary for him to create and invent his own solutions to problems.

The Importance of Creativity. Why is it important to know something about the creative process? At the present time we are faced with widespread, deep, and rapid changes in our society and changes in our ability to control our environment. This is a time of change. It is a time when we can rely less and less on tradition and on precedent.

An understanding of the creative process is important because of the assistance it can give us in handling difficult problems associated with this kind of change. Insight into the process of invention or innovation can increase the effectiveness of the adult intelligence. It is important that we examine ourselves to see how our own possible fear of change or fear of deviating from the group may be keeping us from achieving genuine creativity or self-realization. The strength of our nation has come largely from the pioneering or inventive nature of its people. The decay of our nation, according to some contemporary writers, may very well follow from man's reluctance to continue these pioneering, creative efforts.[18]

The Growth of Creativity. In scientific studies on the stimulation of creativity, it has been found that creativity emerges in a situation of informality and in an atmosphere of acceptance and freedom rather than in one of criticism and rejection. Characteristics that seem to be highly related to the growth of creativity are a basic personal security, intelligence, flexibility, spontaneity, humor, originality, ability to perceive a

[18] Alvin Toffler, *Future Shock* (New York: Random House, 1970).

variety of essential features of an object or situation, playfulness, radicalness, and eccentricity. Traits or characteristics which appear to be opposed to the development of creativity are thoroughness, excessive concern with neatness, personal rigidity, too much control, reason, logic, respect for tradition and authority.

Creativity is a process of (1) *preparation,* (2) *incubation,* (3) *illumination,* and (4) *verification.* Certainly before creative work can be done, much preparation must precede it. No artist ever painted a masterpiece without years of hard work and preparation. No inventor ever created a new device without much basic preparation in his field. In the same way, the executive cannot expect to be creative in business without *thorough preparation* and a sound background of knowledge in both the technical and human areas.

Creative individuals report that when they are trying to solve a problem or create something new, there is often a period in which they feel somewhat confused, indecisive, or at least in a state of suspended decision-making. There seems to be a need to "lose themselves" or somehow relax and not try too hard to drive toward a solution. The word *incubation* fits this state of mind. It is a time when the individual is able to be free in his thinking and free of restrictions and criticisms.

The third step in the creative process, *illumination,* is illustrated by the fact that we often grasp the solutions to problems or think of an idea quite spontaneously. We "see the light." Haven't we all had the experience of waking up in the middle of the night with the solution to a problem we had been trying to solve during the day? The more spontaneous an individual is in his behavior and thinking, the more likely it is that he can allow *his unconscious thought processes* to work for him and to help him achieve creative effort. Creativity through a process of deliberate, conscious, calculated effort seems to occur rarely. The well-ordered, plodding individual who follows established routine may achieve fair success in life and may avoid mistakes, but he may also avoid the discovery of new solutions.

The last step in the creative process, *verification,* is the step which permits constructive creative gain, rather than simply a hare-brained notion. The new idea, once created, needs to be tested or subjected to systematic observation (as through the scientific method) to make sure that it is a true advance over tradition rather than rebellion against existing authority.

The Right Atmosphere. The business manager can help his employees become better and more creative problem-solvers if he will listen to their ideas objectively and with understanding, help them find workable ways of putting the ideas into action, and do this with an absence of petty criticism or ridicule. To establish an atmosphere which helps them grow in creative ability, *the manager must himself be in the process of growing and developing creatively.* New ideas in business or in solving the needs of a customer are more likely to come from companies headed by a man who is strong enough to try new ideas without being afraid that he will "look silly" if they fail. The manager who follows the rules to the letter and operates his business in the same way it has been run in the last twenty years may not be able to recognize a genuine advance in thinking when it does occur.

Behave Yourself or Be Yourself? From the earliest time that we can remember, we have been told to behave ourselves. Our parents told us that and our bosses (and even our wives) tell us this now. "Behave yourself." What this usually means is that you must stop what you are doing and do what they want you to do. Of course, it is necessary that we behave ourselves, for conformity to standards prevents chaos and inefficiency. But nonconformity can also be quite important! In addition to behaving ourselves, we can probably accomplish far more if we will *be ourselves.* Being yourself means realizing more and more of your potential as a human being. There is a good deal of falseness or artificiality in our behavior, not solely because group pressures demand us to conform, but because we are to some degree afraid, insecure, or lacking in self-confidence.

We are often aware when we are artificial and when we are genuine. But by a curious psychological maneuver, we repress recognition of much of our false behavior. If we do happen to notice it, we put it out of our minds immediately and try not to think about it. If the business consultant pretends an interest in his client that he does not feel, the client is likely to realize this, even if only unconsciously. In any individual's effort to be himself, to realize more of his potential, and to make better use of the creative ability he has, it is important that he practice being honest with himself and with others. It takes courage to be yourself, but the rewards are great!

Being Human

Man has a drive to improve himself, to get somewhere, to amount to something, and above all to become a person who knows who he is and how he fits into the larger scheme of life. Being human means painting a picture for no other reason that just to look at it. Being human means wondering why grass is green and why objects fall down rather than up. Being human means wanting to be with other human beings and at the same time wanting to be alone. Being human means experiencing a desperate urgency to understand others and to be understood in turn. But above all, being human means to want to transcend the limitations of time and space, to rise above the natural restrictions which keep all other animals at the mercy of their surroundings, *to control our destiny rather than be controlled by it.*

Man becomes human in the company of man. Man grows by helping man to grow. Man grows to the extent that he can visualize his potential. Man visualizes his potential to the extent that he can look at himself without flinching, can see what is there, and can share his observations with his fellow man. Man has the choice of growing toward greater humanness or of ignoring his potentialities. Each of us has this choice to make.

SUMMARY

America, the land of the free and the home of the brave: Freedom in any society carries with it a responsibility to one another and requires courage to deviate from the norm in the name of creative improvement. The way we live in our work or family situation is a mixture of conformity imposed upon us by our group memberships and individuality arising from our own unique needs. Seeing the many ways in which human behavior is shaped by the national and local culture gives us more freedom to control our destiny rather than be controlled by it.

Human behavior is the product of the individual personality and the environment in which he lives. Sales are made, businesses succeed, friendships and marriages survive, and individuals reach high levels of self-fulfillment depending largely on the capacity to find a healthy balance between conformity and creativity. Everyone in a culture is a conformist, although a person conforming to one group may appear to be a nonconformist to a member of another group. If we conform without knowing how, when, or why we conform, we lose a large measure of personal freedom. Understanding the problem is a first step toward its solution; seeing the invisible sea of influences which shape us allows us to plan our life in a deliberate, intelligent way.

QUESTIONS FOR DISCUSSION AND THOUGHT

1. If we think we are free but are not, we are more likely to engage in self-defeating behavior. What does this mean?
2. Of how many groups are you a member? See if you can list at least thirty different groups which openly or subtly influence you.
3. What is the importance of status in our society? How does it motivate behavior?
4. "My team is better than yours, my company, my town, my country is better than yours." Does this common sentiment interfere with our ability to understand and work with others? How?
5. What are the implications of the changing role of the American family? How do these changes affect selling, manufacturing, and education?
6. Think of an example of role conflict which you often experience. What are the factors which might allow you to minimize such conflict?
7. What is the function of conformity in a society, business, or family? Is the influence good or bad? Explain.
8. Why is it important to develop our own creativity? What will be the probable result of becoming more creative?

4

SITUATIONAL COMMUNICATIONS

Driving along a Los Angeles freeway one morning commuters experienced a shock, perhaps a laugh, but certainly a challenge. The night before someone had crawled up on an overhead support for road signs to hang a home-made, but official-looking, signboard with the terse message, "IGNORE THIS SIGN." The impossibility of the task and the improbability of the situation provided the humor. If you have placed yourself in that situation, mentally, you are ready to begin the study of communication.

Communication cannot be ignored nor can it be accomplished with anything like completeness. There are many things which we can avoid doing, such as yard work, weekly reports, balancing the check book, washing the car, taking our wife out to dinner, or reading this chapter. But there is no way to avoid communicating. It goes on all the time.

We communicate with ourselves as well as others. We communicate consciously as well as unconsciously. Words are used, but much communication takes place nonverbally. Where we are, and when, adds to the maze of communication networks. Communication, like the sign over the freeway, cannot be ignored, nor will it go away. We're stuck with it!

Communication involves an exchange. What is exchanged depends on the *sender*, the *media*, and the *receiver*, and also on the *situation*. To understand the facets of human communication, where should we begin? "At the beginning and continue until we have reached the end?" That very same suggestion made by the King in Alice in Wonderland sounds reasonable, but like many other things is impossible. You are in the middle of the subject right now because you are engaged in the process itself. If words are used to transmit, or clarify, then the meanings you attach to those words because of years of personal experiences are adding to or subtracting from the intended message. You are in the middle because you already know, or think you know, something about communicating. You are in the middle because you are immersed in a cultural situation which influences you in manifold ways and from which you cannot be completely free; you are in the middle of other events, physical and mental, which compete for your attention; you are in the middle of a book in which human communication is being discussed implicitly and explicity. You are somewhere in the middle of your life span which has been a continuous series of communications. Your life of communications has been a real battle; you have been fighting the battle against confusion.

THE BATTLE AGAINST CONFUSION

A battleground situation involves strategy, tactics, an enemy, perhaps subversive elements in our own camp, a terrain, weather conditions, people, materials, traditions, etc., but, above all, masses of communications. The enemy, *confusion,* is all around us. He is often successful in thwarting us by infiltration, if frontal assault has not worked. In a perverse way, we create our own confusion and place it in our very nerve centers where it can do untold damage. When the battle is particularly severe and we seem to be losing, we may be tempted to dig a deep hole and hide until it's all over or else wave a flag of truce and hope that we'll be treated humanely.

There are times when the clearest of letters you write is grossly misunderstood and a client or other human relationship is severed. Perhaps failing to respond to a question soon enough is interpreted as a rejection, when you were only preoccupied with a totally different matter. Seemingly explicit instructions to the yard man result in the wrong tree cut down. A compliment intended to flatter is seen for what it is, and the attempt to impress backfires. In spite of your best efforts you misread the form and get a call from the I.R.S. wanting to see your records. Confusion is often with us, but retreat usually adds to it. *Confrontation and effort* may not end the battle against confusion but they increase the chances of gaining ground.

Communication confusion cannot be eliminated in daily interactions between people, but it can be minimized. Increasing the number of people involved in a communication attempt increases the probability of adding confusion. The passage of time increases confusion. Individual experiences before, during, and after a communication attempt contribute to confusion. Communication confusion seems to multiply itself so that constant efforts are necessary to keep the confusion level down. Paradoxically, many urgent efforts to reduce confusion only add to it. "Common-sense" strategies frequently add the most confusion and make the battle more difficult because they "seem right" and "everybody knows" what they are doing.

One "common-sense" notion is that the best way to clarify is to simplify. Chaos and confusion are unpleasant; we become nervous, uncertain, and anxious. Our need is strong to bring order out of chaos and understanding out of confusion. As when a bad headache eases, we feel a sense of relief when confusion is ended. The strong need to end confusion can entice us to jump to a conclusion too soon, see order when it is not there, and believe "facts" when they are not factual. A constant source of chaos and confusion lies in the inevitable differences between people. Each person is different, and therefore difficult to understand because of these differences. Differences between people require constant changes in us if we are to communicate effectively with each unique person we meet. Of course, there is similarity between people, but it is the uniqueness which increases the likelihood of confusion. When Joe and Sam seem similar we may explain an idea to Sam in the same way that worked with Joe. When Sam is slower to grasp the idea, we change our approach if we are aware that he is not getting the idea. If we don't notice his difficulty, the explanation that worked with Joe will create confusion with Sam. In fact, the more similar Sam and Joe seem, the more likely we are to overlook their differences.

A favorite gimmick of some lecturers on communication is to write on the blackboard the acronym KISS, the first letters of the phrase, "Keep It Simple, Stupid." This may be accompanied by a few laughs from the audience, if they are charitable, or at least smiles of recognition of the obvious truth of the thought. But "simple" statements are often wrong, often the basis for prejudice, and almost always a source of communication confusion. Sam and Joe may have some characteristics in common. They may look somewhat alike, have similar backgrounds, and work for the same company. It may seem easier to think of them as being similar enough to communicate with in the same way rather than do the additional work of seeing the complicated differences between two unique individuals. But not until we accept the complications and act accordingly will it be possible to decrease confusion instead of increasing it. "Simple" statements are not necessarily clear and "complicated" statements are not necessarily confusing.

Prejudices are maintained because of our tendency to make "simple" statements about racial, ethnic, or religious groups. Prejudice is, literally, a judging of someone or something without sufficient knowledge. Prejudice is shown in making the "simple" statement, "Women are all alike—they're not logical and can't make businesslike decisions." But we know that there are thousands of highly successful women scientists, judges, executives, legislators, educators, and other professionals. It is more complicated to determine the particular ability of each female we meet but it is the only way to be clearer about what we communciate about them. It is discovering and mastering the complications of a person or situation which help us wage successful war against confusion; simplistic thinking leads too frequently to defeat.

A Strategy for the Situation

Conversation often seems so casual that we are unaware of the careful and deliberate plan we follow in devising a communication effort which accomplishes our aims. A strategy is a broad plan followed in order to achieve ends, but this plan is not necessarily conscious. Sometimes we are aware that a statement as simple as "My, you look pretty in that dress," is made so that a special advantage can be gained at some later time. The mutual fund salesman who knows his prospect well comments "casually" on the prospect's good judgment in the past in seeking the advice of an attorney, hoping that later in the conversation he can urge the prospect to rely on the professional judgment of investors. The parent looks for opportunities to praise his child when he reads something other than comic books, thinking this will "motivate him to do better in school." It is not being cynical to recognize that we often think long minutes, hours, or days ahead when we talk to each other and plan our words according to a strategy which we think is known only to ourselves.

We plan communications well in advance, we say some things "on the spur of the moment," and many other communications take place by unconscious intent and without awareness. Our plan of attack is incredibly complex, although we may be aware of only a part of the strategy. The increased awareness of *what* we do and *why* gives us more real control over our lives and greater freedom as individuals.

Communications take place within a *situation;* this situation influences what the sender of the message communicates and what the receiver understands. The experienced sailor knows that wind and water currents influence the vessel as well as the set of the sail, the position of the rudder, the shape of the hull, etc. Similarly we send out a word vessel upon a sea with uncertain currents and unpredictable winds, sometimes having to tack and steer away from our objective in order to move forward; without considerable sailing skill we may even capsize! Some of the events in the situation can be controlled and predicted by the initiator of a message, but other events can only be guessed at and poorly handled. The more the helmsman of a vessel or the sender of a message knows about the total situation, the more often he meets with success.

A communications situation includes the sender, the media, and the receiver. But the situation is more than this. The preceding chapter examined the multiple influences of our *culture* on individual behavior. Communication efforts are part of the behavior influenced by the cultural situation. The *relationship* between the two or more people involved in a communication effort is part of the total situation. This relationship is made up of past experiences and future expectancies. It is affected by the roles the participants decide to play; socioeconomic class positions, education, intellectual capacity, sex, race, religious beliefs, the time of day or month of the year, all play a part in determining the total communication situation out of which come individual attempts to exchange information.

Devising a communication strategy which helps in fighting the battle against confusion depends, in part, on recognizing all these elements that make up the situation in which this battle takes place.

Communication Reconnaissance

The professional military man who fights the real battle depends on information gathered during an exploratory survey of the situation to plan broad strategy and devise specific tactics. He reconnoiters the territory so that his moves will be effective and surprises will be minimized. The professional burglar "cases the joint" for the same purposes. Both men differ from the amateur in that they recognize the importance of understanding the situation before blundering into unforeseen obstacles and pitfalls. We become more professional in our everyday communication efforts as we follow the same plan. We must look ahead, understand the people and situations we will be dealing with, and plan accordingly if we are to make headway in minimizing enemy confusion.

One of the most important conversations we ever have is that which takes place when we apply for a job or when we hope to persuade someone to do business with us. The inexperienced job seeker will probably approach the employment office and say, "I need a job. Do you have anything I can do?" He'll be asked, "What experience do you have?" When he says, "None," the refusal will probably sound like, "Sorry. We don't hire inexperienced people. Come back when you've had some work experience." Admittedly lack of work experience is a sizable handicap in applying for a job. But imagine a different applicant who understands more about the situation. He, too, has no experience, but he begins a reconnaissance long before applying for a job. He knows he has no employment record, but he assesses other kinds of experience he has had such as skill in home or mechanical repair, chairing a committee in school or club, writing term papers, persistence in learning to play an instrument, budgeting and buying supplies for a Scout campout, etc. It is not possible to be without experience, although one may not have a formal employment record. Our knowledgeable applicant would then investigate the organization in which he is interested. The suppliers of goods and services to the organization have valuable knowledge to give, as do the company's salesmen, clerical workers, etc. Knowledge about many large companies' operations and scope usually can be found in the public library. Customers of the company's products or services can give a different point of view. The "inexperienced" applicant is then in a position to approach the company armed with insight into the company's needs, past successes, current opportunities, but, most important, armed with the "language of the situation." He can use words and phrases which pertain to the specific work he wants to do. In fact, the applicant for a job can easily acquire more information about the company and its business life than most of the present employees have. Not only is the knowledgeable applicant in a stronger position to state his case, but his awareness of the company and their "publics" may so favorably impress those who do the hiring that a job may be *created* for him.

The same strategy is useful no matter what the level of job experience or sophistication of work. The account executive of the new business department in a bank may have minimal success in adding deposits if he canvasses the offices in a large office building without first doing his "homework." Other officers of the bank may know some background details of a particular branch office the account executive is to call on. Unfortunately, the rivalry between officers may prevent or minimize such exchange of information. Before calling on a branch office, the account executive can become aware of the general market conditions affecting his prospect, the internal trends in the industry, the unique problems of the specific company in the industry, the jargon used, and of course some personal information about the branch manager. All of this information makes up the communication situation affecting both the account executive and the prospect for bank services. Some banks arrange briefing sessions for the account executives before they make calls to assemble as much as is currently known and to indicate facts which should be obtained *before* the first word is exchanged with the prospect either by letter or in person.

Reconnaissance must continue during the conversation or interview itself. The person making a call can ask himself questions regarding the situation even while in that situation. For example, what is the prospect's situation *as he sees it*? What distractions are dividing his attention? Does he show signs of fatigue? Does he seem preoccupied? What is he likely to want to hear? What words does he use and what do they mean to him? What biases or blind spots is he likely to have? What must my presence mean to him?

At four o'clock one afternoon in May, a life insurance salesman was waiting in the outer office of the company's president to go over a proposal based on the fact-finding interview the previous week. The president was finishing a telephone conversation with his wife, who was calling from the emergency room of the hospital. His son had been hit by a car, but his only injury was a broken arm which was already being put into a cast. "You don't have to come over here, dear," she said. "Timmy's a little scared and shook up but he'll be all right soon. We'll see you when you come home for dinner." He hung up, feeling a mixture of relief and concern. Rather absently he turned to the salesman just coming into the office and went through the motions of shaking hands and saying, "How are you?" The salesman, trained to reconnoiter, noticed the faint signs of distraction and impulsively asked, "Well, how has your day been going?" His voice showed concern and was not flat or stiff as is often the case in the perfunctory exchanges of greeting. The president briefly mentioned the telephone call, but said, "My wife is there so I guess I don't need to go.

Let's take a look at your proposal." The salesman's assessment of the situation was rapid and because he had learned to overcome his own self-centeredness in a genuine concern for others he interrupted. "You know, I'd want to be there if it were my son, just to give him a little added comfort. Let me take you there. My car's right outside. We can talk on the way if you want to."

Because he was then doing something which would help relieve his apprehension about his son, the president could listen attentively as the pension consultant outlined the plan. At the hospital, another situation presented itself. Wisely, the salesman waited outside the emergency room while his prospect, wife, and son had an intimate family moment. This was an awareness that his presence could be inhibiting to the free, emotional communication within his prospect's family. The ten-minute ride back to the president's office was enough to make the final arrangements and a sale was made.

Fortunately, the salesman could see that staying in the prospect's office physically would not keep his prospect from mentally drifting away to think about his son. The absent son was as much part of the initial office situation as the physical objects of desk, chairs, papers, etc.

Of course, this example may seem like a coincidence. But it does indicate the possible favorable results from an attempt to be sensitive to the situation which influences communication effectiveness.

Self-Created Communication Confusion

Millions of GI's were involved in World War II, the Korean *conflict,* and the Viet Nam *struggle* (let those who were there define them). The acronym SNAFU reflected a general observation that in a military operation a number of self-created barriers, inhibitions, obstacles, pitfalls, mistakes, goofs, etc., made it seem amazing that any resemblance of a military operation could be carried on at all. Snafus appear in all organizational life. The businessman often realizes that his most difficult problems are created within his own organization. Certainly in a communication situation it is common that the greatest communication barriers or obstacles are created by the sender of a message himself.

One of the chief problems which prevent effective and accurate communication is that we are all essentially self-centered. We are the center of our own universe. Our behavior is based on the way we perceive things, and our perceptions are based, in turn, on our own past experiences. Our perceptions are really our own personalized interpretations of reality. No two of us see the same events in exactly the same way. It is quite amazing that people can communicate and cooperate with each other as well as they do in view of the fact that (1) each of us perceives the world in his own personal way, (2) we have our own personal meanings for the symbols which we call words, and (3) each of us has slightly different goals for which we are striving.

Most of us would like to be considered unselfish, as we usually mean that term. The most unselfish of us, however, cannot "get outside ourselves" or be independent of our own fundamental and very personal desires. It is likely that our most unselfish tasks are largely motivated by very personal satisfactions which we hope to obtain. Because there is this broad and often unrecognized tendency to be self-centered, *we can improve the effectiveness and accuracy of our communications to others if we begin making a greater effort to understand the other person.*

We have not really communicated a message to another person until that person receives the message and takes some kind of physical or mental action as a result of it. If the message is received in a distorted form, we, as the sender of that message, must be the first to take the responsibility for any distortion. We should be ready to say to ourselves, "I don't believe I've made myself clear," and then try again to send a clearer message. A natural but self-centered tendency is to assert that our listener is simply a "dodo" if he has failed to "get" our message. We assume that because the words we use are perfectly clear to us they should be clear also to the listener, and if they are not, it is the listener's fault. This kind of thinking is further evidence of our self-centeredness.

This preoccupation with ourselves blocks communication in still another way. Much of the talk in which we engage is really talk about ourselves. We talk about *our* point of view on foreign affairs, *our* opinion as to how someone else should be doing his work, *our* interpretation of how a job should be done, etc. We reveal a great deal about ourselves as persons simply by talking, but this is likely to keep us from listening to others, thus causing a block in communication. There is the occasional individual who is not only afraid to reveal himself but afraid to get too close to other people. He may resort to one of the most effective ways known of blocking communication both ways: he may avoid saying anything of value and avoid listening, by simply talking, talking, and talking some more. Such individuals seem to follow the dictum that "the best defense is a good offense," for they produce a veritable barrage of words inundating all those around them and producing a kind of numbness which paralyzes exchange of information. Just as one can be the most lonely while in the midst of a huge crowd, so we can avoid saying anything by the simple technique of producing a great volume of prattle. While some individuals seem to use this method of noncommunication almost exclusively, we would make a mistake if we thought that all of us do not occasionally engage in such a maneuver. We have all had the experience of steering a conversation away from a subject which would be bothersome to us by the simple expedient of talking rapidly about some other subject. The salesman does this during a sales situation in an unconscious attempt to prevent the prospect from saying no. It is, of course, a self-defeating mechanism because it also prevents the prospect from saying yes.

Constructing verbal walls not only protects the individual who is unwilling to communicate with others, but also camouflages the weakness of an individual who simply lacks knowledge. We are likely to get the longest and the wordiest explanation from people in the areas of knowledge where they are the weakest. The classroom instructor will take much longer to explain a concept that he doesn't understand than he will in dealing with a familiar subject. Abraham Lincoln is reported to have said that if he had more time he would write a shorter letter. We can use our language to express ideas precisely and succinctly, or we can use words as a cover-up for a lack of knowledge and as an effective bar to mutual enlightenment.

THE LEVELS OF COMMUNICATION

Communication is the passing of information from one place to another. Communication must involve (1) a sender of information, (2) the information or the message itself, and (3) the receiver of such information. Without all three of these elements, communication does not take place. If we attempt to speak to a deaf person, we may in fact send an intelligent message, but if it cannot be received, then we have not communicated. Errors and misunderstandings can occur in all three elements of communication. We communicate with other individuals because we expect to effect some change in their behavior. If we do not see the expected behavior change, we must carefully inspect each of the three elements of communication for sources of error.

For example, if we have made an appointment with an individual through his secretary and he is not in at the appointed time, there are several questions which must be asked: Did we really say the date we thought we did? Did the secretary write down the message and give it to the person? Did he read the message as his secretary wrote it or did he misread the date? Did he choose to ignore the message? Before we get all upset about being "stood up," we should at least try to find out where the communication failed. The most common reaction, however, is to assume that our message did not get through only because the receiver or listener was at fault in not understanding the message or because he was willfully ignoring it.

Most of the material in Chapters 4 and 5 deals with the role of these three elements in the success or failure of communication. We spend much of our working day communicating with people. It is vital that we understand not only the sources of error but also the steps by which we can improve the effectiveness of our communication. But not all our efforts to communicate are with others. We also communicate with ourselves. This communication with ourselves is potentially the most disruptive because the sources of error and the effect on our own behavior are far less obvious than when we communicate with another individual.

Communication between one person and another takes place on a *verbal* and a *nonverbal* level and on a *conscious* and an *unconscious* level. All four forms of communications are used as we present ideas to others. We may be conscious that we use words to sway others. We may be unaware of the fact that certain of our mannerisms offend them and make persuasion less likely. It is possible that the unconscious, nonverbal (non-language) communication is more powerful and a greater motivator of human behavior than the conscious, verbal communication.

Verbal Communication

Within the first year of life, the infant may begin making sounds which are words or which sound like words that stand for the things he wants or needs. The beginning of verbal language is a matter of trial-and-error learning. The child makes a sound when he wants his milk and may or may not be understood. The closer the child gets to the sound of the word "milk" the faster it is probably given to him. The child soon learns to associate certain sounds he makes or his parents make with an actual object of value. This is communication on a verbal level.

The enormity of the child's task in learning to speak his native language can be better understood if we imagine ourselves suddenly dropped into a foreign country with a language we had never before heard. We would go through a period of confusion and would undoubtedly try to use some kind of language to indicate to the native our various desires. The task is even greater for the child, because he must *also* grasp the complicated concept of language itself, that is, that sounds or words are symbols for things and ideas.

As the child learns his native language, he naturally makes many mistakes of interpretation. Even as adults we use many words, though we may not be entirely sure of their specific meaning. The English language contains about one million words and most of us in our lifetime learn to use only a small fraction of this number. There is a close relationship between an individual's general level of intellectual capacity (I.Q.) and his ability to acquire and use a great many words. The learning of a language is a private affair. Each of us acquires the use of the hundreds of symbols that we call words because of the experiences we had with words and the things for which they stand. Because we learn words according to our own experiences, it is no wonder that each of us attaches slightly different meanings to the same word. Such individual interpretation of the common words that we use can become a formidable barrier to communication. This will be discussed at greater length in Chapter 5.

There is one other tremendous obstacle to communication involved in the verbal transmission of ideas. The *words* that we learn to use for different experiences we have had or for different objects *never completely describe the experiences or the objects for which they stand.* When we are concerned about what a word does stand for, we normally resort to the dictionary as the authority. But the meaning of a word or phrase is not only its dictionary equivalent but is also the effect its use has in any given situation. We have certain emotional reactions to words which are not included in their dictionary definitions.

Nonverbal Communication

We have seen how the child learns to acquire human characteristics through his ability to learn and make use of verbal symbols or language. Communication on a nonverbal level is just as important, if not more so, in shaping the early behavior patterns of the child and the later experiences of the adult. Andrew Carnegie is reported to have said, "As I grow older, I pay less attention to what men say. I just watch what they do." One of our clichés expresses this same idea: Actions speak louder than words. Even silence is often more eloquent in meaning than words.

Referring to one's associate as "an old buzzard" will mean one thing when said with a smile and quite a different thing without the smile. As we talk, we emphasize or modify the meaning of our words by our facial expressions, our bodily movements, gestures, pauses, inflections, and even significant omissions of certain words. Researchers in the field of non-verbal communication estimate that our *gesture language* may include around 700,000 distinct and different signals. Our largest dictionaries contain fewer words than this.

Contained in every spoken word there is always nonverbal communication: the *pitch* and *timbre* of an individual's voice, the *speed* with which he speaks, the way he *pauses* between words. People who have made a study of speech patterns and habits find that they can tell much about an individual's emotions and thoughts simply from the sound of his voice. A person who is blind frequently compensates for this deficiency by becoming more keenly attuned to the voices of others and the emotional qualities that are revealed. Just as we can "read between the lines," so we can hear between the words. When we are attempting to communicate with a blind person, we often feel some uneasiness. Possibly this is because we realize that the blind individual can "hear" more as we talk than can most people.

When we talk, we use facial expressions, gestures, bodily movements, etc., to augment and supplement what we say with words, These bodily expressions are often used as a kind of camouflage to hide our true feelings or thoughts. We all probably have at one time or another said to someone that we are very glad to have met him even though we didn't mean this. We have attempted to prove our pleasure by smiling broadly, and shaking his hand, making it a point to look very much pleased. A person who could not see this physical show of apparent interest might very well detect in our voices the actual distaste or disdain that we really feel.

Nonverbal communications, such as the way the businessman wears his clothes, the way his desk looks, and his personal mannerisms such as biting his fingernails or squinting his eyes, all affect the total message that others receive. A man's clothes and the way he wears them literally "says something" to those who see him. His clothing tends to say, "Look at me. I'm successful," or it might say just the opposite. If, when a manager is meeting with an employee, he allows himself to be interrupted by phone calls, he will unwittingly communicate to his employee that these interruptions are more important to him than is the employee.

It is probable that the successful businessman does a better job of communicating and understanding communications on this nonverbal plane than the unsuccessful man does. The successful person seems to "know" when others are ready to understand or cooperate. This same person may find it impossible to explain to someone just how he "knows" when this moment is at hand. It is likely, however, that he is picking up faint clues from the behavior of the person which indicate his general mood and feeling.

The manager communicates nonverbally a great deal to his leading salesman when he gives him a private office. He communicates even more when he authorizes him to have a rug in his office. The salesman who makes an evening call on a prospect in his living room, and who in an unguarded moment looks aghast at the dust and dirt that he observes, might just as well pack his briefcase and leave. He has communicated something to his prospect on a nonverbal level that probably can never be corrected on a verbal level.

The physical distance we maintain between ourselves and others is also a part of nonverbal communication. Generally speaking, we get close physically to individuals whom we like. We maintain much more distance between ourselves and those we dislike. Let us assume that a salesman has decided to make a call at the home of a prospect. After he knocks on the door, the woman of the household may answer. If he happens to be standing very close to the door at this moment, the woman may feel threatened or disturbed, either consciously or unconsciously. If, as the door is opened, he takes a step backward as he is announcing his name, this may relieve any anxiety that the woman may feel. This, of course, would be especially true if she happened to be alone in the house. In a standing conversation, the distance between the two people may either facilitate or disrupt communications. Perhaps all of us have had the experience of meeting someone for the first time and having him stand too close to us as he talked. If someone does stand too close to us, according to our own frame of reference, we are likely to feel vaguely uncomfortable even though we may not realize exactly why.

The desk in a man's office is a very real psychological barrier as well as a physical barrier. The desk in the office is an important status symbol. It represents authority, position, accomplishment, prestige, protection, etc. In entering a man's office you may attempt to sit beside him in a chair very near his, behind the desk, feeling that you can get closer to the prospect emotionally as well as physically. This, however, can be interpreted by him as an invasion of his own private space. As a result of this invasion, his defenses may be raised to the point that it is impossible to get through to him. It is likely, however, that if he *invites* you to sit behind the desk with him, he will probably be more receptive to what you say than if he asks you to sit across the desk and away from him.

We are all aware that we can mislead people and state an untruth through the use of our language. We can also be deceptive in our nonverbal communications. The man who walks by throwing out his chest and swaggering may be trying to convince people that he is a sophisticated and poised fellow, even though within himself he may feel quite uncomfortable and inferior. Just as we are often tripped up in our verbal lies, so can we be discovered in our nonverbal deceitfulness. Attempting to prevaricate in nonverbal communications may make our behavior so artificial that an observer may mutter to himself, "Boy, is he a phony!"

Some managers place great emphasis on hiring people who are dominant personalities. They feel that a man's natural dominance is an important factor in his ability to sell or manage. Undoubtedly there is much truth in this. It is likely that a dominant individual may control others not so much by what he says as by the way he says it. The dominant person has usually had a lifetime of experience in compelling people to action. He usually feels strongly that others will do as he says. When we are in the presence of such a dominant personality, we often unconsciously do without question whatever he wishes us to do. Of course, like anything else, if a dominant personality exaggerates his behavior and becomes a domineering person who attempts to bully those around him, he may find that he is antagonizing people so much that they will not follow his "commands."

Conscious and Unconscious Communication

To complicate the matter of communication futher, nonverbal expressions may be conscious or unconscious. The person who is tense and ill-at-ease may appear on the surface to be poised and relaxed. Others, however, may detect this tension and become quite uneasy themselves. One of the fascinating things about the human being is that he can detect such unconscious signals on the part of someone else without even being conscious of it himself. Two individuals can communicate with each other without either of them being aware that communication is taking place. It is probable that many conversations go awry because both individuals unconsciously react to each other with hostility and are dimly aware of dislike and lack of confidence but can't put their finger on why.

At this point you may very well ask, "If I don't know that I am creating a negative impression, how can I do anything about it?" The answer is not simple. But it can be said in general that the more an individual does to advance his own personal growth and development, to free himself from prejudice, stereotypes, false pride, etc., the more likely he is to be able to have a genuine *self-regard* and a genuine *regard for other people*. A genuine regard and respect will be communicated just as readily as tension or hostility. The more we are aware of the *possibilities* of conscious or unconscious communication, the more effective we can be in using techniques of communication to influence others.

PROBLEMS OF LOGIC IN COMMUNICATION

Everyone likes to believe he is reasonable. In fact, in an argument or disagreement both disputants are likely to accuse the other of being irrational or illogical. Because we tend to assume that problems of logic are to be laid at the other person's doorstep, we are not on the lookout for illogicalities in our own camp. It is the unexpected traitor or saboteur who can be most effective. A logical fallacy can be fully as disruptive in communication efforts as any other kind of distortion or deception. Some common logical fallacies are: confusing levels of abstraction, overgeneralizing, and dichotomizing.

Confusing Levels of Abstraction

The words we use do not accurately describe the objects to which they refer. A map of a region does not accurately describe that region, although it does describe certain salient features. Words are something like maps.[1] Just how correct and accurate a map is depends on the amount of detailed information supplied and the purpose for which the map is to be used. A flight map of a state looks quite different from a road map. Both are maps of the same territory, but they describe different aspects of that territory. When we drive from one city to the next, we use a road map of the state. But when we enter a large city we find our way by using a street map of the city itself. The words we use in daily conversation are symbolic maps of territory. No matter how detailed a map may be, it still does not

[1] The comparison of words and maps was suggested by Alfred Korzybski, *Science and Sanity* (Lakeview, Illinois: Institute of General Semantics, 1948).

describe the territory with complete accuracy. In the same way, words do not describe an object or a person with complete accuracy.

If the map we use conflicts in some way with the territory that is supposedly described, then the map must be considered in error, not the territory. In the same way, a word we use to describe a person may be in conflict with the person as he actually is. Here again we must consider that the word is in error, not the person about whom the word is used. Because a man is *called* a thief doesn't mean that he *is* a thief. This seems obvious, but we often accept the word which describes a person as being more true than the person himself. We may believe that a person is incompetent because we use the word or label *foreigner* to describe him (if *foreigner* is associated with *incompetence* in our minds) without bothering to check whether or not actual incompetence exists. Whenever confusion results from an attempt to communicate, the confusion can almost always be resolved if both parties are wise enough and patient enough to test their respective maps or beliefs with objective reality. Prejudices, biases, and unrecognized cultural influences keep us from checking our perceptions with reality.

When we use a word or a series of words to describe an external reality, we are engaged in the process of abstracting. We do not describe everything there is to say about the situation, but instead pick out what to us seems most important. *There are different levels of abstraction,* however, and it is important to recognize the effect on the accuracy of communication of confusing one level of abstraction with another. If, for example, we were to attempt to describe where a person is at the present time, we could begin at a low level of abstraction by saying that he is seated at his desk at the east end of the room that he calls his office. We could become more abstract, that is, we could move up a scale of abstraction by saying that he is located in a suite of offices on the seventh floor of an office building. We continue on up the level of abstraction by stating that he is generally located on Peachtree Street in- the city of Atlanta located in Fulton County in the State of Georgia in the United States of America on the continent of North America located in the western hemisphere, etc. With each separate level of abstraction, we are describing his relative position in more and more general terms.

Using higher-level abstractions permits us to make generalizations, to form principles, and to see overall relationships. The higher we go in our abstracting process, or the more general we become in our description of a situation or object, the less accurate or precise we shall be in describing any *particular* object, situation, or individual. We lose accuracy because we leave out details in our description. Each level of abstraction has its own proper use in communication. The *danger comes when we confuse one level of abstraction with another.* If we wanted to locate the person whose position we were just describing, it would not be enough to learn that he is a resident of Georgia. We would need to know much more detail down to and including the specific room number of his office.

As we describe an individual with certain words or abstractions, we must be careful that we are not misled into thinking that we have accurately described that specific individual when we use a high-level term. The high-level abstraction *Southerner* is a useful term as a generalization, but it says very little about a specific Mr. John Doe who happens to reside in the South. The term *Southerner* as a term is excellent to describe a person who lives in the South. We dare not go beyond this level of meaning as we listen to or use the term *Southerner* without being in great danger of vague, inaccurate, and dangerous communication. *We are confusing levels of abstraction,* or jumping to a false conclusion, if we think to ourselves that the term *Southerner* describes personality characteristics, attitudes, biases, etc., of all people who live in the South. We are all individuals!

High-level abstractions do help us understand and predict the behavior of people. The scientist makes many observations before generalizing that "people with low self-esteem are more likely to be influenced by persuasive communications than are those with high self-esteem."[2] While this may be a good guide for the manager who wants to persuade his subordinates to change their approach to a new EDP system in the office, he may find that some of his employees who seem to have high self-esteem are more resistant to his persuasive efforts than those with low self-esteem. But the very opposite may also be found. A generalization may be a good guide, but the great individual differences which appear in industry may lead us to follow the generalization or abstraction rather than be sensitive to the individual we may be working with. *While such high-level abstractions,* or generalizations, may apply in a majority of cases, *they do not necessarily apply in each particular instance.* If we blindly assume that any generalization is always true, then we are very likely to misperceive reality.

We must be aware of this tendency to confuse higher-order abstractions

[2] Berelson, Bernard and Steiner, Gary A., *Human Behavior, an Inventory of Scientific Findings* (New York: Harcourt, Brace & World, Inc., 1964), p. 548.

with lower-order abstractions. One customer may say to himself that when he has listened to one sales pitch he has listened to them all. He may feel that one product is about the same as another. Unless the salesman is aware that his prospect is making this false generalization, he will not be in a position to do anything about it.

We all form higher-level abstractions about people in many ways. Regardless of our background, we are likely to have rather definite pictures which come to mind when we use the term "management," "labor," "Catholic," "Irishman," or "truckdriver." We form our own high-level abstractions in an effort to understand better the similarities and differences among people or groups. *If our high-level abstractions suggest various possibilities or approaches to solving a problem, then they are useful. If, however, we think we are describing accurately a particular unique individual, then we are in difficulty.*

The tragedy of confusing levels of abstraction in our daily life is almost too enormous to be described. What talents are being wasted when we refuse to hire a person just because that person happens to be a *woman* or a *Jew* or a *Negro* or a *Baptist!* Nations fail to understand each other in the same way. Wars, persecutions, lynchings, and elaborate programs of mass extermination occur because of confusion between levels of abstraction. Whenever it is at all possible, we should look at the reality of a situation to see whether or not the *facts* are what the label or words imply. We must examine each individual situation to see how it is unique or different and avoid overgeneralization just because we notice *some* similarities to other situations.

A Generalization Is Not a Specification

It is against the law to put a label on a can of peas or a tube of ointment which does not describe it accurately. Unfortunately, we have no such laws which apply to the labels we use to describe people. The manager who describes all his employees as "selfish, ungrateful people" will probably do a poor job of managing or supervising them because he is failing to notice the various *important individual differences which make each person what he is.* Things which appear to be the same are never really the same and the actual differences may be more important than is recognized. The father coming home from a business trip with toys for each of his children may think that the toys are exactly the same. It is likely that his children will point out to him just how wrong he is.

The manager may make serious errors in his selection decisions because of his tendency to apply inaccurate labels to the candidates whom he interviews. For example, he may interview a candidate and discover that when he was thirteen years old he got his first job, started making his own money, and bought his own clothes. The high-level abstraction or label "worked hard at an early age" occurs to the manager and he thinks that his candidate is a lot like Mike, the star producer of the company. The manager may get excited, say to himself, "I think this is going to be another Mike," and hire the candidate without much further evaluation. The candidate and "Mike" have certain similarities and because of this the manager forms a high-level abstraction in his effort to evaluate the candidate and solve his selection problem. Unfortunately, the label he has formed and applied to his candidate does not necessarily conform to the actual facts.

This tendency to accept hastily formed labels as actual descriptions of the real object or person blocks effective communication in the selection interview, just as it does in the sales inteview. No two candidates are exactly alike or even very much alike. No two sales prospects are alike, either. As we listen to a businessman, we may notice that he uses poor grammar. We may then in our minds apply the label "not very bright," and make an obvious attempt to talk down to him. If, by chance, he happens to use bad grammar but also happens to be quite intelligent, he may resent our apparent patronizing attitude and decide never to do business with us. We would have made the mistake of noticing one element of the man's behavior and forming a high-level abstraction or label of "not very bright" which, in this case, was a far from accurate description. A real block in communication is the result. We might add that in such a situation we may be the last person to know that we have grievously misjudged him!

The Weight of Authority

The fact that we accept the word as being more true than the thing itself is a reason for widespread prejudice among human beings and for the popularity of scapegoats. Why do we make such obvious mistakes in our thinking? Why do we accept the label for the thing as being more accurate than the thing itself? Perhaps it depends partially on the way we are taught as children. Are we not taught to accept the authority of our parents without question? Are we not taught to accept what the teacher says without question?

When we see something in print, we are likely to believe it is true without questioning its validity. When we hear gossip about an individual, the tendency is strong for us to swallow, without even chewing, the information rather than to check it for ourselves. We may even commit the atrocity of regurgitating this gossip in the presence of someone else, without knowing or caring whether we are speaking the truth.

Blind acceptance of labels describing people, and blind acceptance of statements by an "authority," can be real blocks to our own personal growth and maturity and blocks to communication. Would Einstein have achieved his brilliant results if he had not questioned authority? Many inventions exist because someone did challenge the "truth" of what was being said in the classroom or written in books. Of course, inventions frequently result from a *new* combination of previously established facts or truths.

Progress is made precisely because someone has dared to question persons of authority rather than merely accept their pronouncements. Unless we can resist this tendency to accept labels blindly, we shall continue to make gross errors in our observations of the world, and, at the same time, make gross errors in our attempt to communicate. It is sometimes more pleasant to maintain a fiction than it is to discover reality or the truth. What child does not struggle to maintain his belief in Santa Claus? It takes real courage to be honest with ourselves and with others. It may be convenient to maintain a belief in a label or high-level abstraction than to discover the facts. Maturing as an individual and collectively as a nation will not follow unless there is a concerted effort to examine one's beliefs (and thereby one's language) to see if they do, indeed, need to be modified.

Whenever we run into a snag in our efforts to communicate with each other, or even to live with each other, a common reaction is to shrug our shoulders and say, "Well, that's human nature." We sometimes carry this one step further and say, "Let's just rely on common sense and everything will turn out all right." But contemporary writers tell us that we had better start changing human nature, or human nature will eliminate itself in one more large-scale war or world-wide pollution. The way we think has much to do with determining human nature and also the kind of behavior which we accept as common sense.

The Either–Or Problem

Our present civilization (and therefore our language and system of communication) is based on a system of logic or reasoning formulated by the Greek philosopher Aristotle, who did what seems to us now to be a simple thing. He merely observed how men behaved and how they thought; then he formulated some laws to describe this behavior. Aristotle said, in effect, that men act as if a thing is what it is, that anything must be either a particular thing or it must not be that thing, and that something cannot both be a particular thing and not be that particular thing.[3] In other words, a chair is a chair, any particular thing is either a chair or is not a chair, and something cannot at the same time be a chair and not be a chair. What Aristotle observed about men was that they think in an "either–or" way about the world in which they live. Either something is the truth or it is not the truth. Something cannot at the same time be the truth and not be the truth. This was the beginning of our formal system of logic and to us today it simply sounds like "common sense."

Expressing things in an either–or way is known as *dichotomizing*. A dichotomy is a division of something into two parts. In logic it is a division of a class of things into two opposed subclasses as, for example, real and unreal. There are many things which can be logically dichotomized. People are either male or female. A woman is either pregnant or she is not pregnant. We either go for a physical examination or we do not. But there are many things with which we deal every day that cannot be logically dichotomized. Because this is so, either–or thinking can become a real problem if it is applied indiscriminately.

Many things are not black or white, but instead are shades of gray. Much of nature consists of a series of gradations rather than of things which can be reduced to an either–or status. The difficulty in communication and in all human relationships comes when we attempt to apply either–or thinking to a many-sided or multidimensional situation. We might say, for example, that failure is the opposite of success. We may think that either we have achieved success or we have failed. We may also feel that we cannot succeed and fail with a particular project at the same time. There is probably nothing more potent than this kind of thinking in causing maladjustments among men. The tendency in our culture to see success and failure in either–or terms invariably gives rise to frustration and to gross feelings of inferiority.

---

[3] For the interested reader, these three observations are known respectively as (1) the law of identity, (2) the law of the excluded middle, and (3) the law of noncontradiction. A discussion of Aristotelian logic and its implications will be found in Alfred Korzybski, *op. cit.*

What is success? Ask one of your friends this question and you are likely to get an extremely vague and ill-defined answer. A man may not know what success means to him, but will drive himself relentlessly for years in an effort to seek it. Success is, for some men, like the carrot dangled in front of the donkey. We know that there is something "out there" we are trying to reach, but we may never feel completly sure that we have reached it. If, because we have never reached success, we feel that we are, therefore, "failures," our life is likely to be a series of never-ending frustrations. It seems more realistic to measure success and, failure, not in either–or terms, but as a succession of minor successes or minor victories. Success is relative rather than absolute. We can achieve partial success as well as partial failure. It is the inability to accept this simple fact of life that leads many people to serious mental and emotional maladjustments.

Making inappropriate either–or judgments about ourselves not only contributes to maladjustments and errors in communication, but keeps us from seeking help for our maladjustments. What individual likes to think of himself as mentally ill? The assumption that most of us hold is that either we are mentally ill or we are not. But this just doesn't make sense. If we will think for a moment in terms of physical illness, it will be easier to recognize that mental illness is a matter of gradation or degree. We can easily admit to ourselves and others that we can have minor physical aches or pains and that we are slightly ill. With afflictions of a more serious nature, we can be moderately or grossly ill even to the point of being almost incapacitated. In precisely the same way, we are all, at some time or another, slightly, moderately, grossly, or completely incapacitated by mental illness.

Either–or thinking about matters which are not black or white undermines our communication with each other (and especially with ourselves!) and makes it difficult for us to learn. Common words that can tip us off to the fact that we are thinking in either–or terms are the words "always, never, all, none, completely, forever," etc. Our use of high-level abstractions, or labels, to describe people is frequently dichotomous in nature. The manager who states he wants to hire a dominant employee is implying that such a person is always completely dominant in all situations and is never submissive to or controlled by other people. If this is what he is searching for, he is likely to be continually disappointed. If he were to look, instead, for a man who has the ability to control individuals more often than not, then he is more likely to find the individual he wants. A manager who thinks in an either–or fashion about dominance while he is interviewing a candidate and discovers that his candidate has once behaved in a way which does not indicate dominance, may jump to the conclusion that the candidate is not "dominant." It is more reasonable to attempt to determine *under what circumstances* and *in what situations* this particular candidate is able to control people, and to what degree. The difficulty with this kind of careful thinking is that it does not permit us the "luxury" of putting people into pigeonholes. But people do *not* fit neatly into pigeonholes.

SENDER AND RECEIVER COMPLICATIONS

Understanding the complications of communication situations may help us clarify what we can do individually to exchange information more effectively; inappropriately simplifying the situation very often leads to confusion. As a sender of a message, a first tendency, if things go wrong, is to blame either the media or the receiver. As a receiver of a message, if things go wrong, the first tendency is to blame either the sender or the media. The result of these mutual and very human tendencies is to lean back and point an accusing finger at the other when instead we should lean forward and bend a listening ear. Understanding the complications in both sending and receiving a message will not necessarily eliminate communication errors, but perhaps it will start us in the right direction in understanding and improving our sometimes feeble efforts to transmit an image from one brain to another.

The sender and the receiver of a message have similar problems. Both are involved in an abstraction process, both are dealing with codes (languages), and both are involved in misleading and deceiving not only the other but himself as well. Both have limited awareness of what is transpiring. Both have a point of view and a set of values they are defending. Both are maximally interested in changing the behavior of the other and minimally interested in changing his own behavior. Both are faced with the problems of finding the right words or signs to convey a message. Both are convinced they will not really be understood by the other and both want not to be fully understood by the other. The enormous amount of energy we expend to deceive, mislead, manipulate, or otherwise control the perception of others is evidence that we share the common conviction that if others really understood us they wouldn't like us very much. For both the sender and the receiver, this last factor may be largely unconscious.

Abstracting—Encoding

When we have an image we want to convey to others, we abstract certain things from the general and often vague mental image and then search for words which come close to expressing these vague thoughts. The words we choose certainly do not contain all the feelings and complex thoughts in our minds, but we hope they come close. A young man in love (or an old man, for that matter) may feel a bursting sensation of delight, wonder, and awe as he looks at his beloved, but reared as a "typical American" feels inhibited in fully expressing what he feels. What may come out is, "Wow! It certainly is nice to sit here and put my arms around you!" By no stretch of the imagination do these few words express all there is to say about his feeling for his girl. But these are the only words she hears. She cannot read his mind nor can she always correctly interpret the gleam in his eye. If she had hoped to see a certain movie and he had forgotten it, what she hears may be, "I don't care if you want to see that movie or not . . . it's cheaper to stay at home." Wouldn't he be surprised, then, if she said, "Oh, you're so inconsiderate! You never think of how I feel or what I might want to do!" Perhaps it was this kind of communication error which prompted Shakespeare to write, "The course of true love never did run smooth."

Not only does the sender of a message have a problem putting his mental images into the right words, but he has to decide how much of his image he is willing to share. Each of us has a built-in censor which scans the messages we are about to send out so that "secrets" (or that which we feel the other person wouldn't really understand or accept) won't slip out. But, on the other hand, there are times when we want something to slip out so that we can test the effect of the message on someone else. Politicians do this all the time to measure the pulse of their constituents. If an unfavorable reaction follows, it can always be denied that the information "leaked" was correct. Or in a private conversation we can always say, "That's not what I meant to say."

Decoding—Generalizing

If we are the receiver of a message, we have the problem of interpreting the words used (using our own frame of reference based on past experiences) and deciding on the general idea the sender is trying to convey to us. The following chapter examines the difficulties in interpreting words and the errors in meaning which are almost inevitable. Since we as the receivers will invariably give different meanings to words than the sender of the message did, it is easy to see how confusion can multiply. The sender of the message doesn't say exactly what he means and the receiver doesn't hear quite the same things said by the sender.

In addition to these problems, the receiver has his own censor at work. Some of the information coming in he wants to hear, but some he wants not to hear. His desire to defend himself from certain recognitions leads to *selective perception*, to screening out unwanted information, to inattention, misinterpretation, or even "hearing" things which were not said.

Many distractions compete for the available attention of the receiver while he is in a communication situation. His own needs to perceive, unconscious protective mechanisms, fatigue, a desire to talk rather than listen—all introduce possible sources of confusion. As we will see in the next chapter, listening is an active skill which takes concentration, energy, and above all an ability to go beyond the self-centeredness which so drastically interferes with communication effectiveness.

SUMMARY

We cannot *not* communicate. Communication is going on around us all the time on a verbal, nonverbal, conscious, and unconscious level. Every situation we are in communicates something to us and influences the outcome of our efforts. The more we can see what the communication situation is, the more facts we have in planning how to communicate in order to obtain the desired results. There is no way to avoid distortion in communication, but we can minimize this distortion by understanding its sources and causes. The way we think has much to do with the accuracy and appropriateness of our communication efforts.

When we communicate to and about people it is easy to overgeneralize and thereby encourage prejudices and misconceptions. The common tendency to use simple words to describe complicated situations makes us lose sight of important individual differences and creates self-perpetuating communication errors. Recognizing when and what to question in a communications situation allows us to make more effective use of the language tools at our disposal.

QUESTIONS FOR DISCUSSION AND THOUGHT

1. "One 'common-sense' notion is that the best way to clarify is to simplify." Why is this not always the case?
2. What are the major factors which are part of every communications situation?
3. What is an example of self-created communication confusion? What can be done about it?
4. What happens when a verbal and nonverbal message contradict each other? Give an example of this from your own experience.
5. Confusing different levels of abstraction is a major cause of communication confusion. How can this communication difficulty be identified?
6. A person in a position of authority may not always be correct in what he says. Why is it difficult for many people to doubt an authority and to think for themselves?
7. "Either you're for me or you're against me!" How would you analyze this kind of thinking in order to improve communications?
8. Needs determine perception. What are the implications of this for the person who wishes to improve his own communication ability?

5

LANGUAGE TOOLS

tool: ... an implement or object used in performing an operation or carrying on work of any kind; an instrument or apparatus necessary to a person in the practice of his vocation or profession (a barber's chair, a photographer's camera, a scholar's book are all tools); something that serves as a means to an end; an instrument by which something is effected or accomplished (words are the tools with which men think).[1]

picnic: ... an excursion or outing with food usually provided by members of the group and eaten in the open; ... a pleasant or amusing experience; a time free of ordinary cares and responsibilities.[2]

These are two of the nearly half-million words defined in one of our largest dictionaries. They also happen to be two words whose meaning almost no one looks up. They are such common words that we easily (?) understand the financial consultant who talks about a recent interview. "I made a presentation to the board of directors, but the controller who will make the decision was really a dull tool. This sale is going to be no picnic, believe me!"

Words have tremendous power. Words permit us to transmit knowledge

[1] *Webster's Third New International Dictionary* (Chicago, Illinois: G. & C. Merriam Co., 1966).
[2] *Ibid.*

from one generation to another. Words help us become civilized. But words also lead marriages to the divorce court and nations to war. We tend to be prisoners of words. Words allow us to love and hate each other. Words allow us to build societies and to destroy them. Words can be "mightier than the sword." Word sounds are only vibrations in the air, but they make us think or behave in certain ways. Words mean something to us because we give them meaning.

LANGUAGE IS DISTINCTLY HUMAN

Webster Says

When we come across a word we don't know, we invariably turn to the dictionary. Webster says that the word *definition* is:

1. The act of defining, determining, distinguishing, or explaining. 2. A brief description of what a thing is. 3. An explanation or statement of what a word or phrase means or has meant. 4. A putting or being in clear, sharp outline.[3]

Referring to a dictionary gives us only the barest notion of the full meaning of a particular word. The meaning of a word or phrase is not solely its dictionary definition but is also the hidden or obvious reaction that its use brings about in any particular situation. We use words to interest people in what we are doing, to threaten them, to protest, etc. Words are tools which can be crude or refined, which help or hinder getting something done, which please or hurt, depending on how we use them.

We may use the right word at the right time, or the wrong word at the wrong time. Either way we recognize that human effort is successful or not, depending largely on the adequacy of the word tools we use.

It's a fine May weekend and you and your family are excited about last-minute preparations for a picnic. Food is quickly thrown into the basket and off you go. There's a stream and a grassy area a few miles off the main highway north of town, but where is that side road you took before? Rummaging through the glove compartment you find no map

[3] *Ibid.*

(tool) of the area so it's a matter of guessing where to turn. You're in luck! The first turn was the right one and here you are in your favorite spot. The children are thirsty so you consent to their drinking a Coke. But where is the bottle opener (tool)? You forgot it! But with considerable effort you manage to get the top off a bottle by jamming the top against the edge of a board (tool) you found in the weeds (this is after chipping a tooth [tool] trying to pry off the top). Now where is the can opener (tool) for the beans? No can opener! Give the trunk keys (tools) to your older son and ask him to look in the trunk for the hand axe (tool) you think is there. Maybe you could get the can open with the axe. No axe? Well, ask your son to look in the glove compartment for a screwdriver (tool). He doesn't have the keys to the car? He dropped them in the weeds on the way back? Oh!!!

Tools are important to the animal known as "man." In fact, with the exception of very crude tools used by the chimpanzee and perhaps a few other animals, man is the unique tool-user in the animal kingdom.[4] He invented the wheel to transport heavy items more easily. He invented the use of fire, metal, chemicals, and words to transcend the physical and temporal spatial limits of all other animal brethren. He uses the word tools to communicate with past generations and avoid some of their mistakes. He communicates with future generations and thereby contributes to "progress." Through word tools he has found weapons against disease, invented institutions such as schools, churches, and governments, and overcome the limitations of gravity, temperature, and seasons. Man has achieved his unique position among animals because of his superior ability and desire to formulate a system of abstractions and symbols called language.

There is nothing more human than the speech of an individual or of a group of individuals. Lower forms of animals apparently do have an ability to communicate some kinds of meaning through their natural sounds and bodily movements. But man is the only animal that can communicate abstract ideas and transmit them from one generation to another in order to avoid costly trial and error and advance what we know as civilization. Lower forms of animals are bound by time, that is, there can be no communication about things that happened in the past or will happen in

---

[4] The chimpanzee "manufactures" tools to fish for termites, uses sticks as weapons and levers (!), chews up leaves for use as sponges, uses leaves for toilet paper, etc. A long term field study of chimpanzee social and tool-making behavior is reported by Jane VanLawick-Goodall in *In the Shadow of Man* (Boston: Houghton Mifflin Company, 1971).

the future. Man, of course, is able to do this. Lower forms of animals can communicate only about things or objects that actually exist. Only the human animal can communicate about abstract ideas and concepts which may not exist in fact or reality. The uniqueness that man enjoys in the use of language is not that other animals are incapable of forming the basic speech sounds. Other animals and even birds such as the parakeet are able to make individual sounds which closely resemble words. But man's unique language ability stems rather from his innate or inborn capacity to use symbols to represent things and to use his imagination to find meaning in these symbols.[5]

Language is the cement that binds people together. Language is what makes us human. It permits us to form societies and allows us to learn from the mistakes and successes of others. Language is one kind of cultural behavior and one which is learned. Language is, in fact, the reason that cultures or societies continue to exist.

Symbolism and Imagination

A symbol is something that stands for or represents a thing. For example, the cross is the symbol of Christianity. Words are symbols which stand for objects, qualities, or ideas. Man's ability to use symbols allows him to form *bridges of understanding* between his fellow creatures of the same generation and from one generation to another. But the use (or misuse) of these symbols can become insurmountable barriers between men. Many of mankind's problems occur because we don't all "speak the same language" in either a literal or a colloquial sense. We have the power to determine whether the language we use becomes a bridge, allowing us to transcend frustrating conditions, or a barrier to our own growth and development as individuals and as a society.

Language is not the only form of symbolic expression that man uses, but it is the most important form. Without speech there would be no human social organization. Without language, we would have no laws, few rules of behavior, no science, literature, music, or religion. It is the continued use of this ability that makes it possible to perpetuate our

[5] Chimpanzees have been taught to use a sign language similar to that used by deaf human beings. Through the use of sign language, and the use of plastic symbols for words, chimpanzees have been taught to speak in sentences. The use of symbols or signs in communicating with chimpanzees is reported in: R. Allen, and Beatrice Gardner, "Teaching Sign Language to a Chimpanzee", *Science,* Vol. 165, 1969, pp. 664-72.

culture. Without the use of symbols, there would be no culture, and man would not be much different from other animals.

Just as symbolic behavior which we call language has made mankind "human," so each individual, as an infant, becomes human only as he learns to make use of symbols or language. Until the infant learns to use speech, his behavior cannot be distinguished qualitatively from that of an ape or baby chimpanzee. As we have seen, the family is the chief teacher of culture to the child. The child learns about his culture through the use of language as a means of communication.

Man's unique ability to make use of symbols in his efforts to communicate gives him an advantage of incalculable value over all other animals. However, this same advantage can become a tremendous disadvantage because of the very nature of symbolic expression. A symbol represents or stands for an actual object or an idea. Note that we say the symbol *stands* for the thing; it is not the thing itself. As we say the word "chair" the listener will invariably form a mental picture of some kind of chair, possibly the one he is sitting in. The word "chair" is a symbol which stands for the real object.

Through the use of language it is possible to transmit images from one mind to another in somewhat the same way that television pictures are transmitted. As we walk into a store and look at the array of television sets for sale, we may see a dozen sets all tuned to the same station and all receiving apparently the same image at the same time. The transmission of images from the television station to the set is accomplished with a minimum of distortion. When one speaker talks to an audience of a dozen people, however, all these people do not receive the same mental images as a result of the transmission of symbols from the speaker to the audience. Instead, these twelve individuals will quite likely receive twelve different images. If the speaker mentions the word "chair," one listener may picture a soft, comfortable, overstuffed, well-worn leather chair in his den, another may think of the device used for electrocution, while still a third may immediately think of a position at a university.

Man's ability to use symbols to represent things can be a source of great understanding, but also a source of immense and sometimes tragic misunderstanding. *In communication between individuals, one of the few things that we can be absolutely sure of is that the receiver will never get exactly the same message that the speaker is attempting to send.* There is no way that we can communicate with another person with complete accuracy.

There will always be a certain amount of distortion in the message picked up by the listener or receiver. Different individuals give different meanings to the same symbol and this is of vital significance to the businessman, who makes his living by motivating men's behavior through the use of symbols.

LEARNING THE LANGUAGE OF SYMBOLS

Just as our culture teaches us how to behave, so our culture teaches us the use of symbolic communications, or language. The child learns to speak by imitating his parents. Learning to talk is primarily a matter of trial and error, with many repetitions being necessary before recognizable speech emerges. The child who is born deaf learns to talk only through an extremely difficult process. Because he cannot hear the sounds, he cannot use imitation as a method of learning. Thus, the child who learns to talk without a sense of hearing never completely escapes a harsh, unnatural tone of voice.

When we learn to bat a ball or shoot targets or reach for things and grasp them, we are depending upon an elaborate *system* of feedback of information. As we reach for a pencil, a whole network of muscles and nerve impulses is called into play. If our hand overshoots the pencil, we automatically compensate for this and adjust our muscle effort so that our hand does grasp the pencil. We do this easily and smoothly when we have a constant and reliable source of feedback information. If we close our eyes and reach for the same pencil, we see that we engage in a good bit of groping and poorly coordinated movements directed toward the goal. Even though our eyes are covered, we still have a source of feedback information in our sense of touch, and also in the muscle sense which is called *kinesthetics.* As soon as we touch the pencil, we know that we can grasp our fingers around it and move it.[6]

In the same way, in learning to speak we need the information which comes to us from our feedback mechanism. Feedback is important not

[6] Cybernetics is a science which includes the study of feedback mechanisms and their operation in the machine and in man. Further theoretical background and some practical applications may be found in the following texts: Norbert Wiener, *The Human Use of Human Beings: Cybernetics and Society* (Garden City, New York: Doubleday & Co., Inc., 1954); F. H. George, *Automation, Cybernetics and Society* (Piqua, Ohio: Leonard V. Hill, 1959); and G. T. Guilbaud, *What Is Cybernetics?* (New York: Criterion Books, Inc., 1959).

only in learning a language, but in continuing to speak normally as well. The child tries first one pronunciation and then another until he sees that he is rewarded by his parents. He has then learned a new word. As adults, unless we have a steady feedback of information about the sounds we utter, our speech patterns are likely to become distorted and virtually unrecognizable. We hear ourselves speak when we are talking to someone else. If there is some interference with our ability to hear a feedback of our speech through outside noise, earplugs, etc., our pattern of speech immediately takes on a different quality. Our voice may become higher pitched, we may speak with greater volume, and we may do a good bit of slurring and mispronouncing of words.

In one scientific study on the effect of this kind of feedback information on the quality of speech, the subjects were asked to speak into a microphone which was plugged into a tape recorder. As the speech was recorded on the tape, the message was immediately played back to the subject through the earphones that he was wearing. The pickup head of the tape recorder was arranged so that it could be adjusted along the length of tape as it passed through the recorder. In effect, this allowed the experimenter to delay the return of the speakers's voice to the speaker's ears. When the subject spoke and he heard the sound of his own voice delayed for just a tiny fraction of a second, this delay in voice feedback was enough to cause a complete breakdown in his ability to speak at all. At first, the subject reacted by gradually slowing his rate of speech. Then he either stopped completely or continued to verbalize a single word by stretching it out so that it became a wail or almost a scream. This study had to be done with care because of the very upsetting psychological conditions which it presented to the subject. Many of the subjects became extremely disturbed and remained so for some time after taking off the earphones.

We have illustrated the importance of a feedback mechanism in terms of the actual presence of sound which comes back to the speaker. This we might call *phonetic feedback*. But another kind of feedback is important in learning a language, and that is *semantic* feedback. We learn to use our language by speaking it and then by seeing the effect of our speech on people. If we cannot see how people react, or if we are too insensitive to notice how they react, distortions may occur in our ability to communicate which are just as severe and dramatic as those discussed in the above paragraph. Learning a language is much more than memorizing the dictionary definitions of words. Words mean much more than the simple explanations in the dictionary. An individual may feel that he has already learned to speak and to use his native language. But learning to speak and communicate with others is a skill which must be learned and relearned and refined on a daily basis. Through this process we eliminate sources of error in communication and become more effective in motivating others.

Words have a *denotation* and a *connotation.* The denotation of a word is the direct, explicit meaning or reference to an object, especially as it may appear in a dictionary definition. The connotation of a word is an idea which is *suggested* by or *associated* with a word or a phrase. We define the word "mother" as meaning a female parent, but the connotation of the word "mother" is that of love, care, and tenderness.

When we use words to communicate, we usually do not stop to consider the various possible denotations and connotations they may have. The attorney may explain to a client and his wife that a certain trust agreement should be chosen so that the wife will have a monthly income rather than having to invest a large sum at the death of the husband. The connotation that this may have for the wife could be a feeling of being overcontrolled or restricted and lacking freedom to do any financial planning of her own. She may feel unfavorable toward the advice of the attorney and directly or indirectly block the completion of the arrangement. If the wife verbalizes this connotation further explanations and adjustments can be made so that a much-needed trust will be created. If, as is often the case, the client or his wife have private connotations which they do not reveal (possibly because they are not even aware of them), the attorney may have inadvertently said something which will confuse the issue and may be powerless to correct it. These nonverbalized objections are sometimes called "hidden objections." As we shall see in a later section, active and intelligent listening on the part of the professional adviser can help him discover many of the personal connotations his clients may have in response to the verbal communication between them.

Loaded Words

A word can have the impact and shock of a rifle shot. Daily we read about people who are injured or killed by the handling of a gun that was thought not to be loaded. We often injure another person by the use of a certain word even though we might afterward say, "I didn't know it was loaded." Words can have what is called an *emotional loading.* Certain words carry with them an emotional response for the listener. The words "female parent" do not have nearly the emotional loading that the word "mother" has. A word acquires an emotional loading through association. If we use a word or hear a word used at a time when our emotions are aroused, the emotional tone of the situation can then become attached to the word itself. We react much differently to the sentence, "My boss and I had a misunderstanding and we both decided it would be better for me to move on," than we do to the words, "I got fired."

Our language is full of euphemisms, which are words or phrases that are less expressive or direct and are considered less distasteful and offensive than other words. The disadvantage of being indirect in what we say is that our real intent or meaning may be lost "in translation." Many a manager has failed to get his point across to an employee because he used a roundabout or inaccurate way of expressing himself. Depending on the situation, it may simply be more effective for the manager to pound his fist on the desk and say, "Get out of this office and go to work!" rather than to hint gently that the employee might do a better job if he were to find a way to process more forms each day.

We live in a culture in which it is not always acceptable to be completely accurate in our communications. One school of thought on how to get along with people says that we must at all costs avoid being offensive or disturbing. We are taught that it is polite and even right to tell a "white lie" to spare someone's feelings. With this kind of cultural pressure affecting us, is it any wonder that we have great difficulty in our simple efforts to communicate with each other?

Slippery Words

The same words mean different things to different individuals and the same words can have different meanings at different times. The meaning of words can vary according to the *group* we find ourselves in and according to the *individual* to whom we are speaking. On the back of a bakery truck, there is the slogan, "Good Pies Like Mother Used To Make." How do we interpret this slogan? It is likely that some of our mothers made excellent pies while other mothers made pies not fit for consumption. Because of our individual personal experience with pies made by mother we have individual and personal interpretations of this slogan. As a matter of fact, the word "good" which appears in that slogan is itself quite a slippery word. What does that word mean to us? If your boss tells you that you did a "good" job, he may mean that he has never seen a job done in quite as excellent a fashion. On the other hand, you may feel that since he did not say that you did an *excellent* job, he is really not rating you very high.

Words like "good," "pretty," "valuable," and "intelligent" are words that not only are difficult to measure and define adequately, but vary in meaning depending on our personal experiences, our level of education, and the way these words are placed in a sentence. When we speak, we can give different shades of meaning to a certain word by the way we say it, by our inflections, by a slightly lifted eyebrow, etc. When the word is written, the author cannot control the meaning of a word; he cannot use a tone of voice or a facial gesture to shade the meaning.

Words which are especially slippery in meaning, that can mean so many different things at different times for different people in different situations, are words such as "they," "we," and "that." As we make a statement about a certain matter the listener may say, "I don't agree with that." It is very likely that he will mean one thing when he refers to "that," while we may interpret his statement as referring to something quite different. If the discussion continues long enough, this confusion may resolve itself. One or the other party in the conversation may suddenly get an insight and say, "Oh, I think you and I have been talking about two different things." What is just as likely, however, is that if there is a difference of meaning attached to the word "that," the discussion may not continue long enough for the uncertainty to be cleared up. It is imperative, in any attempt to communicate, that such vague words be pinned down to a more specific expression. We are fond of saying, "They tell me that . . . "when we are attempting to advance our own argument. We may avoid this difficulty if we will try to restate what we think he is saying by using words that can be less easily misunderstood.

The Word Is Not the Thing

Many of the words we use we have learned by hearing the word and seeing the object to which it refers. When the infant first sees a chair, it does not know what the object is or what it is for. It learns about the chair only by sitting on it, by falling off it, by bumping into it, by chewing on it, etc. As the infant experiences the chair and at the same time hears the word "chair" he acquires the ability to use the word "chair" as a symbol for the actual thing.

The word "chair" is not the actual object itself. The word is only a sign or symbol which stands for the object. This may seem obvious, but quite often we confuse the word or label with the actual object. This simple confusion of words and objects causes trouble in our attempts to communicate. We make this point about words and things for two reasons. One is that *no word ever completely describes or tells everything about the object to which it refers.* The language we use always contains a great amount of built-in inaccuracy. The second reason for emphasizing the nonidentity of words and objects is that, while we may all agree that certainly the word "chair" is not the actual chair itself, *there are many times when we act as if the word were the object.* Many individuals need only to hear the word "cancer" and they react with fear and apprehension. We react to the word as we might react to cancer itself. Too often, an individual avoids using the word "cancer" or even thinking about it, for fear that somehow talking about it might even make it happen. Because of this reaction toward the word, thousands of individuals avoid periodic physical examinations and even avoid consultation with a physician when some of the well-know danger signals make their appearance.

If this kind of thinking seems strange to you, just remember all the times that you have said, "I've had good luck so far—I'd better knock on wood." Well, consciously we might deny that we believe such a superstition to be true, but there is plenty of evidence to show us that unconsciously we react as if the superstition were true. Many a man hesitates to talk about his business being profitable for fear that something might happen to this profitability. This kind of false identification of the word with the object causes difficulty in communication. We blush and are embarrassed at the mention of sexual objects, and especially the four-letter sex terms, in much the same way that we might if we were actually exposed to the objects or acts themselves.

We need to elaborate on the idea that a word or a phrase never completely describes the object or situation to which it refers. We can never say *all* there is to say about an object such as a chair. This is probably because we can never know all there is to know about any one object. Because we cannot completely describe reality with words, and because any attempt to do so is too time-consuming, we take a short cut. We *abstract* what we think is probably the most important or prominent characteristic of an object or aspect of a situation and this is what we put into words. We make only *partial statements* about any object or situation.

Words Are Abstractions

As abstractions, words describe only parts of what we are talking about. Because there is almost always more that can be said about any given subject, experts working in the field of *general semantics* suggest that we might remind ourselves of the incompleteness of our language by frequent use of the words *et cetera*. If we say that the chair upon which we are sitting is made of wood, is upholstered, is green, is made of oak, is comfortable, is handmade, we can indicate that more can be said by simply adding the words *et cetera,* or *etc.* The real danger to communication comes when we use a certain word and then forget that more could be said while assuming that we have said everything there is to say. If we say that an employee is not productive because he is "lazy," we are in trouble if we think that we have completely described the situation. Much more can and needs to be said to communicate the problem fully.

IMPROVING COMMUNICATION WITH WORDS

As mentioned before, words are slippery things in the sense that their meaning can change according to the person using the words, according to the time, the group, etc. The language we use is exceedingly inexact. Not only are words quite inadequate to describe situations or to convey information accurately, but the way we use them contributes to this inexactness of language. Many words we use to describe people are general in nature; they could apply to any one of a number of people, but we often use them as if they were specific and accurate descriptions of the particular individual we have in mind. When we use such terms as "lazy," "dominant," "money-motivated" to describe anyone, we are in danger of introducing gross errors in our communications. Because the word "lazy" is such a general term, the mental picture it creates in one person's mind can be far different from the mental picture in someone else's mind. Using this kind of term blocks clear thinking about the individual. We may either consciously or unconsciously say to ourselves, "That guy is lazy, and he's always going to be lazy." The term "lazy" has a ring of finality about it and implies that there is no necessity to think further about him.

To clarify our communications and also *to remove blocks in our own thinking about that individual,* it would be better to substitute for the overgeneralized term "lazy" an operational definition of the individual's behavior. We might say instead that "he doesn't work hard enough." This comes closer to describing his actual behavior, but in addition it sets the stage for some kind of action which we might take or which that individual might take to overcome the problem. But we need to go still further. If we are going to attempt more accuracy in our communications, we must *refine our operational definition.* We might then say, "That individual, according to my standard, is not completing as many projects as I think he should, is not starting his work day early enough, and is not using his spare time in the evenings or on weekends to get more work done." In defining the term "lazy" in terms of the actual operations or behavior involved, not only have we done a better job of describing his behavior, but we also have listed some possible causes and solutions for the problem. We *decrease* our understanding of people when we use broad labels to describe them. We *increase* our understanding of people when we strive to formulate operational definitions of their behavior.

The manager who maintains that he looks for a "dominant" individual, without formulating in his own mind what a dominant individual does, is in danger of never finding such an individual and consequently of making poor selection decisions. No one is dominant in all situations. The manager would be more accurate in communications, not only with his assistant but also with himself, if he were to state that he was looking for a man who had demonstrated an ability to control or strongly influence the behavior of others under certain specific conditions. Unless he does this, he is in danger of never going beyond a rather hazy or vague notion in his mind as to what is a "dominant" individual. He is likely to make the mistake of hiring someone who is rebellious and who speaks up and talks back, but who is not competent in actually swaying people's behavior.

The term "money-motivated" is another such general, loose term which is often used but rarely understood. We cannot tell that an employee is money-motivated simply by listening to the man's statement that he wants to make a large amount of money. There is really no way that we can measure his inner motives in this regard. But we can come close to measuring whether or not he has made money in the past or whether he has gone out of his way to make more than a usual amount of money in the past. His *statement* as to his drives is less significant than his *demonstrated past behavior.*

Thus, we will do the best job of communicating if we describe the actual behavior of an individual. As we use operational definitions of events rather than loose, vague labels, we will find that we are communicating with each other with much more precision, and there will be much less chance of being misunderstood.

THE LISTENING PROCESS

Communication is, after all, the transfer of knowledge *and* understanding from one person to another. While we agree that attempting to communicate orally with a deaf person is difficult or impossible, many of us with normal hearing ability turn a "deaf ear" to what other people attempt to communicate to us without realizing what we are doing. One of the most effective tools we have to help us be successful in selling or persuading is our own effective listening ability. If, in listening to a person, we hear only the words he uses but fail to understand what he is trying to say, then communication is not taking place (and we have lost a great deal of our ability to motivate behavior changes in people). Hearing is a physical activity, but real listening is an active attempt to understand someone else's viewpoint which may differ from our own.

Whom do we choose as our friends? We like people who listen to us. This isn't the only reason for choosing friends, but it is an important one. With whom do we like to work? Again, we enjoy most working with people who listen to us and apparently show interest in us. By whom are we most likely to be influenced? Aren't we usually more responsive to someone who has demonstrated his desire to listen to us and to consider our feelings carefully? Listening is one way of showing our real interest and regard for people. But how often do we really listen to someone else? We like to be listened to. We like to have people show interest in us. We like to feel important and worthwhile and we hope that others consider us to be important and worthwhile. But just how good a job do we ourselves do as listeners?

Listening Is Rare

We shall not make the mistake of overgeneralizing about businessmen who deal with the public, but we can observe that a great many are poor listeners. Each of us as we go about our daily business has various worries and concerns with which we are *rather naturally* preoccupied. We worry about our production record, bank account, our marriage, or our children. Because of this preoccupation with ourselves, real listening is relatively rare. We cannot listen too well if we are overly concerned with ourselves and our own problems.

If we expect to become better listeners, we need to be less preoccupied with ourselves and more genuinely interested in others. That is, of course, a tall order and not something that can be accomplished merely by resolving to do so. If we are truly interested in being more effective in communicating, then it should become important to make gains in our own maturity and ability to focus interest and attention on others rather than mostly on ourselves. Real gains in listening ability will come only as we become mature enough to minimize our selfish motives and find real satisfaction in contributing something to others.

Why is it that good listening is so rare? There are several other reasons. When many of us were children, we were often told, in effect, that "children should be seen and not heard." When parents apply undue pressure upon their children to mold them into obedient and attentive listeners, the children in self-defense may actually learn to block out much of what is said to them. Demanding that the child listen may force him to react by not "hearing." If the parent combines great pressure for the child to listen to him with a failure to listen sympathetically to the child, the child does the only thing he can do: he doesn't listen. He resorts to the unconscious mechanism of "psychological deafness." The child can unconsciously block awareness of his sensory impressions; he can be disobedient to his parents and at the same time avoid conscious feeling of guilt for his disobedience. In extreme cases this can result in a kind of deafness which is as impressive and as total as actual physiological deafness.

Probably nothing facilitates listening more than an atmosphere of sympathetic appreciation and acceptance on the part of the parent. Parents can do much to help their children grow in listening ability by making the child feel that his viewpoint is appreciated at least part of the time. The child who grows up without having sympathetic listeners around him is more likely to indulge in passive activities such as television, radio, or movies. Parents who force their children to listen may lead their children to face painful life situations by "turning off" their listening mechanism instead of by listening for ways to solve problems.

Another reason for our lack of effective listening ability is the way we are taught in school. Much of the emphasis, at first, is on learning how to read and on acquiring reading skill. New words to be learned are written on the board or are presented on flash cards. Even instructions from the teacher are written out on the board, again with emphasis placed on learning to read the instructions rather than on listening to them. In addition to this, verbal instructions in a classroom in the first few grades of school are almost always repeated many times by the teacher. This repetition of instruction makes it less necessary for the child himself to take the responsibility for really listening and understanding the spoken instructions the first time. This may cause the child to develop the habit of not really listening to what is said because he knows that if it is important it will be repeated. This kind of instruction probably teaches the child how *not* to listen.

Why all this emphasis on how children learn to listen? The habits formed then appear to be the same habits that continue into adulthood: as an individual engaged in some form of business enterprise we may think and act like an adult but listen like a child. This material on eliminating blocks to listening and finding ways to improve our listening skill may appear naïve and elementary to many, but observation in organizations reveals many highly educated and sophisticated executives engaged in the crudest kind of listening. In business activities much pressure is placed on writing memos rather than relying on the spoken word. While there are good reasons for writing down important information, dependence on writing rather than on speaking or listening gives us little real practice in learning better how to listen.

Blocks to Listening

It is hard for us to listen because to listen attentively to another person's ideas or opinions means that we ourselves become vulnerable to the possibility that our thinking may need changing. Change is uncomfortable. We may, indeed, live in a time of constant change, but this apparently does not make it any easier for us to accept change. We reach a kind of personal equilibrium where we have learned how to act and behave so as to avoid punishment and to gain praise. Once having achieved that delicate equilibrium, we are loath to change it.

Really listening to a person, then, is an acknowledgment that he may have something to tell us that we don't already know. This arouses the often-feared possibility that we must make a new adjustment based partly on the new information we have just received. If someone says something to us with which we disagree, we are most likely to say, "You are wrong." It takes courage to admit to ourselves that possibly we are wrong.

Many people do not really want to understand others or to be understood completely. We hide many of our true feelings. Perhaps most of us are engaged in daily self-deception as well as in the deception of others. This human tendency is a further obstacle to acquiring real skill as a listener. Because of our reluctance to reveal ourselves to people, we tend to be satisfied too quickly with the external details of things and the external characteristics of others.

There is often a fear of deep personal involvement with others. In most of our conversations we like to talk and listen only if the conversation does not go too deep or does not become too intimate. Thus, we keep ourselves at an *emotional arm's length* from others. Effective listening cannot take place between two people holding each other off at arm's length. The poor or ineffectual listener is likely to be on the defensive while he is "listening." He is likely to be waiting until the speaker stops so he can express his rebuttal or somehow attack the speaker. The businessman will often be presenting his proposal to others who may be poor listeners. This obstacle to communication and to understanding is compounded if the speaker himself also happens to be a poor listener. In a conversation involving *two poor listeners,* we can expect that little behavior change will occur.

Empty Listening

Much of what passes for listening is instead an empty compulsive effort to maintain self-esteem. How often have you laughed at a joke you really did not understand? Were you not trying to hide the fact that you did not understand in order to avoid the implication that you weren't very intelligent? *Much of our communication is rendered ineffective because of our unwillingness to ask questions or somehow indicate that we have not understood the conversation.* This kind of *empty communication* is what keeps nations worlds apart. For some reason or another, we rarely permit ourselves to become emotionally involved with people or with the world around us. Perhaps we are afraid of being hurt, of losing our self-esteem, or losing our status, but whatevever the reason, this fear will keep us from really listening to others.

Listening Is an Active Skill

There is nothing passive about effective listening. Listening can be an active tool to use in a sales or persuasion effort. Like most skills, listening can be improved with intelligent practice. Note that we say "intelligent" practice. We are used to hearing and believing that "practice makes perfect," but this, of course, is not true if we practice the wrong thing. Listening does improve with practice, but only if the practice is intelligently planned. The practice must involve some way to measure its effectiveness and some plan for systematic improvement. It is not enough merely to be silent as someone speaks. This is not neccessarily listening.

The good listener listens "between the lines." One of the reasons we listen so poorly is that we think at a more rapid pace than we hear. When someone speaks to us, we have a lot of spare time for other thoughts to creep into our minds and provide competition with the speaker. *Effective Listening is hard work!* The easiest thing to do is to listen to only part of what the speaker is saying, listen only to the things we want to hear, or in some way distort, modify, and censor what the speaker is saying. To be listening actively means we must be constantly applying all our spare thinking time to what is being said. This constant active awareness that is demanded in effective listening infers an awareness that not only what *is* said is important, but also what is *not* said. Sometimes silence can speak more eloquently than words. A word omitted or an idea not mentioned can be as significant as something said. If the husband compliments his wife on each of the separate items she has prepared for dinner but says nothing about the biscuits (which are rock hard), she is more than likely to "hear" clearly the omitted words.

If one hopes to be a skillful listener, it is important to be actively *analyzing* and *weighing* what the speaker is saying. Our immediate evaluation or judgment of what is said, however, can also be one of the greatest obstacles to effective listening. When we listen to a statement made by someone, our first reaction is likely to be, "Do we agree or disagree?" At that moment we probably are not listening simply because we are busy preparing our own rebuttal or argument against the speaker if we happen to disagree with him. *Good listening is something of a scientific procedure.* The scientist carefully observes and records the data he receives, but he is careful that he does not record only the data which is favorable to his hypothesis while failing to record the data which is unfavorable. The scientist does not "listen" only to the data that he wants to hear because he is interested in ascertaining the truth. The good listener must adopt this same attitude.

LEARNING TO LISTEN

The power of real listening is tremendous. Good, effective listening is so rare that when it does occur the speaker is likely to feel extremely warm, friendly, and cooperative toward such a listener. Managers, salesmen, teachers, attorneys, etc., are given much training in how to present ideas and how to overcome resistance or objections. The experienced person has discovered that sensitive and intelligent listening can be the very device which will encourage the listener to talk himself into agreement. *Great pressure* can be placed on the listener either to *overcome his own objections* or to *come to a decision to cooperate* simply through the device of listening. More pressure can be brought to bear through sheer silence than through a barrage of arguments.

How can we improve our listening ability? How can we control the behavior of other people by listening? How can we be sure we will get our points across if we spend more time listening? We can improve our listening ability only through hard, conscientious work, but there are some specific techniques which can help.

When we are listening to what someone is saying, it is useful to try to *restate in our own words* what we think the speaker has just said. This technique does two things: first, it forces us, as the listener, to greater awareness of what the speaker is saying; and second, it indicates to the speaker that we have really been listening. The ability to *catch the meaning* behind what is said is of the utmost importance in guiding that person toward agreement. Experienced and successful persuaders often use the listener's own statements about his needs, opinions, and beliefs to convince him that he should comply.

If we are to improve our listening ability, we must listen longer, listen more often, listen with respect, listen with feedback, listen without premature evaluation, and listen critically. This may sound like a lot of work, but the businessman has not attained his present status without a good deal of hard work, and if a little additional effort helps him to use his ability more effectively, it will be well worth it.

Listen Longer

Most of the time, as we begin to listen to someone, we are searching for the answer to a problem. We examine the first few words the speaker says, trying to see if our answer is contained in them. If we get something that approximates the answer we are expecting to hear, our usual reaction is to stop listening. We may stop listening by simply refusing to listen any longer, by interrupting the speaker, or by allowing ourselves to be distracted in any number of ways. The first rule in learning to be a better listener is simply to give yourself more time to listen. There are many things the listener can be doing while he is listening longer. The listener can put himself in the speaker's shoes and try to feel what the speaker must be feeling. The listener may be wondering about the speaker's background and trying to interpret what the speaker is saying in light of what is known about him.

The executive who listens longer, who allows his subordinate to voice his objections, raise questions, and discuss his own situation more fully, may actually be allowing him to solve his own problems. It is difficult for most people to express themselves adequately. Quite often the first few statements that a person makes about any given subject do not contain all the thoughts and feelings he wishes to communicate. If the listener will simply listen longer, he will give the speaker an opportunity not only to express himself more fully but also to listen to himself and thereby to modify his thoughts and feelings and eventually express himself more accurately and reliably. A speaker may begin to express a point of view, knowing full well that later he wants to add qualifying phrases. If the listener breaks in before the speaker has had a chance to amplify his statements, the speaker is likely to feel both offended and misunderstood.

Listen More Often

It takes practice to learn how to listen just as it takes practice to learn any skill. The individual who wishes to become an accomplished listener will take every opportunity to practice listening. He will attempt to listen more often. There are many times when we can practice listening. If we are concerned about the growth of our children, we can practice listening to them at least some time during each day. Really listening to our children can be of immense help to them in their efforts to grow and in our efforts to help them.

The executive who is married may find that his wife is a valuable asset to him not only personally but in his business. His wife is almost certain to be more enthusiastic about her husband's business if he consistently makes an effort to understand and appreciate her by simply listening to her. Here is another opportunity to practice listening. A problem that many managers have is getting subordinates to listen during training or field activities. The employee may feel he can establish his independence only by doing things his own way, rather than by following the advice of his manager. Someone printed a humorous sign for an office wall, which states, "When all else fails, try doing it the way the boss says." Is it possible that valuable advice or insight may be lost by not listening more often to one's manager as well as to colleagues?

Listen With Respect

The financial adviser provides a service to people by helping them plan toward financial security. Such men are often dedicated to the idea that they should be professional. One way of defining what is meant by the professional approach is to say that the interests of the client become paramount. The adviser interested solely in his own financial gain has lost or perhaps has never found the concept of providing in a professional way the program which best suits his prospect. Such a person may find it difficult to listen to his client with respect.

Much of what man achieves depends upon his ability to understand others, and this in turn depends upon his ability to verbalize his thoughts and feelings. *Real understanding* between people comes when there is an *implicit agreement that each individual recognizes the basic right of another individual to his own integrity and worth.* Effective listening, therefore, depends on our ability to see others as unique personalities with their own beliefs, thoughts, and values. Listening and understanding are based on the *interest* of the listener in recognizing the integrity of others. Without a deep and genuine regard and respect for the person, listening will be shallow and ineffective.

Some of us have learned to *pretend* that we are listening. we have coached ourselves to sit with bright eyes and a rapt expression, apparently taking in every word that is uttered. This is false listening, that is, listening without a genuine motive of wanting to understand. It is likely that the only person who is fooled is the pseudo-listener himself. In addition to being unable to listen, such a person adds insult to injury because he seems to say by his behavior that the person to whom he is apparently listening has so little intelligence that he cannot see through this sham. It is a rare individual who does not recognize this kind of contempt on the part of a fake listener.

Listen With Feedback

Anyone who has ever learned to throw a ball knows that you gain skill only by being able to see how far off target the throw is each time. If we were to practice throwing while we were blindfolded, probably no learning would take place. The learning of anything requires that we have an adequate system of receiving feedback information to provide for necessary changes in our behavior. In learning to listen, there are really two kinds of feedback. One occurs *within* the listener or speaker and the other occurs *between* two or more people. When we listen, and when we speak, we can be reflective about what we are saying or hearing. When we listen to a speaker we can be forming hypotheses in the same way a scientist does, and these hypotheses can be tested continuously. When we do this, we can say to ourselves, "In the light of what he has just said, he must feel this way. Let me check on that possibility by listening to him some more."

Some have learned to sit through a conversation with an almost immovable "poker face." Apparently, it is important to this person that he not reveal anything of his own personal reactions during the conversation. This can be extremely unsettling to anyone speaking to him. Such a person may indeed sit in silence and give the speaker plenty of time to express himself; but if he does not give some indication of how he is responding, this kind of listening can disrupt communication. If the listener will occasionally respond with an "Uh-huh" or "Oh, yes, I see," he will do much to encourage the speaker to express himself more eloquently.

Listen Without Premature Evaluation

Nothing blocks communication, and especially listening, more effectively than prejudices or premature evaluation of the person to whom we are listening. There is a natural tendency for us to listen to and remember the things which support our own biases and prejudices. We may feel that a new acquaintance is a pretty fine fellow when we discover he is a former member of our old college fraternity or voted for the same presidential candidate. We listen to him differently now that he is "one of us." The person who forms conclusions about a speaker that are based on prejudices and on premature evaluations of him is likely to be about as effective in his listening as the batter who swings before the ball is pitched.

JUDGING RATHER THAN LISTENING

It is natural that much of our attention is centered upon ourselves. It is just as natural that we tend to *evaluate* and *judge* what others say in terms of how their statement may affect us or in terms of our personal opinion about the statement. While this is a natural tendency, it becomes one of the major blocks to communication.

If one of our friends happens to say to us, "Boy, I could really go for a steak smothered with mushrooms," we might say, "Ugh, I can't stand mushrooms!" When we say, "I can't stand mushrooms," we are really talking about ourselves and our preferences rather than listening to and trying to understand our friend. We judge what our friend has said, not from his point of view, but from our own. What he has said stimulates in us a desire to *talk* rather than a desire to *listen further* and communicate with him more clearly. When we approve or disapprove of what an individual says, we tend to be not really listening to him but instead thinking about ourselves. The speaker senses this, either consciously or unconsciously, and is likely to react with displeasure and with a feeling that he is not really being listened to.

Perhaps there is little that we can do about our natural tendency to be concerned about ourselves, and to see the world in terms of our own frame of reference. But there is something we can do to overcome the block in communication caused by our tendency to reply to statements by others with immediate and obvious approval or disapproval. Carl. R. Rogers, world-famous because of his professional contributions to methods of psychotherapy, suggests that many misunderstandings can be eliminated in conversations by following a simple rule. After someone makes a statement, *we must withhold our comments or our viewpoint until we have restated accurately the ideas and feelings expressed by the speaker in such a way that the speaker is satisfied with our summary of his message.*

Before we present our point of view we must truly and genuinely understand the *frame of reference* of the speaker and understand his message from *his point of view.*

If it is important for us to *think before we speak,* it is no less important for us to *think while we listen.* We have, in language, a tool which can promote the continued rise of our civilization or destroy it. This same tool helps us make either more or less use of our innate and learned capacities. The proper use of language and of listening can give us greater control over our own behavior and that of others, or it can become a sticky web of confusion which limits our effectiveness and shuts us away from growth experiences.

SUMMARY

"In the beginning was the word . . . "and certainly the word is the beginning of human civilization. We take words for granted and thus overlook the potential of these language tools. Unless we can agree on the meanings of words, our language will create communication inaccuracies and human problems. Words have dictionary definitions and also private individual meanings. It is these private meanings which create communication barriers, barriers which are powerful because they are so subtle. A word is only a symbol and does not tell all there is to know about the thing or feeling it refers to. It is up to us to discover the hidden meanings of words, the meanings others intend but do not or cannot say. Otherwise, we assume understanding when it is not there, and chaos is the result.

Listening is an active process which can be improved if we are willing to practice. As we increase our skill as listeners we can more often hear what a colleague or customer is really saying, what he is not saying but intends to say, and what he does not know he wants to say. If effective motivation depends upon knowing what people need and want, then effective listening is the first and most important step in discovering those wants. Our attitude toward ourselves determines our ultimate listening skill.

QUESTIONS FOR DISCUSSION AND THOUGHT

1. What do we mean when we refer to language as a tool?
2. "There is no way that we can communicate with another person

with complete accuracy." What are the implications of this statement for those engaged in business, family living, or international politics?

3. What is the role of feedback in effective human communications?

4. Why are understandings of connotations of words important for effective interpersonal relationships? Give some examples of different connotations for words such as "security," "loyalty," "hard work," etc

5. "... Quite often we confuse the word or label with the actual object." Give an example of this kind of confusion and discuss the implications.

6. Write down an operational definition of "success" from your own point of view. Explain this definition to someone else. Notice whether it helps or hinders understanding.

7. What are some major obstacles to effective listening? How can these obstacles be reduced?

8. How can we discover someone else's frame of reference?

6

IF ONLY

What? What kind of title for a chapter is that? If Only? If only what? Maybe the best explanation for using the title "If Only" can be found in a nursery rhyme:

> Twinkle, twinkle, little star,
> How I wonder what you are,
> Up above the world so high,
> Like a diamond in the sky.

Do we have your attention? Fine! At least now we are well on our way to discussing the perplexing but pertinent subject of human motivation. Motivation does start with an attention-getting signal, and a twinkling, blinking light rivets our gaze to the spot. Human motivation arrests the attention of every one of us, whether we are conscious of it or not. It is a subject which is incredibly complex, and yet is often discussed as if it were very simple. "Just find his *hot button* and you can sell him." Many a salesman or business manager would say just that. And nothing could be further from the truth.

But what's with this nursery rhyme? It is a rhyme often said to the young child, but probably said without realization that it tells the story of evolving mankind. Man is indeed the imagining animal. He is certainly the tool-user, but he is even more the animal with imagination. He thinks. He wishes. He dreams. He wonders. He hopes. He is curious.

Over the millions of years the animal *man* rose from the ooze and slime to become truly a creature sublime. He evolved from a four-legged animal to a two-legged one. Standing upright on his two legs must have made it easier to look up at the stars at night and wonder about the recurrent and changing patterns of light. When was the last time you looked at a clear sky at night, undimmed by city lights, to see the brilliant display? Doesn't it make you wonder? Just imagine those many years ago when there was no artificial light and man wondered (was curious) and wandered (explored) by following the lights in the sky. Two very human characteristics are revealed as a man looks at the sky: he wonders about those twinkling, unreachable orbs and he has a strong need to give *meaning* to them. The imaginings of early man showed him patterns of light he saw as a bear, bull, crab, winged horse, lion, bird of paradise, and dozens of other configurations known as the constellations. It was self-centeredly human that man thought that his life was controlled by the arrangements of stars. It was equally human that he thought that special appeals or prayers to the gods in the sky could give him relief from the troubles which this same imagination often presented to him.

The same imagination which wonders about a star also wonders how to motivate employees, customers, children, and politicians. The same imagination which results in putting a man on the moon also creates problems which don't exist. What does Thoreau say to us when he talks about a flower?

> I saw a delicate flower had grown up two feet high between the horses' feet and the wheel track. An inch more to right or left had sealed its fate, or an inch higher. Yet it lived to flourish, and never knew the danger it incurred. It did not borrow trouble, nor invite an evil fate by apprehending it.[1]

The mountain folk of a north Georgia county would warn against "borrowin' trouble" and thereby give us profound advice if only we would heed it. Creative man invents labor-saving devices but he also invents

---

[1] Henry David Thoreau, *Journal,* September, 1850. Quoted in John Bartlett, *Familiar Quotations* (Boston: Little, Brown and Company, 1955), p. 589.

anxiety and apprehensions which are unnecessary. It is human to wonder about the future, and this can save lives, but what of the future imaginings which show us our own deaths and the anxiety which this creates? The same ability which allows man to achieve excellence also paradoxically leads to self-destructive, self-defeating patterns of behavior. The self-conscious individual who wonders if people will laugh at him if he asks a question has already defeated himself because he has decided not to ask the question and thereby escape the ridicule and laughter he has imagined he would receive. He defeats himself because he denies himself the oppor-tunity to gain knowledge while he strives to avoid discomfort. The call-reluctant salesman who fears rejection decides that the prospect would not be interested in his sales presentation so he does not make the call. This surely avoids any possibility of a refusal, but at the same time it eliminates acceptance. Every one of us is an imagining animal. We are thereby achieving and self-defeating animals. HUMAN MOTIVATION IS INDEED COMPLEX.

"How I wonder what you are" is really the essence of motivation. The person contemplating suicide, the businessman facing tough problems, the salesman after a day or week of steady rejections, the mother remembering the recent death of her child, the bank president facing a ten-million-dollar bad loan write-off, all raise the question, "What is life all about?"

"What does it all mean? Why me? Why me?" Life is confusing and the behavior of people more perplexing than understandable. When things go the way we want them to go, we seldom think of "heavy" things like, "Why do people do the things they do? How can I succeed more often? What is success, anyway?" But when things go wrong, we think long and hard about what motivates people and what we can do to make others do things which would be more satisfying to us.

AN "IF ONLY" PHILOSOPHY

The young child spends much time on unrealistic wishing, and this does not entirely disappear in adulthood. The child thinks or says, "If only I could stay up later and watch the TV special. If only I had a drink of water I could go to sleep. If only I could eat a snack now instead of waiting for dinner. If only I didn't have to do homework. If only my parents would understand me and stop pushing me to do things I dislike. If only . . ." Each parent reading this can supply his own list of demands made by his children which often seem unrealistic. But what of the adult? What of *you*?

One of the authors, a consulting psychologist to top management groups, is frequently asked for advice on business problems involving people. What do you think is the most frequently asked question? While it is different in the way it is expressed, the most frequent question posed to a consulting psychologist is, "How can I get 'him' to be different?" The "him" may be a salesman, a manager, a prospect, a wife, a child, or almost anyone who is needed or is important to the client. "How can I get my salesmen to work harder and get off the plateau they're on? If only my wife would keep the house cleaner, our marriage would be so much better. If only my husband would understand my needs to do something signifi-cant, he would let me work part-time. If only my daughter were less interested in boys and more interested in her studies. If only my son were less of a bookworm and would start dating some girls. If only my executive vice president would delegate more of the work and stop killing himself by trying to do everything himself. If only my partner would spend less time on the golf course and more time on the business. Should I dissolve the partnership or is there some way I can get him to see the light?"

The common denominator in these varied requests is an implied or sometimes explicit statement, "*If only* he (or she) were different, my life would be so much better." The psychologist is most frequently asked for advice on how to get *other people* to change. His reply is usually to work with the client (or patient) to help him see that wishing others to change is usually symptomatic of his own immaturity or ignorance.

A member of a tribe of a primitive culture will dance for rain when his more knowledgeable cousin in a more advanced culture will dig an irriga-tion ditch to provide the needed water. The sick, neurotic, alcoholic patient will blame his mother, his wife, his job, or the "hard" economic times for his drinking problem. The frightened salesman will blame the time of day, the month of the year, or the production schedule of his company for his poor sales records—blame anything but himself and his self-defeating fright.

The rain dancer, the alcoholic, and the scared salesman all believe in a kind of magic. Perhaps we can call the human being the "magic animal," too. He believes that evil spirits of nature (or maybe he will call it "bad luck") block him from his goals, and he also believes that certain rituals (the rain dance, wearing a "lucky" tie, crossing fingers, knocking on wood, etc.) will produce satisfactions. Many popular books on motivation stress magic, too, when they discuss "the seven secret steps to successful motivation" or the effectiveness of certain "Power Phrases" guaranteed to close the sale. How many eager salesmen try these "magic" steps only to find that while they may have worked for the author they do not automatically produce sales for him.

A quick look at three giants of thought and their experiences demonstrates how resistant people are to new and potentially freeing ideas, and how much they cling to magic and self-centered notions of man's power. Nicolaus Copernicus, a sixteenth-century Polish astronomer, taught that the earth was not the center of the universe, as self-centered man had believed for centuries; he was placed under house arrest and forced to recant his findings. Charles Darwin taught that man was not a totally unique creation but instead was related to the rest of the animal kingdom; self-centered man in 1929 convicted the high school biology teacher Scopes of teaching the heretical theory of evolution. Sigmund Freud demonstrated that the human being is motivated by forces beyond conscious awareness—that he is not in full and totally conscious control of himself. Jokes and ridicule have surrounded Freud's name since his major publishings in the early nineteen-hundreds. Each of these men tried to show that men thought in self-centered terms and they hoped to help man feel more responsible *for* himself and less reliant on the hopelessness of magic. *How much real progress have we made?*

You may be impatient with this chapter so far. You may wonder why we don't get on with the business of explaining how you can motivate people to do things. You would like to know how to use psychology to sell, convince, persuade, motivate, inspire, change, influence, control, pressure, entice, and inveigle desired behavior from others. But if the psychologist is most often asked how to get others to change, his most frequent advice is to help his client see what he can do about *himself—his development, his own adjustment capability, his own self-awareness, his own understanding* of the situation, and *especially his own self-motivation.* The psychologist would say to his client that he cannot really motivate those other people to change. He would say that the client can make attempts to motivate himself, but that it is impossible to motivate others.

CAN WE MOTIVATE OTHERS?

To say that we cannot motivate others is so obviously contrary to "common sense" and seems to contradict our first-hand observations that we become suspicious that only a play on words is involved. "Of course I can motivate others," you would say. But much more than just a semantic point is involved in the concept that all motivation is ultimately self-motivation and nothing more. Motivation is self-motivation only because our behavior is based on *our* perception of the world about us, and that perception is individual and unique.

Perhaps an illustration from the area of field sales will help make this clearer. A sales office in Peoria, Illinois, finished a six-week contest at the end of October. The purpose of the contest was to increase overall sales during a time that was ordinarily considered a slow time of the year for the product involved. But, unfortunately, this was one more contest which had not worked. Sales volume for the region had remained stable; no increase was apparent. One of the men was the winner, however, in that he had the largest percentage increase during the six-week period, even though his increase was not very large. He was the winner of the first prize, which had been announced as a weekend, all expenses paid, at a resort area in Wisconsin to go ice fishing! It should be added that the sales manager who was paying for this first prize loved to go ice fishing. One of the salesmen who "lost" showed a burst of wit when he suggested that second prize should have been *two* weekends in Wisconsin to go ice fishing.

An outsider can see that the first prize did not motivate the salesmen to work harder to increase sales. What a first prize! They were not motivated because they did not value the reward offered for the extra contribution expected. They did not *perceive* that the *goal* would *satisfy* their *needs*. In this last statement are contained four important elements of the motivational process: *perception, goal achievement, satisfaction* and *needs*.

We move ourselves, or are motivated, toward a goal if we perceive that to us the goal has meaning or significance. We do not move in a direction because of the perceptions of others but because of our own. Perhaps the sales manager is motivated by a weekend in Wisconsin to go ice fishing because he perceives it as being valuable to him. Obviously, his salesmen are not motivated because their manager happens to like ice fishing. They do not perceive the weekend as being meaningful to them and are unmoved. We cannot perceive *for* others. Our perceptions, based on our lifetime experiences of joys, sorrows, successes, and failures, give each of us a unique way of looking at things.

Now the sales manager, seeing that things are not going so well during the contest, could change the rules of the game a little by "advising" one of the poorer men, "Either you start bringing in some orders or you're through." Then maybe the contest would have more "meaning" to that one man. But it would be a negative kind of motivation. The goal, in this case, would be to keep his job. It would be expected that under these motivational conditions the salesman would go through the motions of increased effort while he was seeking another job.

These examples illustrate that often we attempt to motivate others depending on factors important to us but not to them. It does illustrate the self-centeredness of the "normal" human being. It is as egotistical to assume that we can motivate a person as it is to assume that we can make a flower grow. We can supply water, fertilizer, proper soil conditions, and enough sun (oops! We can't supply the sun. We can only plant the flower where the sun happens to shine) and then stand back and watch the flower grow.

Perhaps the obvious solution to the sales manager's problem of lagging sales is to offer a cash prize and let the winner use it for whatever he desires. Most contest prizes are in terms of prizes which may be selected from a catalogue or in terms of a medium of exchange: cash. But even a selection of prizes or cash seems not to motivate some. It may be the recognition which comes from being first, it may be status, competition, a sense of challenge or self-fulfillment, or any number of other satisfactions which motivate the individual to greater effort. People are different, and this fact is as clearly illustrated in the world of work as anywhere. The situation must be perceived as *meaningful to an individual* before he will motivate himself.

Just What Is Motivation?

The essence of motivation is finding meaning in what we are doing. The meaning has to be our own. Others cannot give us meaning or significance; it must come from our past. But others can appeal to the needs, wants, and values we already possess.

For the individual who wishes to influence the behavior of others (and this includes all of us) another definition of motivation may suggest a strategy to follow and tactics to try. Our ability to "motivate" another individual depends on our *sensitivity* to his needs and wants. This allows us partially to create the living conditions or the work situation he is in so that it increases the probability that he will motivate himself in a direction we desire. The hobbyist who "grows" roses understands the "needs" of the plant for soil of a certain acidity, the right moisture conditions, the spray necessary to remove aphids, and proper pruning procedures. From that point on is he not helpless to motivate the rose to produce beautiful blooms? Motivating people is no different.

Figure 1 illustrates three basic principles of motivation which help explain the complex process which is constantly going on inside and outside of us and which makes us the unique persons we are. Any person can be seen as a collection of needs which are as varied in their strengths and combinations as a person is different from all others. Figure 1 shows only a few of the perhaps hundreds of needs contained within us, some of which lie dormant and some of which scream for satisfaction. Since these needs are contained within the individual, *we know of their existence only by inference from the behavior of that person.* Inferences can sometimes be wrong, so the inner needs which are the beginning of motivated behavior can never be known for sure. Just because we observe a person making money does not mean for sure that he needs money. A person does not eat always because he needs food. A person may need sleep, but be unable to sleep because of other needs which may not be conscious. Our assumptions about motivated behavior begin, then, with the concept of needs, some of which are necessary for survival and some of which have been learned and therefore are more properly referred to as "wants."

Thus, the first principle is that these needs seem to move the person in a certain direction toward a goal, or some kind of satisfaction for the inner need. Motivation, then, is goal-directed toward need satisfaction.

A second basic principle of motivation is that at any one time many needs exist which push and pull the individual, potentially, in many different directions, some of which may be completely opposite to others. Figure 1 suggests that some needs produce a strong drive (long arrow) toward a satisfaction while others (short-arrow) are less strong. The strength of these drives probably changes from time to time or in different situations; at any moment the person will tend to move in the direction

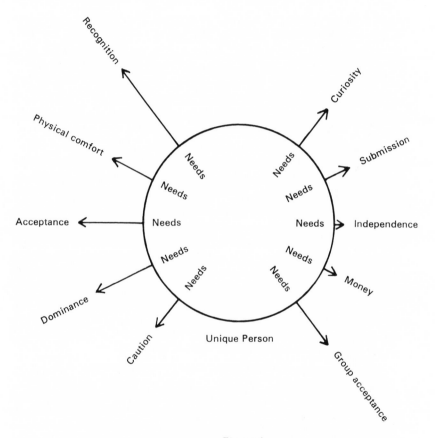

Figure 1
The Motivational Process

which seems to satisfy the strongest of the needs. As an example of different needs pushing the person in opposite directions, look at a new management trainee recently employed right after graduation. He is curious (need) and wants to ask hundreds of questions about his new company, their policies, traditions, fringe benefits, etc. But he is also cautious (perhaps stemming from a need for survival) and has been profoundly impressed by an older trainee, who exceeds him in seniority by three months, and who has advised, "Keep your mouth shut, don't ask questions, and you'll get along just fine." He faces a dilemma! It looks as if he can't satisfy his needs to be curious and cautious at the same time. If these two needs happen to be equal and in opposite directions, the concept of the resultant of forces (borrowed from physics) would make us predict that he would be immobilized. Perhaps the behavior we would actually see would be the new trainee sitting at his desk staring into space with a strange vacant thought such as, "Why do I feel uncomfortable?"

The third basic principle of motivation has been mentioned many times but is repeated once more for emphasis: People are different! One man may enjoy ice fishing; others won't.

The sales manager can provide certain conditions in the evironment of the salesman such as a sales catalogue, travel expenses, a commission schedule, cash bonuses for sales above the quota, exposure to a training program, threats, bribes, promises of promotion to management, etc., but he cannot make the salesman sell. The same idea is contained in the popular cliché, "You can lead a horse to water but you can't make him drink." Why do we persist in believing that we can motivate anyone to do anything? The psychologist would say that this belief persists because of either immature thinking or lack of knowledge or both.

But there is *regularity* in the way groups of people respond to different stimulating situations. Perhaps most people would like to make more money, so the offering of a money prize has a high probability of seeming attractive to the majority. If we offer money to a person as inducement for harder work, we can predict that *if he is like most people* he will respond by working harder for the money prize. But *most* people does not mean *all* people. While we can offer the money, we must wait for the other person to perceive its usefulness to himself and *move* toward it. In addition, the same person who worked harder last week for money will not necessarily do the same this week. It all depends on how *he* sees it!

The main problem in believing that *we can* motivate others is that we think mostly of what *we* want, what *we* want them to do, and what *we* can do to control their behavior. This preoccupation with *our* wants makes it difficult to know the *other* person and what *he* wants. In a small country store, a customer was surprised by a full-grown skunk which had wandered in through the open door. Without a moment's hesitation, he plunged a dime into the vending machine beside him for a bag of peanuts. He walked slowly backwards, dribbling the peanuts in a line out of the door and into the road. The skunk ate the peanuts until he was safely outside. This customer understood the principle of motivation perfectly: he changed part of the skunk's environment in a way calculated to increase the probability that the skunk would *move* in a desired direction. But what would have happened to a skunk not hungry for peanuts? Did the customer *motivate* the skunk to leave the premises? The peanuts were placed by the man, but the hunger was supplied by the beast.

We have referred to *motivation* as *the inner control of behavior* as it is affected by bodily conditions, learned interest, values, mental attitudes, and recognized or unrecognized goals or aspirations. Referring to inner control recognizes that, if we want others to do things, at best we can merely control *some* conditions which then either directly or indirectly are perceived by them and occasionally produce the behavior we hope to see in them. We cannot change people. We can only attempt to control some things that people want and hope that they move toward the satisfaction of their wants. Individual motivation refers to some impulse or urge of the human being to reach for or try to attain a goal or objective, or to avoid an unwanted situation.

We cannot motivate others but we can partially control their environment so as to increase the probability that they will perceive the environment as meaningful and will move in the particular direction we want them to move. Motivation of ourselves is possible; motivation of others is not. Motivation of others is an incredibly complex process of which we can be a part. Our part is to understand the needs of others and plan situations which will be perceived by them as being desirable. But this is such an awkward way of expressing a process which goes on around us all the time. It is so much easier to talk about how we can "motivate others," and we can use this simpler expression as long as we recognize it as a "shorthand" way of referring to the more complex and accurate process described above. From now on in this text, when we talk about "motivating" someone other than ourselves, we will mean the recognition of their needs and the efforts to present conditions or materials perceived by them as so desirable that they will probably "move" toward them.

Motivated Behavior Is Goal-Directed and Persistent

Figure 1 reminds us that wherever motivation is involved, a goal for achievement is also involved. This does not mean that we always know what the goal is toward which we are motivated, for much motivation is often on an unconscious level. This goal may be anything from food, shelter, or sexual activity to wealth, prestige, affiliation, power, or self-fulfillment.[2] Closely allied to this is the further principle that the human being shows persistence in moving toward or searching for goals. Some goals such as food do not seem to be learned, although the specific method of obtaining food may be learned, but many more of our conscious and unconscious goals are learned. We learn to seek certain goals because of the culture in which we were reared. We learn to want certain goals because of the particular pattern of reward or punishment which has accompanied our various past experiences. We learn to seek goals because of our obvious exposure to situations in which the achievement of these goals is possible.

Because motives involve goals, we could increase our effectiveness in creating environments with a high probability of seeming attractive to others if we could find out what they want. This is complicated by three things: a person may not know what he wants; he may know what he wants but be reluctant to tell us; or he may know what he wants but be unable to tell us. If we could observe, undetected, everything a certain person did or said during a period of time such as a week, we could make some valid guesses about the inducements or enticements we could offer him so that he would be more likely to do what we wanted him to do. But this technique of long-term observation is impossible. The next best thing would be to increase the accuracy of our observations of him during a very short period of time, such as a conversation. The educated person trained in background information on human behavior will "see" more when he is with others. Just as an artist is trained to see more color and variations of color in a landscape, so can a business manager, husband, mother, child, etc., learn to recognize more of the wants and desires subtly displayed in gestures, expressions, sounds, postures, and general mannerisms.

---

[2] Abraham Maslow presents his theory of motivation suggesting that certain classes of needs are satisfied according to a hierarchy of prepotency. See A. H. Maslow, *Motivation and Personality* (New York: Harper and Row, 1954).

Our Knowledge About Human Motivation Is Largely Inferential

We can directly observe human behavior. We stress again that we can only infer the presence of the motives which may give rise to that behavior. As we watch a leaf being lifted higher and higher, we can only infer the presence of an upward draft of air. We cannot see the air movement, but can see only whatever is being carried by the air. We cannot see man's motive to obtain food, but can observe only that he does indeed search for food. We do not know that a person is money-motivated; we can observe only that he does many things which result in his making money.

Motivation and Perception Are Intertwined

Learning to "motivate" people is difficult (1) because people are *complex*, (2) because human behavior *is not very predictable,* but especially (3) because we can never escape the ever-present and largely *unmeasurable influence of our own motives.* Our efforts to "motivate" people always involve ourselves and the needs and wants and goals for which we strive. We cannot perceive any event or any example of human behavior without distorting, through personal interpretation, what reaches our senses. We are prisoners of our own frames of reference, often without realizing it. Our past experiences, attitudes, and blind spots are so intimately involved in our efforts to observe people that we tend to lose the objectivity which we must have if we are to observe accurately and have a sound basis for later motivational efforts. The more we know about how motivation works, within ourselves as well as within those we are trying to change, the more we can create the conditions toward which others are most likely to move or be motivated.

THE FUNDAMENTALS OF MOTIVATION

A person has *his own reasons,* based on *his own needs* and *his own desires* and *his own goals,* for doing what he does.

When an individual wants to see only good things in a person or an activity, we commonly say that he is wearing rose-colored glasses. In the same way, all of us can have many pairs of glasses we wear at different times, each pair reflecting our experiences, values, attitudes, etc. If we have on "money-colored glasses" we will tend to see people in terms of their being motivated by a desire for money and of being frustrated and unhappy if they do not obtain it. But if we are not aware that we are seeing things through "money-colored glasses," we are in danger of misinterpreting statements made by someone if he, for example, has little or no interest in money matters. We might make the mistake of oversimplifying the problem of "motivating" him by thinking that he is motivated by just the one motive, money. So many errors and tragedies in human history can be traced to the temptation to assume that *one* motivation, *one* solution is the total and only answer necessary.

Biological Needs and Motivation

What is behind a motive? What is it that impels us toward a goal? What gives us the drive or the incentive or the urge to buy or to sell or to engage in any kind of human activity? The answer is that there are a great many things which impel us to behave the way we do. One of the easiest types of motivation to understand is that which results from physical or bodily conditions.

A need is some requirement for man's adjustment to his environment. Basically, man "needs" to survive. Stemming from this broad need are such needs as water, food, air, protection from danger, etc. We can classify these as biological needs. Biological needs appear to be innate or inherited. We do not seem to have to learn that we have these needs. The infant, shortly after birth, has a biological need for food. He requires food to survive. A need, then, can be thought of as a lack of something which the person must have to sustain life.

In response to a need or requirement, the human being experiences a tension or drive to satisfy this need. Obtaining the goal or object which satisfies a biological need tends to reduce the strength of the tension or drive. When we are thirsty, we start looking for water and continue until we find it. As soon as we have a drink, we have less interest or desire to search for more water. The longer we go without water, however, the greater is this biological need and the stronger is the tension. If we are without water for an abnormally long time, we become frantic in our efforts to find it and may think of little else until we are successful in our search.[3] This relationship between biological *need, tension* or *drive,* and

---

[3] *Ibid.*

reaching a goal illustrates one kind of motivational process. We emphasize that this is only one kind of motivation, for human behavior appears to be a composite of many forces rather than a simple response to a need, as we shall see.

Learning to Satisfy Needs. A major step in the motivational process is the establishment of an *assortment* of learned responses which can act to satisfy the biological needs. The physical need itself impels the individual to activity, but it is through a learning process that he discovers the most efficient ways of satisfying his needs or reducing their tension. It we are discussing the need to satisfy hunger, we can see that food may be obtained by growing it, by exchanging money for it, or by stealing it. There are a number of ways, then, that we might go about satisfying our need for food or our other biological needs. The motivational process also entails the location of a goal-object and the decision as to which of a number of possible activities might be used to reach the goal. Because these physical needs reoccur at periodic intervals, the repetition of need-reducing activities results in these activities' becoming stamped in or *learned* as a habit. The strength of any habit will ordinarily be greater as the strength of the need and the frequency with which it must be dealt are increased.

Maintaining Equilibrium. Much, but not all, human behavior stems from the existence of basic physiological or bodily needs. Our motives for providing ourselves with food, rest, shelter, and sexual activities have the function of maintaining an internal balance or equilibrium. The specific way in which we satisfy these bodily needs is determined by our culture. The cyclic or wavelike rise of tension and the satisfaction from a decrease in tension which characterize these basic needs act as almost automatic motivational processes. This mechanism of maintaining a balance is called *homeostasis.* This means, literally, maintaining things as they are. The temperature of our blood, for example, maintains itself within a few tenths of a degree most of the time. When the internal body temperature begins to go up, we automatically begin perspiring and the evaporation of the perspiration tends to cool off the body. When the internal body temperature goes down, we automatically begin shivering and shaking and the heat generated from this muscle activity moves the body temperature back up where it should be.

As the intensity of the need increases, our general activity increases and usually stays at a high level until something happens to satisfy the need.

Just as the wall thermostat controls the operation of the furnace according to the temperature in the room, so we have literally thousands of "thermostats" in our body which help to regulate needs and drives. These are feedback mechanisms which operate very much the way a heat thermostat works. As the furnace warms the room, the heat activates the wall thermostat, which sends an electrical message to the furnace telling the furnace to turn off. The gradual cooling of the room again activates the thermostat which again feeds information to the furnace, this time telling the furance to turn on and supply heat. As long as there is fuel and a source of electricity, this cycle of action and reaction will constantly strive to maintain the equilibrium in temperature which is also constantly being unbalanced.

Emotional Motivation

To understand how emotions can act as motives, we need to be sure we know exactly what emotions are. One is likely to have at least two reactions to the question of defining an emotion. The first is likely to be, "Why, of course. I know what an emotion is! An emotion is the feeling of fear, anger, love, or disgust." A second reaction to the question might be, "Defining an emotion by saying that it is fear, anger, love, etc., is really only giving it another name. It is really not a definition at all." Certainly this second reaction is more likely to lead us toward the kind of questioning about emotions that will allow us to understand and even predict the role emotions play in the motivation of human beings.

Referring to *definitions of emotion* implies that there is more than one way to understand emotion. It suggests that we may be dealing with a kind of human behavior which is so broad and all-encompassing that a single definition would not begin to tell us all we need to know to understand the concept of emotion. An emotion is something of which we often are very much aware. Emotions may interfere with the normal, rational way of behaving. While we are experiencing emotions, there are various external and internal reactions of the body, such as blushing, "butterflies in the stomach," pounding heart, and the like. But what, really, *is* an emotion?

Emotions are generally thought of as rather destructive, undesirable displays which must be somehow controlled or concealed. We may tell an excited friend, "Don't get so emotional—cool off and keep your head." Emotion in this sense is thought of as a general disorganization which occurs within an individual and makes it difficult for him to relate to someone in a predictable and acceptable manner. Emotions can be defined as complex disturbances that are recognized and named, in terms of the stimulus situation that arouses them and the adjustments that we make to this situation. We are familiar with the predicament of the young boy who had memorized perfectly his part in the school play, only to become completely speechless when he is pushed onto the stage on the night of the performance. Something that he is experiencing, which we call emotion, has somehow interfered with his otherwise adequate abilities. Our definition of emotion, then, must surely include the concept of disruption or disorganization. But love is also an emotion and we cannot feel entirely satisfied in describing the emotion of love as a disorganizing and disruptive influence. Certainly love includes a desire to care for and to appreciate another individual as he or she is. This emotion of love is responsible for some of the most deeply satisfying and uplifting human experiences we can know. Emotions, then, are states of psychological being which act also to facilitate or enrich human interactions.

Emotions can also be thought of as an awareness of pleasantness or unpleasantness. This definition of emotion refers to mental activity within a person without regard to his external behavior or the effect of this mental activity on his behavior. Our awareness of pleasure or displeasure depends upon our past experiences. Emotion used in this sense becomes our conscious awareness of the evaluation we place upon a perception of events which may be taking place. Used in this sense, the word *emotion* means an interpretation of present experiences based on past experiences.

Emotions Motivate Behavior. Emotions motivate behavior in some of the same ways as do biological or physical needs. The presence of an emotion tends to give rise to a tension or drive toward or away from an object, situation, or person; and obtaining this objective satisfies that emotion and helps restore a balance. Just as biological drives move the individual toward activities which assist in his survival, so emotions aid in the survival of the human being. The emotion of fear, for example, helps keep the individual out of potentially threatening or fatal situations. The emotion of anger serves to direct our activities and mobilize additional strength to help us overcome a difficulty or obstacle. Emotions, like physical needs, act as drives to motivate the individual toward action. If one kind of activity does not lessen the tension, the force of the emotion acts to motivate the human being to try other methods of reducing the tension.

Emotion Can Become Generalized. An important fact about the learning of emotions and the development of emotions as motivating forces is that an emotion can become generalized from one situation to another. An individual has learned to be afraid of many things by the time he is old enough to be employed. If he has had a particularly bad experience with a dentist as a child, he may always feel uncomfortable in the dentist's chair. The child experiences many frustrations and punishments in the process of growing up. In response to these frustrations and punishments, he may experience the emotions of anger and fear. To the child, a parent is seen as a source of authority. As the child grows, he meets other adults who are also authority figures. These might include his teacher, the policeman, his sergeant or superior in the Army, and even his employer. The anger or fear first experienced with the parental authority figures can become generalized to other authority figures. The salesman may have the same emotional reactions to an older fatherly-looking prospect that he originally had to his father. He may thus be afraid of calling on anyone in a position of real authority. This could be a president of a company, a judge, a city or state official, or even a school teacher. Perhaps all of us experience a certain amount of discomfort when we are in the presence of a high-ranking official such as the mayor or governor. It is probable that some of the discomfort we feel is an earlier learned fear which has generalized from our parent-child relationship.

Another example of the way emotions can become generalized from one situation to another can be seen in again discussing our reactions to authority figures. In the literally hundreds of learning experiences we go through as children, we receive punishment or praise from our elders. Most of these experiences take place while we are with our parents and are literally looking up to a person who appears to us to be a giant in terms of size. We thus associate correction or punishment or fear with the presence of something above us. Later in life, whenever an individual is physically above us, we may tend to react to him as to an authority figure and experience the earlier learned emotional reactions of fear, anger, or respect. A speaker stands on an elevated platform. The judge in the courtroom sits high above the defendant. The physical relationship, especially the vertical distance between the two people, may have much to do with the creation of fear and respect. In an office, even such an apparently superficial thing as the height of the chairs may affect the outcome of a business conference. The person sitting in a lower chair may feel somewhat subordinate, or inferior, although usually on an unconscious level. The boss who rises from his chair to lean over the desk of his vice president while making a point may gain some authority in the eyes of his subordinate and may "motivate" him more than if he were to remain seated. Unfortunately, he may also feel intimidated by this and have a negative reaction to his boss. Most of the time these physical relationships with their emotion-arousing effects operate unconsciously on both persons involved.

The manager who himself experiences insecurity may unknowingly transfer some fear of making decisions to his men. The clerk may "learn" from his supervisor to be afraid when otherwise he might not have known fear. This works the other way, too. The manager who is secure and confident may also transfer a similar feeling of confidence to those he is supervising.

Similarly, the individual who is tense as he enters someone's office may very well cause others to feel uneasy, uncomfortable, and even afraid. We show our fear in many ways, in our facial expressions, our bodily posture, and in a slight, almost unnoticeable tremor in our voice. The fear that we may feel becomes a self-defeating mechanism. The employee may unconsciously feel the manager's apprehension or fear without realizing that he does so. He is not likely to say, "I don't want to avoid decisions because you make me feel uncomfortable." He is instead likely to say something like, "I want to think about it," and the manager may never be the wiser.

The Role of Emotions Is Often Overlooked. We live in a culture where men are supposed to act in a reasonable, logical way and avoid giving signs of feeling or emotions. It is almost unthinkable for a man to cry or even show signs of distress when he experiences disappointment, sadness, or despair. We feel that emotional behavior, while it may be appropriate for a woman, is inappropriate for a man. Because of the way society looks upon emotions and the expression of feeling, it is likely that men tend to overlook the role that this important source of energy plays in our daily behavior. It is becoming increasingly recognized that many of our decisions are made for emotional reasons rather than for rational or logical ones.

The person who cannot allow himself to express genuine feeling or behave in an emotional way may deny himself a most potent way of influencing behavior. Obviously, this can also be overdone. We cannot give unrestrained vent to our feelings, but if we try hard to cover them up we lose effectiveness as a persuader. If we avoid any emotional expression, we are less likely to establish a motivating atmosphere, less likely to use the force of an emotional motive, less likely to be in tune with others, and less likely to sense the emotional motives of others.

We need to find a balance between being too emotional and too suppressed or neutral. A younger man will often mistakenly think that he will look older, more mature, and more sophisticated if he maintains a poker face and an air of studied indifference. It is more likely that he will be seen as the artificial person he is. Rarely do we fool other people when we try to behave in ways we don't feel. We may think we fool others, but we usually don't.

Social Needs and Motivation

As we have seen, the operation of physical needs and the drive-reducing activities which result from them act in a *relatively mechanical way*. "Persuading" people to behave in certain ways because of what we say to them is a much more complex and less easily controlled activity. Social motives, as the term implies, have to do with the normal desires of the human being to associate with others. The human being cannot be truly isolated from the influence of society although he may withdraw and seem not to react to it. Much of what he does as an individual is related to this apparent need to be an acceptable member of society. We *learn* that it is important to get along with people and that many of our satisfactions can come only from others. It is true that we could live as isolated individuals by becoming hermits, but most individuals choose to live in a group and sacrifice some personal freedom for the immense gain that comes from group activity. Man is a conforming animal. Man also has purely personal impulses and desires. In each individual there must be a *fusion* between his individual and personal needs and the needs of the group of which he is a member. Out of this conflict between the individual and his group(s) grow *social* motives. We have previously referred to a mature interaction between people as *interdependence*.

For survival we do not need a twelve-room house, a Cadillac, a boat, a

TV set, a life insurance policy, etc. But *we learn to need these things*. We are now using the term "need" in a different sense from before. A physical or bodily need is a requirement for survival. As we talk about *social motives* being based on an individual's need for association with people, we might better substitute for "need" the words *want* or *desire*. Often an individual feels that he needs something which an impartial observer can see that he only wants or desires. In our daily activities we do not generally make a distinction between what we need and what we want. We need a haircut, not for survival purposes, but because we have learned that being neatly trimmed makes us more acceptable to others, and this is something most of us *want* very much.

By the time we reach adulthood, we learn to want or desire an almost infinite variety of things. As with any learning, we tend to learn first or best the things which seem to lead to reward. The basic principle of learning, called the *law of effect* states that behavior which *seems* not to lead to reward or seems to lead to punishment tends not to be repeated. We use the word "seems" here because we usually act on the basis of what we believe to be true and not necessarily of what is objectively true. As we go through life, some things we do result in approval and affection from people around us and other things we do result in punishment. *Learning what to want or desire is essentially a part of the process of assimilating the culture in which we live.*

Desire to Be With People. The infant is totally dependent upon his mother or some other adult for survival. He goes through periodic cycles of experiencing hunger and discomfort which are relieved by something that the mother does for him. Being in close contact with an individual is thus pleasurably associated with the satisfaction of needs and wants. It seems natural, then, that all of us early in life learn to desire the company of people. For the child, a punishment worse than spanking is to be made to stand in the corner or somehow to be isolated from the family. The most unpleasant punishment for prisoners, short of death, is solitary confinement. One of the outstanding symptoms of mental illness is the tendency of the patient to isolate himself from others. A patient in a mental hospital will frequently be seen to stand apart rather than engage in some group activity. *The social motive to be with people* is one of our first learned motives and probably continues to be the strongest motive influencing our behavior throughout life.

Desire to be Accepted. Closely related to this social motive of desiring the company of people is the social motive of wanting to be liked and to *be accepted and respected.* The strength of this motive will vary according to the importance to us of the other person or group of persons. We are concerned about being wanted and respected by people who are *important* to us, in the sense that they control things that we want, such as love, money, or status. If we can identify ourselves as being members of the same group of which a new acquaintance is also a member, our reception is likely to be much warmer. The desire to be liked is so important that some will frequently work harder to gain the approval and friendship of their manager than to earn more money. The desire for companionship, approval, and acceptance plays a very important part in all business activities.

Desire to Help Others. Another social motive is the desire to be affectionate toward people and to take care of, or to help, others. It is socially acceptable to do things for the welfare of people. We learn that it is pleasurable to receive the kind of recognition which accompanies an apparently unselfish desire to care for others. The desire to help others or to be altruistic probably cannot be separated from a more selfish desire to help ourselves. We often do things for others because it makes us feel good. That this is so only illustrates again that our behavior is motivated by more than one desire or need at a time. While we may discuss motives one at a time, we must not make the mistake of thinking that any one motive ever exists entirely by itself. The person who does not have this desire to help may be thought of as cold or hostile. When this desire or social motive becomes too strong, however, the individual may find himself spending so much time providing service to his customers that he does not do enough searching for new business.

Desire to Make Money. The desire to make money is a social motive that perhaps has more importance in our American culture than it does anywhere else in the world. The worth of men in our society is frequently measured by the size of their paycheck. The definition of success which most businessmen give is in terms of money or financial security. The desire for money may be stronger in a man who grew up in a family of little means. But a man from a well-to-do family may also have a strong desire for money in order to maintain his socioeconomic status. Money to many people becomes almost the equivalent of affection. Many a man who has been denied normal affection as a child or who has an unhappy marriage has attempted to compensate unconsciously for this by striving for money to an unusual degree.

Giving gifts is an example of how money can be equated to affection. Many people purchase the most expensive gifts for those they like the most. The recipient is likely to interpret the gift's probable cost as an indication of the degree of friendship or affection the giver has for him. How much life insurance a man carries, for example, is often considered a measure of his money-making ability as well as of his concern for his family. Some men have bought policies of several hundred thousand dollars in face value because of the underwriter's statement that "this puts you in a very élite class and shows how much you love your family." When a company stops their tradition of giving a free turkey to every employee at Christmas time, a first reaction may be, "Our company doesn't care about us any more." For many, money and affection become very closely tied together.

Desire to Dominate. Another important social motive is the desire to control or influence the behavior of others. We learn to desire *dominance* because we have found satisfaction in "controlling" the behavior of others. A strong desire to dominate may be established in a child when he discovers that he is much more likely to have his desires satisfied when he is controlling the situation rather than being controlled by it.

Most businessmen attempt to control the behavior of people, even to the extent of encouraging them to take action which they may actively resist. The desire for dominance, like all social motives, varies greatly according to the individual. One with a strong need and desire to dominate will be much more interested in changing the opinions, attitudes, and behavior of others than someone with a minimum desire for dominance. Such individuals are often regarded as "natural" leaders and are looked up to. An individual with a strong desire to dominate who has learned techniques of "controlling" behavior of people may often seem to *compel others to action by his very bearing or manner.*

Influence over people is frequently achieved through physical size or strength. In our culture a tall person is generally more respected than a short person. The size of the person will affect (but does not completely determine) the degree to which he can be dominant. A man small in stature may work much harder (overcompensate) to overcome any disadvantage he may have or thinks he has because of his size.

On the other hand, a person with a very strong need to dominate and control may be so self-centered that he loses sensitivity to the needs and desires of others. His very attempt to control may be self-defeating if others see him as being indifferent to their wishes.

Desire to Submit. In addition to the motive of dominance, there is perhaps the equally common *motive of submission.* These two contradictory motives exist to a certain degree in all of us. To cooperate in a society we must of necessity be submissive in certain situations, as in obeying traffic regulations or tax laws. While we all must submit to the general rules and laws of our society, in some individuals the desire to submit is a very predominant motive. Life can be seen as a series of never-ending struggles to survive and to accomplish. We are constantly confronted with change, and change is often uncomfortable. The persuader, whether he is a manager, salesman, teacher, or parent, is trying to induce change in others. He may ask some vital questions which require a decision to be made. There will be in many people a strong (although unconscious) desire to submit and have the authority make these decisions for them. The desire to submit will be stronger, of course, if the authority figure is respected and liked. There is a certain amount of pleasure to be gained from giving in and being submissive to another individual. It eliminates the necessity for struggle and exertion in decision-making.

Military service was emotionally satisfying to many men (although perhaps hotly denied) because a great many of life's decisions were made for them. The strong manager can discourage the growth of strength and confidence in his employees if he exerts too much control over them. The manager who tries to force his subordinates to respect him and to follow the rules of the office to the letter and without exception may be building a group of relatively submissive employees. Dominance and submission are learned reactions. We are not born dominant or submissive. While it is not likely that we can change completely from being predominantly submissive to becoming predominantly dominant, it is possible to become more effective in working with others toward mutual satisfaction.

Desire to Compete and Win. Closely related to this motive of dominance is a learned desire for healthy aggressiveness and rivalry. The desire to compete and win is frequently strong enough in some men to motivate them more highly than financial rewards might. The desire to "keep up with the Joneses" or perhaps to excel the Joneses is a common characteristic in our culture. A conversation may be a competitive situation in which both people attempt to "sell" each other an idea or opinion. Both may be attempting to sell the other that he is "right." The issue may not be as important as who can emerge as the "winner." It is obvious that a need to compete and win can block true understanding.

The Motive of Self-Actualization. After the human being has satisfied his basic needs for survival and for protection from danger, he begins to respond to a higher level of motives. This higher level of motivation includes the desire to achieve satisfaction and comfort from people in the form of love, affection, and the pleasure of being part of a group. When this level of motives is reasonably satisfied, a still higher motive asserts itself. This highest level of motivation is referred to as the motive of *self-actualization.*

Man seems to have a drive to make full use of his capacities or abilities. He apparently needs to grow, to develop, to improve himself, and to make the best use of his particular and unique talents. Unlike the biological needs and the social motives, the motive for self-actualization seems only to increase in strength as it is satisfied. While we stop searching for food when we satisfy our hunger, and we relax somewhat in our search for affection when we become a loved and respected member of a group, we seem to want even more growth as we succeed in growing.

Growth means something more than normal physical and mental maturing. It means the expanding ability of man to make use of the qualities which make him unique among animals. Growth or self-actualization is the creative, building urge in the human being to deal with his fellow creatures on a more mutually satisfactory level. Human growth involves becoming a responsible, self-directing, self-knowing person who moves toward becoming everything of which he is humanly capable.

Growth implies a direction. But what is that direction for each of us? If self-actualization means reaching the height of our capacity or achieving an ultimate purpose, what is that purpose? What are our goals in life? Do we not need to achieve a better understanding of who we are in terms of our chief talents in order to move toward realizing the full use of those talents?

"What do I want from life?" may seem like a senseless question to some, and to others a terribly hard but necessary question to answer. But do we not need to answer this question to achieve a sense of direction in realizing our potential? These questions are worth reflection and thought. The answers *you* find may change your life.

SUMMARY

Wishing does not make it so, but we often act as if we could wish something into existence. Wishing that others would do what we want them to do is a way of escaping personal responsibility for our own behavior. We cannot motivate others but we can create an atmosphere or climate which increases the probability that they will react to our efforts as we want them to. We will be more effective with people if we can discover how they are different and what they want. This obvious fact is ignored if we are concerned mostly with what we ourselves want.

Emotions are not to be feared but to be utilized in understanding others and predicting how they will behave. Emotions motivate behavior; but if we are afraid of our own feelings we will engage in a great deal of self-defeating behavior. Learning what to want or desire is essentially a part of the process of assimilating the culture in which we live. Being sensitive to what others desire is directly related to our success in cooperative efforts with others. To see meaning in what we do or what we ask others to do is the essence of motivation.

QUESTIONS FOR DISCUSSION AND THOUGHT

1. Why was the title "If Only" chosen to begin a discussion of human motivation? Think of an example of "if only" behavior you have engaged in.
2. Define motivation. How does motivation depend upon perception?
3. How do we learn to satisfy needs? Does our culture help determine how we react to various situations? Explain.
4. Emotions and physical needs do not motivate in the same way. What are the differences?
5. Emotions which become generalized often inhibit our success. How does this happen?
6. Can an individual desire both dominance and submission? What would be a possible result of this?
7. "People are different." Does this mean that we cannot use the same sales procedures with all customers or the same educational methods with all students? _
8. Can we know what motivates another person? Can we know what motivates ourselves?

7

THEN HOW???

If only I could be more effective in motivating people to do what I want
them to do. But you say I can't motivate others? *Then how* can I sell,
teach, manage, command, order, coach, train, persuade, urge, lead, show,
counsel, coerce, compel, force, entice, push, cause others to do what I
want them to do? O.K. . . . O.K.! You say I can't do these things. But how
do I get things done with people? How can I get my customers to see the
real value in my product? How can I convince my boss that he should give
me a raise? How can I make sure my secretary will finish this report
accurately while I'm out of town? How can I teach my children the value
of money? How can I . . . how can I motivate people if I can't motivate
them?

ANSWER: There is no answer.

· · · · · · ·

There is no answer because there are many answers to the questions we
have raised. There is no *one way* to provide the right stimulus to which
others will react as we want them to. There are many ways because of the
uniqueness of people, the variability in situations, and the constant uncertainty of outcomes. Machines operate in much the same way every time
we push the button to turn them on. But even machines sometimes
become "obstinate" and "refuse" to function. People are different from

machines; as far as we know, a machine doesn't brood because its neighbor receives more attention than it does. A machine doesn't pretend to operate one way and then secretly operate in quite a different way. It is true that when a do-it-yourselfer hits his finger with the hammer, he shouts at it and may fling it across the room almost as if it had a life of its own. The sports car buff may caress his new Mercedes with a loving care ordinarily reserved for a member of the opposite sex. The weekend gardener who pulls the starter rope on his mower for the twentieth time without the reward of a single cough may glare malevolently at the cold machine with the faint suspicion he is engaged in a personal duel he is losing. We can imagine human characteristics into a machine, but that does not make it human. Similarly we can imagine push-button, machinelike, automatic-response characteristics in the person we want to motivate, but this does not mean the person will jump when we push his button.

There are three principles of motivation: people are different; people are different; people are different.

Of course, there is more to motivation than the simple observation, "people are different." And based on the general observations of motivation in the preceding chapter we will take a close look at some of the general ways in which people respond to the various stimulus-situational conditions we create. But whenever we mention a generalization in the area of motivation it will be with the explicit assumption that a certain approach or technique works *often* but not *all* the time. Eighty percent of a certain group may respond favorably to a standard sales slogan or approach, but when we deal with one person at a time from that group, we do not know whether he is one of the eighty percent or one of the twenty percent who are repelled. A study of high school freshmen in one town may show that eighty percent eventually are graduated. Twenty percent may fail to be graduated because of illness, delinquency, boredom, pregnancy, or some other problem. At the present time it is impossible to predict which students will fail to be graduated. Intelligence testing may successfully predict *some* of the nongraduates but it cannot predict *all*. Identifying the socioeconomic status of the entering freshman's family will predict *some* but not *all* of the failures.

The more information we obtain about any individual, the more likely we are to predict how he will behave in the future. The more the manager finds out about his employees, the more he can predict which one will grow in responsibility. The more the teacher finds out about his students, the more he can devise learning conditions which will optimize their learning achievements. The more astute the used car salesman is in noticing the subtle reactions of his customer as they walk through the lot, the more he can select the car which will seem most attractive to the buyer. The husband who is sensitive to his wife's moods, needs, fears, and preconceptions can more readily choose the gift which will most delight or the jab of a comment which will most infuriate.

ACHIEVING GREATER SENSITIVITY TO PEOPLE

Motivation is not making people do things; it is being able to predict how people are likely to react to the things we do. People have minds of their own; and it is their perception of the world which makes them decide to move or not move, to be motivated or not motivated, by the few things we can do to influence their environment. It follows that the more we can know about people and how they are likely to behave, the more effective we can be in introducing factors into their environment toward which they will move. The more sensitive we can be to others, the more we can know how they see themselves, how they see us and the things we say to them or offer to them. Sensitivity, then, is an ability we all have, but to different degrees. People vary in their sensitivity to others in the same way they vary in other human abilities. Some of us are extremely sensitive to the feelings and predispositions of others, some are moderately sensitive, and some are minimally aware of how others feel, think, or are likely to behave.

Sensitivity is like any other word: it has different shades of meanings and different connotations, depending on our past experiences or how we have used the word. Sensitivity, sometimes expressed as hypersensitivity, may mean an inappropriate emotional reaction to a situation. "Don't be so sensitive," we may be told, when our adviser means we should not let our feelings be hurt. Sensitivity, used in this sense, means being "thin-skinned, easily upset or embarrassed, or crushed" by frank or crude comments. But *sensitivity*, to the researcher eager to give us reliable knowledge about how people behave, means simply our ability to be so aware of a person and his predispositions that we can *predict* his future behavior. *The more sensitive we are to a particular person at a particular time, the more accurately we can predict how he will behave at a particular future time and situation.*

Various researchers on sensitivity point out that it is not a general ability but is instead quite specific to the person, the situation, and the perceiver of those people and situations, himself.[1] For example, the chief operating officer may be able to predict which engineers are more likely to develop patentable products but may not be as able to predict which sales managers will be able to market the product for a profit. The sales manager may show great accuracy in selecting the recruit most likely to succeed in selling, but be inept in selecting a secretary. Sensitivity seems to be specific, rather than general. We can probably be more sensitive to those most like us than to those who are quite different. If we characteristically tend to see the best in people, we will be more sensitive to the individuals who tend to be above average in various abilities. It is not surprising that we are more aware of people who are most like ourselves. People who are alike tend to have similar values and attitudes; since behavior is a function of attitudes, we will be more successful predicting the behavior of those who share our attitudes.

Greater sensitivity can be learned. Perhaps it would be more accurate to say that changes in our attitudes and general needs in relation to others allow a greater sensitivity to emerge. The advantage of increasing our general sensitivity is that we will be more aware of the things in others which prompt them to be motivated by events in their environment. The old sage who said, "You ain't learnin' when you're talkin' " had a greater awareness of the psychodynamics of interpersonal relationships than he could have verbalized. The individual who is strongly expressive in social situations tends to be less aware of others than one who is more reserved. Fiction and autobiographies frequently suggest that a person who has suffered a great deal and has had to fend for himself develops a greater awareness of others than one who has had an easier life. These kinds of early experiences may lead to a high level of sensitivity in later life if the early trauma has not produced a neurotic or self-centered pattern of living. The more we worry about ourselves the less awareness we seem to have of others.

The aggressive, dominant person is frequently sought by recruiters to be a salesman. The lore of the sales field pictures the ideal salesman as a strong, aggressive, dominant, forceful, independent person who is smooth

[1] For research information on sensitivity and the factors affecting our ability to understand each other, see L. J. Chronbach, "Processes Affecting Scores on 'Understanding of Others' and 'Assumed Similarity,' " *Psychological Bulletin,* Vol. 52, 1955, pp. 177–193; and H. C. Smith, *Sensitivity to People* (New York: McGraw-Hill Book Company, 1966).

with words, is cool and detached in his analysis of the objections, and knows the appropriate "power phrases" to close the sale. Research on sensitivity would suggest that these characteristics interfere with the ability to know and understand the potential customer. But the strong, aggressive salesman and the forceful, dominant manager do frequently see that success follows their efforts. As we discussed in Chapter 6, some individuals have a need to submit or be controlled. If this salesman is dealing with a submitting individual, sales are likely. It could be argued, however, that some people will buy anything; some employees will put up with almost any kind of working situation or unfeeling treatment from their supervisor. On the other hand, it might be somewhat deflating for some salesmen to realize that occasionally a person will buy from them *in spite* of their pressures and attempts at dominance.

It would be unrealistic to assume that we must understand each person we deal with before they will respond favorably to our words or actions. A thirsty man will buy a cold drink from the nearest boy at the game; in times of high unemployment a widowed mother of three will do her secretarial work well in spite of the most oppressive supervisor; a pedestrian stopped by a "con" artist may buy a "three-hundred-dollar watch" for "only" twenty-five dollars even though he suspects it is stolen and the peddler is a scoundrel. Since we are self-motivated, we will move toward whatever seems attractive to us. It is possible that the other party to the deal will erroneously think that he has "motivated" us!

Becoming more sensitive to others allows us to predict more often how they will react. It does not, however, guarantee that we can create conditions to which they will automatically react as we wish. Increasing the accuracy of our predictions even a little can have large and favorable consequences in the satisfactions we experience.

IMPROVING OBSERVATION SKILLS

Increasing our sensitivity means that we make improvements in our ability to observe what is going on, what is said both with words and without words, and what kind of total situation we are dealing with. Observation is a skill which most of us take for granted.

Give yourself a little attitude test right now. What is your own power of observation? Don't you believe that if you "see it with your own eyes" you are seeing reality? Don't you believe that you are rational, reasonably mature, and generally objective? If you witnessed an automobile accident and told about it later, wouldn't you believe that what you saw was what actually happened? If you have answered "yes" to these questions then you have passed the test and can consider yourself "normal." So far, so good. Now, there were two other eyewitnesses at the scene who also will pass this test of attitude toward their observational skills. But there's a difference. What they report they saw is not the same as what you said! The three versions are different. All three of you can't be right! All right. Confess! Which one of you is irrational, immature, and lacking in objectivity? None of you will admit to this? How odd!

Adult man assumes that he is rational. He can find much evidence that others who do not share his views on politics, religion, sex, finance, automobiles, etc., are not entirely rational in their thinking. But he believes that what he buys is bought wisely (except for an occasional impulse purchase . . . but after all he's only human). He believes that his political candidate is better than the others. He is sure that other drivers take chances and frequently drive recklessly. He sees more fouls by the other team go unnoticed by the referee, who seems a little bit biased against his own. It seems to be quite human that we think of ourselves as being realistic observers when compared to others who differ with us. Changing this one attitude can do much to increase the real accuracy of our observations.

Careful research on how people observe indicates that we frequently "see" what we *want* to see, what we *expect* to see, and what we have *learned* to see. We "see" what fits with our previous beliefs about a person rather than what may actually be true about him. We observe characteristics of a person until we have him "pigeonholed" and then tend to overlook other characteristics which conflict with our neat perception. We frequently "see" in a person not what *he* feels but what *we* feel; this projection is usually unconscious. We tend to "see" in people the things they can do for us or the things we can get from them. It is rare that we "see" what they feel, they need, they want, they believe. Margaret Mead, from her broad perspective as an anthropologist, observes that man more often sees and remembers longer the negative, the weak, and the inadequate things in others.[2] The newspaper sells bad news more readily than good; a man's one major mistake becomes public property while his

---

[2] Valuable reading for the concerned and bewildered adult trying to understand what is happening to our perceptions in this changing world, especially in the younger generation, is Margaret Mead's *Culture and Commitment: A Study of the Generation Gap* (Garden City, New York: Natural History Press, Doubleday & Co., 1970).

lifetime of accomplishments and good goes unnoticed or unappreciated. *The careful observer will recognize these tendencies in himself and will make urgent efforts to overcome them to achieve a more balanced, fair, and accurate perception of people.*

Observation is a skill which must be practiced if we hope to become more proficient. Changing basic attitudes is important, but specific exercises can be practiced daily. Use a tape recorder during a conversation with a friend or during an interview with a recruit, prospect, colleague, or employee (with his knowledge and permission, please). At the same time, take notes as carefully as you can, trying to write down all the facts, ideas, phrases, or points of view being expressed. Then listen to the recording while scanning your notes to see what you failed to write down or forgot to note. Notice the differences between what you "heard" and the tape recording. Analyze the kinds of information you seem to overlook. Ask a friend to listen with you so that he may point out things you are overlooking. Even more help is available if it is possible to video-tape your participation in a conversation.

Go with two or three friends or business associates to a meeting, a lecture, a shopping center, or anywhere people are doing things. Concentrate on what the speaker, customer, or clerk does, says, seems to feel, think, or believe. Take notes separately, write up your observations in detail, and then compare notes with your fellow observers. Notice what you all saw, what only you saw, etc., and analyze the similarities and differences with the aim of understanding yourself better as an observer, a distorter of facts, a forgetter of details, a twister of meanings, a projector of feelings, etc. Hard work? You bet! Worth while? Certainly! Confusing and frustrating? Of course! Humiliating? Probably!

The next time you meet someone you "instinctively" do not like, try to find qualities in him you admire, ideas you can agree with, and values you share. Abraham Lincoln (and probably thousands of other notables) said that when he met a man he did not like, he figured he had to try to get to know the man better. If we can be aware that we tend to jump to conclusions, then we can practice delaying our judgment of others. If we know that it is typical that we "see" only the things we want to see, we can practice searching for facts which might destroy our argument or for qualities in people which might not support our prejudices. The concept of the "Devil's Advocate" can be used to practice better observation. If you believe something, search for reasons why your belief might be wrong. If you favor a candidate for office, see why he might not be qualified. If you think your son is lazy and uninterested in anything but TV and comic books, try to find times when he is highly motivated to do something or is interested in current events, etc. Force yourself to look for things you may not want to see.

Discipline means, first of all, guidance.[3] Self-discipline means guiding yourself toward greater satisfaction and self-actualization. Scientists, as we discussed in Chapter 1, develop a spirit of inquiry which dictates that they observe and record *all* that is there, not just what they might wish is there. The scientific method is rigorous self-discipline; our daily lives can be scientific in this sense *if we choose.*

VALUES, ATTITUDES, AND BEHAVIOR CHANGE

Figure 2 shows a relationship between values, attitudes, and behavior. If we let the three concentric circles represent the most important aspect of

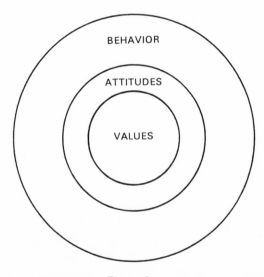

Figure 2

---

[3] Discipline: "3: training or experience that corrects, molds, strengthens, or perfects especially the mental faculties or moral character. . . ." *Webster's Third New International Dictionary* (Chicago, Illinois: G. & C. Merriam Co., 1966).

our psychological being, we see that the core of values plays a central role in determining the behavior we observe in ourselves and others.

Values are the things we feel are right, good, important, or desirable. It appears that for most of us our parents are the first teachers from whom we learn to value certain things, and this teaching process probably begins from the moment of birth. We are not necessarily aware of learning these values or even conscious of what they are. Depending upon the values we hold, certain attitudes are formed which act as mental sets predetermining the behavior patterns most likely to occur.

The first values we learn are absorbed into our personality even before we learn to talk. The child whose first human experiences are with warm, loving parents will value *closeness to others;* an opposite experience of neglect or severe rejection may lead the child to value *caution* or *emotional distance* from others. The latter child may highly value being cared for by others, but finds it difficult to feel comfortable with intimacy, since previously intimacy has led to pain or indifference. It is quite difficult to know for sure why one child tends to move *toward* people as he grows up while another tends to move *away,* but such early experiences as mentioned above probably are the beginnings of such values. The mechanism of developing early values has been tremendously simplified here, but it illustrates how values can be formed on an unconscious and preverbal level.

We tend to gravitate toward the same religion, political views, social life styles, and general behavioral patterns of our parents. The rebellious youth may make a dramatic attempt to cast off the values of his parents because of his growing needs for independence, but after a flare-up of rebellion the life style of the child-adult is remarkably similar to that of his parents. The cultural conditioning of early youth tends to continue to form the pattern of adulthood with few exceptions.

The core of values held by a particular person may include the value of using *force* to get what he wants, the value of *white supremacy* (over nonwhites), the value of using *untruths* for personal advantage, the value of *hoarding* rather than sharing, etc. With these values as part of the basic core, it would not be surprising to see attitudes develop from them that include the attitudes that peaceful demonstrations of a contrary view should be beaten back, legislation supporting racial segregation should be voted for, and false rumors should be spread to discredit the opponent's political candidate. With these attitudes prevailing in that person, we would predict his active participation (*behavior*) in swinging a pick handle at the demonstrators, running for or voting for the segregationist candidate, and being careless with the truth in public and private statements. Still another person could have learned to value *cooperation, truth, equality of opportunity, sharing* of goods and services, etc. His behavior, based on the attitudes of joining with others to work honestly for legislation guaranteeing equal opportunity, would be dramatically different.

The core of values produces attitudes which influence behavior. Change the values, and the attitudes are more changeable, leading to changes in behavior (buying, voting, marriage, child-rearing habits). Values are more general and more highly resistant to change, attitudes are more specific and less resistant, and behavior is most easily changed. But because behavior is relatively easy to change, it seems to change back again if there has not been a fundamental change in the value-attitude basic core. Change a value and the behavior change resulting from it will be relatively permanent. So often we attempt to change behavior without even attempting to understand the attitudes and the more basic underlying values. Forcing employees to behave in a different way by making them punch time clocks so that they come to work on time will not necessarily change their attitude that "you can't get ahead even if you break your back working so why try?" In fact, the new time clock may go counter to a basic value of self-determination, and the reaction may be a subtle work slowdown.

Values and attitudes cannot be directly observed. Referring again to Figure 2, we can think of the outer layer of behavior as the external pattern of behavior of a person—that which is visible. The inner values and attitudes must be inferred. We infer values and attitudes from the only thing we can observe: behavior. But inference is not always reliable. If we observe that a friend works overtime, has a part-time job on the side, and reconditions furniture in his basement for resale, we might infer that he is "money-motivated." The truth of the matter, if we could know it, may be that he has an unhappy home life and values spending all his time away from home or secluded in solitary activity. We may observe someone standing by himself at the company party and remember that he eats lunch alone at work and does not "go out with the boys for coffee"; our inference is that he is snobbish and thinks he's "better than the rest of us." But is it possible that he is shy and frightened of new relationships?

Inferring values and attitudes from observing behavior is a valuable talent if we are to be effective in the motivational process. Our discussion of the scientific method in Chapter 1 applies directly to the problem of achieving more validity in our inferences from behavior. The more often, and in more different situations, we observe the same kinds of behavior, the more we can rely on the inferences we make. If we observe that an individual makes many contributions each year, gives of his time to help out in church, charity, or civic efforts, goes out of his way to help a friend, etc., then we are fairly safe to infer an attitude of being active in helping based on the *value of worth* in other humans. If, on the other hand, frequent observations show us that his giving is done only with considerable fanfare and never without publicity, we might infer the attitude of helping only on the condition of self-gain, based on the values of a *hostile world* and *poor self-esteem*.

If we could know the basic core values held by others, we could design an environment (offer rewards, punishments, give or withhold information, etc.) which would have a high probability of producing the behavior we desire in them. The purchasing agent who values thrift will listen more readily to the salesman who emphasizes the long-range low unit cost of a product as opposed to its relatively high price. The head of a household who values security will be more interested in life insurance than in a speculative stock (but this depends on how the salesman and prospect define "security"). The consumer who values athletics and has a favorable attitude toward organized sports will be likely to purchase a season ticket for the local team. Valuing education and holding favorable attitudes toward personal reading will make a potential buyer more open to the presentation being made about a new encyclopedia.

We are motivated to support the things which agree with our basic values and to attack those which are in opposition. What an advantage to be able to "read" what others value! The more we can be sensitive to the individual uniqueness of each person we work or live with, the more effective will be our efforts to participate in the attitude change of others.

ATTITUDE AND BEHAVIOR CHANGE TECHNIQUES

Avoid Arguments

In ordinary conversation when we meet anyone who expresses an attitude or opinion different from ours, and we wish to change it to correspond with our own thinking, our usual reaction is to begin arguing.

If a Democrat and Republican are discussing politics, their argument usually leads to such evaluative phrases as, "You're crazy," or, "You don't know what you're talking about." There probably is no more effective way to muff an opportunity to change an attitude than to begin a personal argument. And yet many businessmen react to an objection raised by a colleague by immediately trying to argue him out of his objection. One principle of persuasion is to avoid becoming involved in an argument.

There is probably nothing more effective in taking the wind out of someone's sails than to say simply, "Yes, you're right." After you have said this, you can always say, "But I wonder if you have ever thought of this . . ." If we force a person to defend his attitudes he may become firmer in his defense. But if we can use a "Yes, but . . ." approach, he is more likely to think that we are an agreeable fellow and listen to our proposition.

When someone brings up an objection to something we want to do we might handle this effectively and set the stage for persuading him to change his attitude by merely saying, "I can understand what you feel. I'm interested in what you mean. Could you tell me more about it?" After he has run the full course describing his reasons for thinking the way he does, we might then ask him to repeat several of the important points he has made. By the time he has had this much opportunity to verbalize his negative attitude or opinion he frequently will tone it down so much that it hardly resembles his initial assertion. We demonstrate our interest in others by requesting a fuller explanation of the initial statement. In many cases he will realize his initial objection needs to be revised—a benefit of good listening. He will have been "softened up" and be more ready to adopt a different attitude.

Review and Revise Beliefs

Before attitudes and opinions can be changed there often needs to be a change in the person's beliefs or knowledge. A person may feel that renting an apartment is ideal because he avoids maintenance and yard work. A real estate dealer may point out that it is really a form of investment to own real estate and that rent is of no investment value. This new information may be enough to help him see it in a different light and perhaps change his initial attitude toward owning real estate.

Establish Rapport

Most people are quite open to suggestion. When a person we like wears a new-style suit, we are more likely to buy a suit of the same style, even though we may have felt a few days before that it looked "funny." The more highly the persuader is regarded by those whom he is attempting to influence, the more effective will be his efforts to change attitudes and opinions. The speaker who attempts to "sell himself first" is essentially raising his esteem in the eyes of his audience. If he is seen as being more believable and a rapport has been established, then the information conveyed will more readily be accepted. When the speaker and listener can establish a common ground or perhaps can share a joke or an understanding, the situation is much more favorable to a change in attitudes and opinions.

Establish Credentials

The persuasiveness of a speaker will depend largely on how expert the listener feels the speaker is. Even such a simple thing as a minor mistake in arithmetic can raise doubt about the expertness of a loan officer. The counselor (attorney, priest, teacher, manager, etc.) can create in the mind of his client the impression of competence by rapidly and accurately grasping the full significance of his problem. Somehow indicating to the client that the counselor has certificates, awards, that he has handled other complicated problems, that his office employs various specialists or experts in planning, etc., all help convey the impression to the client that the counselor is both *willing* and *able* to be of help to him. Of course, this kind of information coming from a third party (satisfied "customer") is more effective than if it comes from the counselor himself.

The third-party influence of a satisfied client can be of more help than is often realized. The new client who has just been satisfactorily advised by the consultant will perhaps never be more enthusiastic about him and his company than he is just then. This client is often more willing to give referred leads and even to "build up" the consultant to these referrals than the consultant may suspect. But the client may not know just what to say to the friend to whom he would refer the consultant. If the consultant can do a careful and appropriate job of "coaching" his client on what to say, the client will appreciate it and can in turn be of great help in establishing the consultant's "credentials" with new prospects. Obviously, the client will not want words put in his mouth, but he may want to hear how other clients have introduced the consultant in the past.

Establish Similarities of Interest

The more ways we can show that we hold many of the same views held by another, the more likely that there will be changes in some of his attitudes and opinions. It is important to find as many areas of agreement or similarity as possible. We feel influenced more by someone we like or feel is sympathetic to us than by someone who is unsympathetic. In this regard, humor can be very effective. Enjoying a humorous experience or story together tends to establish a similarity of interest. The self-centered bigot who uses derogatory racial or ethnic jokes may find himself on the "outside" because he has destroyed rapport!

Use Repetition

The more often we state a point of view, the more likely we are to get it across. Radio and TV commercials recognize this principle and broadcast the same commercial thousands of times, with the net result that the consumer is "convinced." If we are disturbed or upset by the statement, however, repetition will only increase our aggravation.

Repeating a point or an idea may be more effective if the statements are made in slightly different ways, varying the wording while expressing the same idea. Simply repeating a memorized sentence may give others the feeling that you are talking down to them or underestimating their intelligence.

Request More Change Than You Expect to Get

In "influencing" or changing the attitudes of others we are frequently effective in "producing" the desired change if we initially try to obtain a greater change in attitude than we actually expect. This technique is used effectively in negotiations between governments and in the give-and-take involved in bargaining over the price of an object.

Every teenage boy knows that if he wants to "touch" his dad for ten dollars for a date, it is better to ask for more than that. Generally, the greater the shift in attitude or opinion we ask of a person, the greater the change is likely to be.

Use Group Pressure

An individual is definitely swayed in the direction he thinks a group of which he is a member is moving. A vice president of a bank is more likely to be influenced by the EDP consultant who can say, "More than 5,000 bankers have already purchased this." A person may also be swayed by the opinion of a group of which he is not a member but to which he would like to belong. Undoubtedly, many people have bought an "executive" item who were not themselves executives but who like the idea of being associated with that group.

Use Physical Contact

Physical contact between two people can be an element of persuasion. The simple act of throwing our arm over a person's shoulder actually says a lot. Ordinarily, we do not touch people unless we like them. Shaking hands is a custom and is done automatically. But other kinds of physical contact, such as placing a hand on the prospect's arm, have been useful techniques of persuasion when used appropriately, and with care.

Standing *too* close to the prospect or touching him *too* soon, however, can be threatening and may disturb what has up to that time been a growing relationship of warmth and trust. The company representative who knows his customer well can, at the moment of decision, hand him a pen and say, "John, sign that order!" To a friend this is not being offensively overbearing, but shows only genuine regard and an effort to help him overcome his indecision. Remember that any professional adviser should have a sincere conviction that the decision is a correct and wise one for his client before he uses any effort to motivate.

Ego Building

There is no one more important to the prospect than he himself. In most conversations we look for an opportunity to have our say, or search for something in what others are saying that affects us directly and personally. The human being seems to have much of his interest and attention focused on himself most of the time. If we deliberately exercise certain techniques to enhance the feeling of self-importance in others, we will be in a better position to apply persuasive influence.

A simple way of helping a person feel more important is the judicious use of his *name*. *We like to hear the sound of our own names.* It adds a personal touch if someone begins a statement to us by speaking our name first. We probably come closer to touching a person's emotions if we refer to his children and wife by name also, rather than merely saying "your children" and "your wife."

Everyone has this very human desire to feel important. If we can spot things a person has done that really are important, a conscious effort to refer to them and to compliment him *sincerely* on his accomplishments will do much to place us in a more powerfully persuasive position.

Assemble All Possible Objections to Attitude Change

In applying persuasion to an individual we are essentially answering objections that he is posing for us. Often it seems that as soon as we answer one objection, the person always thinks of another one. One technique of persuasion which has been successfully used is to assemble all of the possible objections before answering any of them. It may even be desirable to stimulate him to think of still more objections when it seems that he has nearly finished. When he says that there are no more objections, we can proceed to answer each objection in turn so that at last he feels considerable pressure to agree since he no longer has any more objections. Such a statement as, "If I successfully answer your last objection, will you agree to take action?" puts him in a kind of box from which it is difficult to escape. If the rest of the interview has been favorable, this kind of persuasive influence is likely to result in a change of behavior, if not in attitude.

In any situation of persuasion, anyone is more likely to give in or submit if he can win something for himself at the same time. The person who has successfully proved a point *to* us may be more inclined to accept suggestions *from* us.

Avoid Being Too Smooth

The more believable the persuader appears to be, the more effective his efforts will be in changing attitudes and opinions. TV announcers who use flawless English and rattle off a prepared pitch appear less effective that those who stumble a little, as many of us do in a normal conversation.

When we listen to a person who is too smooth, we are likely to get the feeling that he has memorized what he is saying and that he is insincere or is not really talking to us personally. The skillful persuader will pause, appear to consider objections before answering them, and avoid too quick or automatic an answer to an objection. Otherwise, the listener may feel that the speaker is not considering his objections carefully enough.

Especially when we are unsure of ourselves, we may try to dazzle our listener by using big words or a technical vocabulary. But if we are to be persuasive with a person, we must avoid confusing or irritating him. He will be uncomfortable if he does not understand a big word or if he has to ask us what a word means. He may not ask for clarification at all, and we will have lost some persuasive impact.

Present Both Sides of an Argument

There are always two sides to every argument or discussion. A more intelligent person seems to respond more favorably to being given both sides so that he can form his own conclusions. For a less intelligent or less educated person, it is probably better to present only the one side most favorable to your needs. Now the only problem is to decide who is more or less intelligent; the person with the most college degrees is not necessarily the most "educated."

Request a Public Commitment

Once an opinion or attitude has been changed, it seems to be more resistant to further change in a different direction. There is even more resistance if the individual has publicly expressed his changed opinion. It would appear that stating an opinion publicly is a commitment; changing this opinion in an open discussion seems to represent "loss of face" to some.

Expecting Later Use of Information

Consciously expecting to make later use of information being given in a sales presentation or in a lecture in the classroom increases our memory of it. A student expecting to be tested on the lecture material will retain more than one who will not be tested. If a man expects to give product information to his wife later in the evening after his conference with the salesman, he will probably remember more; this is especially true if he thinks he must "sell" his wife on the purchase!

Intelligence and Persuasion

It is not surprising that the more intelligent person acquires more information in any persuasive conversation. A person's vocabulary is a good clue to his general intelligence level, but it is not an infallible one. Many persuasive efforts have backfired because the speaker "talked down" to his audience. Since people are sometimes reluctant to admit that they didn't understand some point being discussed, it is important for the speaker to make frequent efforts to find out what the listener heard.

Self-Esteem and Change

Those who have a low sense of self-worth or esteem are more likely to allow themselves to be influenced by persuasive efforts. It is as if a person who felt inferior were saying to himself, "I can't have any opinions or viewpoints which are worthwhile; I suppose if he says his idea is right, it must be." A person who frequently apologizes for what he says or what he is may be revealing a low sense of self-esteem.

Fear as a Motivator

Saying things to which a person reacts with fear may be effective in changing his attitudes or behavior. If too much fear is aroused, however, it may cause so much tension that the person is more resistant to change of any kind. If a customer is too frightened by what the salesman says, or if the patient greatly fears the physician's statements, the strongest motivation may be to avoid the person making the fear-arousing statements.

A Readiness to Believe

If in a persuasive conversation a favorable reaction occurs early, the likelihood is increased that later efforts will be favorably received, too. If the speaker is perceived as having prestige or as being competent, the listener will more readily believe what he has to say.

Presenting a Rationale

Employees who are given the reasons for a change in policy or working conditions are more likely to accept the change. The fullest acceptance of change usually results from the fullest understanding of it. Employees seem not to be assured with vague promises. If the change can be described in terms of the specific effects on the individual or group, and it is realistic, it will be more readily accepted.

The Impact of Disclosure

Openness and disclosure on the part of the speaker will tend to encourage openness to change on the part of the listener. A high disclosure of information and feelings will encourage others to disclose more, thus facilitating more complete exchange of information.[4]

Annoyance, and Information Obtained

Obtaining information about the person whose behavior you would like to see changed is important in designing a persuasion effort. Expressing annoyance in any form when this information is given will tend to stop further information from being offered.

Change in Status

People do not automatically resist change. Change will seem to be a desired opportunity or a threat, depending on the attitude held. We tend to resist changes which we perceive as lowering our status; we accept those which promise to increase it.

Public and Private Statements

If there is a difference between what a person says publicly and what he believes, he will tend to change either his statements or his beliefs. The more he makes statements contrary to his opinions, the more likely he will be to change his opinions so that there is less conflict.

These ideas present only the barest suggestion of the total picture of ideas and techniques which tend to be persuasive. We have stressed the complexity of the motivational process, pointing out that it is possible to create an environment or atmosphere in which others live or work, but ultimately we must depend on how this environment is perceived. It is not our perception but that of others which counts when we want to see changes in their behavior.

[4] For an important work on the effects of transparency and disclosure in interpersonal relationships, see S. M. Jourard, *Disclosing Man to Himself* (Princeton, New Jersey: Van Nostrand, Inc., 1968).

MOTIVATION AND INTERVIEWING TECHNIQUES

The relationship between two or more people is more important than the techniques used, although each affects the other. Trial and error is one way to find solutions to problems, but it can be costly. It is possible to engage in mental trial and error and thereby avoid wasted time and effort. Thinking about the total situation, the communication efforts, the needs and fears of all the people involved, the obvious and hidden motives, and the intriguing but often baffling difference between people makes the motivational process both an exciting and a frustrating experience. Understanding more about the principles and procedures of effective interviewing may make the motivational process less frustrating.

An interview is a conversation between two or more people for some purpose other than simple enjoyment of the conversation. We interview in order to give information, obtain information, and change behavior. While we may think of an interview only in an employment or fact-finding situation, we are engaged in some type of interview most of the day whether we are at work or at home. If we think of an interview as an attempt to make more accurate predictions about the future behavior of others, we can approach it in a scientific manner; we can try things in order to *facilitate* the fullest possible information exchange, we can attempt to *recognize* all the relevant information, not just that which pleases us, and we can *check on the accuracy* of the information while we are receiving it. The principles and techniques which follow apply equally to the selling conversation, the teaching conversation in the classroom, the husband-wife conversation, the manager-subordinate conversation, and any other face-to-face communication effort.

Build an Atmosphere of Freedom

People will give more information about their preferences and needs if they feel accepted and not judged. Information will be given more freely if they feel no unfair advantage will be taken. The first, and perhaps major, job of the person initiating the conversation is to help the other person feel free to express, question, object, disagree, and of course cooperate in the conversation. Generally, two can more quickly reach understanding if a third person is not present. In a business office, the visitor would have a greater feeling of freedom in talking if the businessman's secretary could not overhear the conversation. Interruptions and distractions also decrease the atmosphere of freedom. While a conversation during lunch or dinner may seem relaxing, the number of distractions make it difficult to maintain full attention to the ideas, feelings, and moods being exchanged.

Perhaps nothing more disrupts a conversation than for one to interrupt by talking on the telephone. While it may be unconscious, the person talking on the telephone in the presence of others who were trying to have a conversation will indicate that he is more important than those present. Many years of consulting with top management groups of some of our largest corporations has convinced the authors of a simple but profound truth: the more important and mature the businessman, the easier it is to talk to him. A man who is really secure and adequate will tend to shut off all telephone calls and indicate to his secretary that he does not want to be interrupted while he is talking to *you*. This kind of man will feel, and will indicate in many ways, that the most important thing on his mind right now is *you*. The "you" interest is extremely important in any conversation, and it *cannot be pretended*.

Create the "You" Interest

Throughout this book we have stressed genuineness, authenticity, and sincerity. The only way to achieve these attitudes is to experience them. Research indicates that attempts to pretend genuine interest, where it really does not exist, are most often seen for what they are: phony attempts to manipulate. But nothing is more powerfully persuasive than real interest in that other person. The ability to lose yourself in another person comes with maturity and security. Assuming that you have developed these human capacities, use them in building effective interview conditions. The more you can genuinely use the words "you, yours, his," etc., in conversations in place of "I, me, mine," etc., the more you will be directing interest toward the other person. If you need to talk about yourself, go see a psychiatrist, psychologist, or social worker! But if you want to help another individual motivate himself in some direction which will be good for him, give yourself the growth-inducing experience of forgetting your own interests and try to understand his interests.

People love to be listened to. Don't you? Listening demonstrates our interest and regard for the person. Listening also enables us to learn a great deal about him as an individual. There is no more important foundation for the motivational process. It is obvious that if *you* need to monopolize the conversation, *you* need attention, care, and affection. Don't we all? But if you want to help others *move* in a direction good for them *and* for you, you had better try hard to put your own interests in the background.

Practice Give and Take

Any interview involves the backgrounds, biases, and hopes of at least two people. Both individuals bring a lifetime of hurts, aspirations, and satisfactions to the conversation. Each wants something from the other. It is the more mature of the two who does the most to see that the conversation is mutually satisfactory. Much of the interaction between two people is carried on by gesture, postures, facial expressions, and other physical behavior. The less self-preoccupied we are, the more aware we will be of what others are saying by the way they sit, lean forward, fidget, squint, cross their arms, etc. Leaning forward in the chair may indicate interest in what is being said, but if genuine interest is not there, it will probably be seen as artificial. In a management–subordinate appraisal situation the subordinate is interviewing the manager just as much as the manager is interviewing the subordinate. It is likely that both are trying to see if they are inferior to the other; both are searching for labels which help explain the other; both are self-centered. Both want the other to understand them, and both are convinced that they do not.

Encourage and Discourage Talking

There are two kinds of people: those who think there are two kinds of people and those who do not. Realistically, we do come in degrees. We engage in conversation with some who tend to talk a great deal but say very little and with some who respond with the fewest possible words. Both over- and under- responding create conversational difficulties which the experienced interviewer knows how to handle. Perhaps silence is as effective as anything in helping others put their thoughts into words. Give the other person time and he is more likely to tell you more about himself. But silence can be threatening, too. The experienced interviewer will use silence to allow others to express themselves more adequately, but he will recognize that silence can be acutely uncomfortable and will not allow it to become a conversational obstacle. Comments like, "Tell me what you mean; how, what, where, why, who," are all simple questions which can help another person convey more about himself or his beliefs and tendencies.

"Could you summarize what you've just said?" is one way to help the person be more concise. Listening to the relevant and being uninterested in the irrelevant is another way of encouraging the other person to stop getting off the subject. "I think you are trying too hard to be helpful; could you be more concise in answering my questions?" could be one way to encourage the roundabout individual to be more direct. "What you are saying is very interesting and I wish we had time to talk about it. But as I was saying . . ." This sentence illustrates the principle that we should recognize the importance to the individual of what he is saying but continue with what is most relevant to our present purposes.

Avoid Embarrassment

Your conversation with others will be more productive if you avoid questions which will embarrass. Your companion will talk more easily if your first questions can be answered easily and without embarrassment. Embarrassment is essentially an attitude toward oneself. In the most literal sense, no one can embarrass us. Only we can embarrass us. Embarrassment means that we see our status diminishing. But this is in terms of our own standards. For some of us, discussing our financial status is more intimate than revealing the details of our sexual life; revealing our innermost needs for security can be more embarrassing than discussing our latest love affair. Embarrassment is an individual matter; we can know about someone else's embarrassments only by being extremely sensitive to his moods and feelings.

Use His Language

It seems obvious that we will communicate with others only to the extent that we use words which they know. It *is* tempting to display our extensive vocabulary so that others will be properly impressed. But is it not more important to *express* than it is to *impress?* Unfortunately, people will not always say, "I don't know what you mean by that word." In fact, quite the contrary, we tend to pretend that we understand the big words others use when in fact we don't. William Buckley is seen as a true intellectual, but how many of his fans will admit that they don't understand many of the words he uses? Is he a good communicator if his audience is impressed but uninformed? "What do you mean by that?" is something we can say when we are in doubt but it also indicates that we are secure enough to acknowledge an area of ignorance. There is nothing wrong with ignorance; there is something very wrong with being ashamed of ignorance.

Almost every occupation has its particular terminology. Every activity has a vocabulary which is unique; in fact, those in a given occupation frequently take pride in the fact that outsiders may not understand the lingo of the trade. "Gimme a BLT, hold the heat" is certainly easier to say than "My customer would like a bacon, lettuce, and tomato sandwich, but please don't toast the bread." But is there an element of pride in singing out the jargon of the diner? Of course! The teller who tries to get the customer to buy a "CD" may never know that he doesn't have the slightest notion that a "CD" is a certificate of deposit, and he probably is not going to reveal his ignorance by asking "WHAT?"

The senior takes pleasure in initiating the freshman. But if we're interested in communicating through the interviewing conversation, we should understand what our friend or prospect means by the words *he* uses. "When in Rome, do as the Romans do" makes sense if we want to take the responsibility of mature communication.

Demonstrate Your Understanding

The way in which the interview is conducted can either encourage or discourage communication. Why not try to put into your own words what you think your customer, employee, student, husband, or wife has just said. "As I understand it, you are saying that this approach will . . ." This will not only tell you whether you have been listening, but will give comfort to your colleague that he has been getting through to you. Of course, it can also indicate that you have not been listening; but isn't it better to know, than to remain in ignorance?

We like to be understood. It is rewarding to know that what we've said is understood by our partner in the conversation. *We want understanding so much that we sometimes assume it rather than test for it.* There may be no more important motivation than that of being understood. The good listener in a conversation shows by his repetition of your thoughts in his own words and by his facial expressions that he has understood what you have said.

The Ultimate Goal of a Motivational Conversation

The HOW of the motivational process includes many ideas and techniques, but the fundamental aim is not only mutual satisfaction of the people involved but their growth in maximizing their potential together. Effective interviewing can accomplish two goals: it can help you see the other person's needs, wants, and perceptions; it can help him crystallize in his own mind what his own values and goals are. The individual who is well prepared in his own field *and* in a knowledge of human behavior can experience the dual satisfaction of helping another person while succeeding in his own chosen work.

SUMMARY

The fact of individual differences is a commonly acknowledged but largely overlooked guide to improved interpersonal relationships. Achieving greater sensitivity to those differences is a beginning in our efforts to succeed in motivational efforts. Sensitivity can be increased as we practice the skill of observation, particularly as we learn how to be aware of the hidden values and attitudes which determine behavior. The techniques of persuasion may succeed if we do not forget the emotional and social context in which they are used.

Research findings on attitude change show that people do not automatically resist change: it depends upon what the change means to them. Impinging on another person's freedom seems to increase his defensiveness and resistance to change, even when the change might be in his best interests. In any conversation, helping the other person to feel more free to express himself facilitates the desired change in behavior. Almost everything we do in a conversation can be seen as increasing or decreasing this atmosphere of freedom.

QUESTIONS FOR DISCUSSION AND THOUGHT

1. Discuss various ways in which we can discover what "turns on" someone.
2. Can aggressiveness interfere with sensitivity? Explain.

3. What are the consequences of assuming that man is rational in what he does?
4. What is the relationship between values, attitudes, and behavior?
5. What attitudes in yourself might interfere with your efforts to persuade someone to change their attitudes?
6. If an individual has publicly stated an attitude, it seems more resistant to change than if only privately held. How would you explain this in terms of social influence? What are the implications for the businessman or parent?
7. In achieving persuasive success, "The relationship between two . . . people is more important than the techniques used." Explain.
8. Do we need to help others "save face" if we want them to be motivated by our efforts? Why is this important?

8

WHAT SHOULD
I DO NOW?

The story of human behavior has many beginnings and many endings because of our individual uniqueness. But transcending our differences are common human beginnings and lifetime concerns. "The Tyranny of Our Self-Image" (Chapter 1) pushes us through a process of "Conflict and Decision" (Chapter 2). The way in which we reach sound decisions which minimize conflict is shaped and conditioned by our individual experiences in undergoing the growth of "Socialization and Personal Freedom" (Chapter 3). Our lives are bounded by our understanding of "Situational Communications" (Chapter 4) and the effective use of "Language Tools" (Chapter 5). Of course, we communicate in order to get others to do what would please us, but we are not always successful. It is human to react to frustration by wishing and wondering: "If Only" (Chapter 6) others would do what I want, my life would be so much better.... "Then How" (Chapter 7) can I get them to do so? Each moment in our lives is the last one in the sequence of failures and successes which brings us to *now*: it is also characteristically human that out of despair or hope we utter the silent or audible question, "What Should I Do Now?" (Chapter 8).

It is a clear clue that when we use the words "should" or "ought" we are dealing with matters of ethics. Ethics is a concern with what is right and wrong, good and bad, important and unimportant. Man is concerned not only with obtaining food but also with how food *should* be obtained and what food *ought* to be eaten. It is generally accepted that we should work to obtain the money to buy food rather than steal it. Some feel they ought to eat fish on Friday and some avoid pork products. Man is concerned not only with making money but also with how the money *should* be made. The "drummer" of a century ago sold through misrepresentation and then drove his horse and cart to the next state and beyond to avoid the outraged indignation of the cheated customer. The con man "hits" one city and moves on because he knows he is not doing what he "should" do; he may not care, but he is aware that he is violating the "ethics" of the market place. *Caveat emptor,* or "let the buyer beware," has not entirely disappeared from the modern market place.

Knowledge leads to freedom, and freedom is inseparable from responsibility.[1] When we gain in understanding our own behavior, and that of others, we experience real human freedom: freedom to make choices, freedom to avoid blind tyrannies of our controlling culture, and freedom from self-defeating behavior. The "now generation" of the seventies expresses its philosophy through the lyrics of a Joan Baez song: "Dream one dream at a time, live one day at a time: yesterday's dead, tomorrow's blind . . . live one day at a time." Erich Fromm is over thirty, but he is believed by the young when he says, "Happiness is not the most important thing in life . . . aliveness is. Suffering is not the worst thing in life . . . indifference is."[2] From the Sanskrit come the words,

> . . . For yesterday is but a
> Dream and tomorrow only a Vision.
> But Today well lived makes every
> yesterday a Dream of Happiness,
> and every tomorrow a Vision of Hope.

What *should* I do now? Erich Fromm and Paul Ehrlich are a generation apart, but there is no generation gap. In Fromm's book, *Man for Himself,* he examined the issues involved in the psychology of ethics and concluded that the proper goal of man's efforts to master nature is *man himself.*[3] Paul Ehrlich might properly be called an ecologist, but he also writes about

---

[1] For fascinating reading on the human being, his responsibilities and conflicts, see Rollo May, *Psychology and the Human Dilemma* (Princeton, New Jersey: D. Van Nostrand Company, Inc., 1967).

[2] Erich Fromm, "Do We Still Love Life?" *McCall's Magazine,* August, 1967, p. 57.

[3] Erich Fromm, *Man for Himself* (New York: Holt, Rinehart & Winston, Inc., 1947).

ethics when he pleads that man must recognize his inextricable tie with nature: "If Homo sapiens is to continue as the dominant species of life on Earth, modern man must come soon to a better understanding of the Earth and what he has been doing to it."[4] Both men admonish that we *should* do *now* what will benefit man both now and in the future. Responsibility and freedom are inseparable. The freedom to control carries with it the responsibility to control wisely, or in terms of the continued good of mankind.

Learning about human behavior allows us to exercise more control over that environment or atmosphere, which increases the probability that others will respond as we wish them to. The behavioral scientist who promised that additional *knowledge* of people would allow us to *predict* more often the *behavior* observed in family or colleagues implied that we would increase our *control* of others as a result. Until recently the psychologist and sociologist claimed that their mission was to explain, not to moralize. The scientist aimed to understand human behavior, not suggest what behavior *should* occur. But in the postwar years, modern scientists have realized that they, like all men, *must weigh the long-term consequences of their work.* The scientist must make value judgments about what he does and how his information is used.[5]

WHAT IS ETHICS?

Ethics is concerned with the rightness or wrongness of human behavior. Ethics is a study of the standards by which men live. In studying ethics we are interested in what man feels he *ought* to do and how he makes decisions about what he ought to do. From the time that mankind has recorded his history, we see evidence that he has guided, or attempted to guide, his behavior by following a code of what is the right thing to do. It is equally true that man has often behaved in ways contrary to what he would agree was the right way for him to behave.

If we settle for the definition of ethics as being concerned with what men ought to do, we must immediately raise the question: "According to

[4] Paul and Anne Ehrlich, *Population Resources Environment* (San Francisco: W. H. Freeman & Company, 1970), p. 1.
[5] The reader will find an excellent discussion of the use of knowledge and the value judgments involved in Chapter 17 of Peter F. Drucker's book, *The Age of Discontinuity* (New York: Harper and Row, 1969).

whose opinion or whose authority do we judge what a person ought to do?" Two people or two nations can have two different notions as to what man ought to do. If we say that both individuals or groups can be right, then we are saying that ethics is purely relative and depends on one's point of view. This, obviously, cannot be true, or else the concept of ethics will have no meaning as a general standard or guide for man's behavior.

The Universality of Ethics

Are there universal laws of ethics which tell us what we ought to do? Certainly, human beings from diverse cultures in different parts of the world all behave as if there were some common rules of behavior which should govern all people.[6] Even hardened criminals who flout civil laws still react and conduct themselves as if they believed in a higher code of morality or decency of behavior. One gang member may make a promise to another member, and both will feel that the promise is binding. If one breaks his promise, both men recognize that a standard has been violated. In everything we do, we behave as if there is a universal law of nature which defines good or decent behavior. What one person regards as fairness in interpersonal relationships, another person may feel is not fair; but both would acknowledge that fairness is desirable. There is a remarkable agreement among human beings all over the world that certain ways of behaving are good while others are bad.

In order to study ethics and to understand its role in helping man decide what he should do, we must examine one general assumption which is made by the thinkers and writers in this field: *Man has a purpose for being and he ought to behave in order to realize that purpose.* The assumption continues with the idea that to the extent that man behaves in order to move toward reaching that purpose, he is behaving in a "good" way. To the extent that he behaves in a way which does not advance him toward that general purpose or end, he is behaving in a "bad" way. Most people would agree that there is a purpose to human life, but there is much less agreement on exactly what that purpose is.

A Search for a Purpose

Even the man who declares that there is no purpose to life and sets about trying to convince people of this is himself acting with a purpose. In all cultures and in all ages of history we see evidence that men experience

---

[6] C. S. Lewis presents a good argument for this thesis in his book *Mere Christianity* (New York: The Macmillan Company, 1953).

an overpowering need to understand where they fit into the scheme of things. Even in the most primitive societies the savage feels it important to invent stories and fables to explain his situation. In more civilized cultures, man's effort to find meaning and purpose in life expresses itself in organized philosophies and religions. The great growth of science has given us increased knowledge about the world and what it *is*, but does not tell us what it *means*. Man is exceedingly lonely and because of this loneliness experiences great anxiety. The search for a purpose to life is really his attempt to find a relationship between himself and a larger, more encompassing totality. For many, this larger totally embracing something is given the name *God*. For some, the purpose of life can be summed up in the belief that man's primary aim is to become "one" with God. For others, the word or concept "God" is much too vague in meaning for them to be certain that they can believe in this existence as an end for man. They are disturbed by the manlike conception of a personal creator who administers judgment from above. While they may have a great desire to relate to such an all-powerful, all-present being, they are likely to repress this desire because to them it doesn't make sense.

Especially as one reaches middle age (although also sometimes in youth) and finds that he is halfway through his normal life expectancy, these questions are often raised: "What is the point of it all? Why are we working so hard? Where are we going? Have we done the things that we should have done?" This moment of questioning is an anxious moment for most of us and may lead us to search more vigorously for the truth. If we can discover for ourselves some meaning in life, then we feel some sense of relief from anxiety.

The psychological value of an unshakable belief in a religion is almost beyond measure. The individual who has rejected an organized religion and has not replaced it with a firm belief in some other organized system of values is likely to feel profound despair.

The Importance of Belief

From a psychological, theological, and ethical point of view, *man needs to believe*. The child finds security in full and unquestioned belief in his parents. His early conception of God is likely to be as a kind of glorified father. The child thinks of God in terms of his parents, which illustrates the great responsibility that parents have for the shaping of their children's minds. The child gains security by feeling the firm hand of authority of his parents. The child himself often wants and needs to be punished. This may be his way of "testing the limits" or finding out where he stands with his parents. Parents who are excessively permissive with their children because they believe this to be the modern thing to do may unwittingly create insecurity and anxiety in their children. Too much freedom may not only frighten the child but also convince him his parents do not care for or love him. The child needs to feel the security which comes when people care enough for him to be concerned about what he does. It is exceedingly disturbing for a child to find that his parents have lied to him or even that they are wrong in the information they have given him. The child is disturbed because his faith and his belief in his God-parents is disturbed. In exactly the same way, the adult finds security in relating to a higher authority in which he can believe. And, too, like the child, the adult is profoundly disturbed when his belief is shaken. It is the normal, stable individual who has a well-organized system of belief. The neurotic or disturbed individual is often incapable of constructing a satisfactory philosophy of life.

Man needs to have faith in what he is doing, in his daily activities. Having faith in something means that we believe that it is worth while or good. If a businessman cannot believe in the goodness of building his company or of selling his product, an irreconcilable conflict is established. It is a common observation to see that a newly hired salesman for a firm does extremely well in selling the product for the first month or two but then apparently becomes "burned out." What often happens is that the salesman accepts with faith the statements about the product given him by the managers of the business, but when he begins to find out some undesirable things about the product or begins to believe what his customers say in a negative way about the product, he loses his faith. It is extremely difficult for us to be convincing in selling a product or an idea to a person unless we genuinely believe what we are saying. The businessman who finds himself operating at a low level of productivity often believes that "if I could only get better organized, I'd be more productive." We often come closer to finding the real answer to lack of productivity if we examine our system of belief in what we are doing. The manager who cannot *believe* in the worth and integrity of his top-management team or his company is likely to feel lost, lonely, and unmotivated.

What is Moral Behavior?

The human being consciously uses different, rather definite standards to help him decide what he should do at any given moment. One of the standards that most of us use in our early years is to do what our *parents* tell us to do. But doing what our parents tell us to do is not necessarily doing the ethically right thing. To take an extreme case, the pickpocket who teaches his young son to aid him in this activity is teaching his son the way he should behave in order to get a job done. But inevitably he also must teach his son that this is not the thing that *should* be done morally. No matter what this pickpocket says, he is forced to indicate to his child that they are not *really* doing the right thing because he must explain that they must be careful not to get caught, thereby acknowledging to himself and his son that they are breaking a fundamental rule. We could find many examples to show us that different parents instruct their children in different ways as to what is the right and wrong thing to do. We cannot assume that parental authority is therefore the best or only basis for making moral decisions.

Some may argue that individual parents can be wrong about important moral issues, but that the great mass of people will invariably agree on the rightness or wrongness of ideas or activities. A person with this point of view would hold that what the majority of people agree on would be morally right. People who do the customary thing usually feel that they are in the right. After all, they might argue, when we go against the things our society believes in, are we not either ridiculed, ostracized, or confined? But the same argument for not accepting parental authority as the basis for making moral decisions can also be used in opposing the idea of using *public opinion or custom* as the basis for moral decision. Public opinion on what is right and wrong varies from one country to another, from one state to another, and even from one city to another. In addition to this, customary ways of thinking and behaving change with time. If we grant that custom or public opinion should be used as the standard for making moral decisions, then we must also grant that what is morally right and wrong itself changes from place to place or from time to time.

Public opinion is a powerful influence on how people behave and on what they believe. Many people go through life behaving in ways which encourage other people to grant them approval and acceptance. Their moral decisions are made not on the basis of what may be right in an absolute sense but instead on the basis of what other people may feel is right at the time. The businessman who engages in questionable or misleading practices because "it is good business" and because "if I don't do it, my competitor will" is following the dictates of what he believes to be the custom of the business society. However, other groups of people in the same society are likely to say that these same standards are not right.

Can we assume that if we always obey the law in the strictest sense we will always be doing the morally right thing? Here again, we must conclude that even the "law of the land" cannot be used as the basis for moral living. Laws, too, change from place to place and from time to time. We cannot assume that what is morally right does not also change from time to time or from place to place. In addition, there are many things which can be thought of as being unethical that are not covered by laws. For example, if we break a promise to a friend, we find that this is not covered by law. We frequently hear of cases where an individual violates the spirit but not the letter of the law.

Many of us sincerely feel that if we do what our *conscience* tells us to do, we will be morally correct. Here again, we can easily recognize that what one person's conscience may say very often differs from what another person's conscience dictates. It is true that we often behave the way we do because of the prompting of our conscience, but this is not to say that our conscience always dictates the absolute right or wrong thing to do. The conscience of one person may move him to do his utmost to enforce racial segregation, while the conscience of another equally intelligent and mature individual may tell him that racial segregation is indefensible and must not be supported.

For most Christians and Jews the Ten Commandments are thought to be absolute, unquestionable laws of moral behavior revealed to man by God. To agree that the basis for moral decisions should be this Judeo-Christian heritage, with the recognized beliefs and commands contained in the Old Testament, is a beginning for Christians and Jews, but it is only a beginning in our efforts to understand ethical behavior and how to apply our beliefs to current life problems which daily present themselves. We must still translate these rather general principles and commands into the specific business or personal problems which we encounter. The more one understands the principles of ethics he is following, the easier it is for him to behave in a way which we would call ethical.

"I should do this, but I want to do that." How many times a day are we faced with this basic conflict?

ETHICAL CONFLICT

It is likely that the human being is never free from conflict. Most of us can recognize that we are often confronted with two or more possible ways of acting at any given time and we are faced with the necessity of making a decision. Each of us is faced with many decisions which must be made every day. We must make major decisions like which girl to marry, which job to take, and which political candidate to vote for, and many minor decisions such as what to have for breakfast, what to wear, what kind of automobile to buy. With almost every decision we make there are many reasons we could give for taking any one of several courses of action. We must make a choice. *Whenever a choice is necessary, there is always conflict.* In the case of many minor decisions, habit patterns tend to prevail and we hardly are aware of the choice-making process. But for some decisions, conflict, with its frustrations and difficulties, is a very real and conscious problem.

Some Major Conflicts

Let us look at some types of conflict situations which we are likely to face and in which we find ourselves suspended between opposing pressures. The businessman needs to read and understand a great deal about human behavior, but can't spend all his time reading. The individual needs to be creative and to try new things, but he must not deviate from the expected normal behavior "too much." The salesman needs to be a competitor and yet he must also cooperate with his manager, the company, and even fellow salesmen at times. We are taught to be honest; yet we are admonished to be "tactful" when expressing ourselves to others. The salesman must be aggressive; but he should not become overaggressive. We must maintain a certain level of fear as we move about in our daily activities so that we will keep ourselves out of dangerous situations, and yet we must not let this fear become too great or we will be unable to lead productive lives. We must work hard to "make a name for ourselves" but we must not be so selfishly interested in our own progress that we forget or ignore our family, our fellow man, or society.

We are all suspended between apparently contradictory or antagonistic ideas, concepts, or ways of behaving. How is one to decide how far to go in one direction or in another? The answer to this problem is one of the most difficult ones mankind has ever tried to discover. The attempts we make to find this balance between opposing interests is essentially the story of human relationships.

Man Disturbs His Own Equilibrium

It is important to note that the concept of man's seeking a balance between opposing and conflicting pressures does not explain all of human behavior. Occasionally, we see man seeming to upset his own equilibrium deliberately, in an effort to reach a new level of activity or adjustment. We think we reach a satisfactory level of adjustment or balance only to discover there may possibly be a still better way to adjust. Circumstances change and new adjustments and decisions become necessary. It is a continuous process.

Perhaps the philosopher Socrates was one of the first to question the way man thinks and behaves. While the people in his time were content with their simple, incomplete understanding of the world of material things and even of man himself, Socrates disturbed this pleasant equilibrium by asking, "How do we know these things are true? What do we mean when we use the words we use?" As mentioned previously, great thinkers such as Copernicus, Galileo, Darwin, Freud, Einstein, and many others did not accept the standard answers and understandings with which most men were satisfied and comfortable. They even risked dishonor and death by moving against the tide of public opinion and belief in their search for truth. Without such men to disturb the blissful state of equilibrium in which most of us sleep, we would not achieve greater and greater mastery over our surroundings and ourselves.

RESOLVING CONFLICT

In resolving conflict man utilizes three general methods in making decisions which help him to maintain a satisfactory equilibrium. They may be categorized as (1) the automatic or emotional approach, (2) the rational, problem-solving approach, and (3) the ethical approach. These processes may be either conscious or unconscious, and often all three are involved simultaneously.

We Are Influenced by Automatic Balancing Mechanisms

Imagine yourself trying to walk a tightrope. You take a tentative step forward, only to find that you are beginning to lean too far to one side. Your arms automatically move to help you restore your balance, but then you have moved too far over to the other side and are about to fall in that direction. Again your arms and body seem to adjust themselves in an effort to regain balance. As we walk down the street and are met by a gust of wind, we automatically lean in the direction of the wind to avoid being blown off our feet. In somewhat the same way we walk a tightrope throughout our lifetime. We maintain a balance between opposites or

extremes. We have seemingly automatic and instantaneous emotional reactions to various pressures and forces around us. Our immediate, spontaneous, automatic reactions serve us well, for they help maintain our
equilibrium, help us "keep our feet on the ground," and help us resolve
conflict situations.

Let us consider an example of how our constantly reacting and often
unconscious emotional responses can help us move toward some kind of
equilibrium. An employer was interviewing a recruit. In any selection
interviewing situation, the employer attempts to ascertain and evaluate
both the good and bad points of the recruit. In making his decision either
to hire or not to hire, he must decide that the good points outweigh the
bad points. If he sees an equal number of good points, he will be caught in
a dilemma because the decision will be difficult. During this particular
interview, the employer was undecided about hiring the recruit until it was
revealed that he belonged to the employer's old college fraternity. Immediately the employer was more favorably inclined to hire him because they
were fraternity brothers. An impartial observer of this interview could
clearly see that, from that point on, the employer did not really want to
hear any more about the candidate's background because he might hear
something negative. His emotional reaction to the recruit helped him
resolve his conflict simply by blinding him to any other facts which might
have tended to disturb the comfortable equilibrium he had now reached as
he made the decision to hire.[7] Psychologists describe this as *psychological
blindness.* Perhaps all of us have "blind spots" in that we fail to see what a
more impartial observer would see. In our courting days when we are
anxious to be loved and in turn to love, we are likely to see only the things
which allow us to maintain our comfortable feeling that this is, indeed,
true love. The idea that love is "blind" or even the concept of "rose-
colored glasses" illustrates the automatic emotional reactions to which

---

[7] This is from an actual example during an interview training seminar in which the
interviewer and the psychologist-trainer were listening to a taped selection interview
conducted by the employer. As soon as the tape was replayed, the "student"
interviewer could see how he had introduced bias into the interview because of his
preconceptions of "fraternity brothers". The training session also included help in
identifying behavior patterns in the interviewee's previous work or school experience
which corresponded with those behavior patterns expected in the subsequent work
behavior of the interviewee if he were hired. A recent research article contains many
excellent ideas concerning how selection interviews can be more reliable and valid.
The interested reader is referred to: Carlson, R. E., Thayer, P. W., Mayfield, E. C. and
Peterson, D. A., "Improvements in the Selection Interview," *Personnel Journal,* Vol.
50, no. 4, April 1971.

human beings resort to avoid unpleasantness or to avoid disturbing the delicate equilibrium that has been established to reduce conflict.

While automatic emotional reactions do help us to escape situations of conflict by reaching decisions and restoring a balance, these same reactions can also produce other difficulties and even greater conflict. Automatic responses which help us feel comfortable at any given time are usually effective only on a short-term basis. The child who tells a lie to escape punishment often finds it necessary later to manufacture even larger fables.

We Use a Rational Problem-Solving Approach

This first general method of maintaining our equilibrium acts in a somewhat blind, automatic fashion. It is a childlike striving for pleasure and avoiding of pain. We are constantly ready to react to any conflict situation or any disequilibrium. Partly because this general approach to conflict situations can easily get us into further difficulty and partly because this method of adjusting to life does not lead to progress or advancement of our civilization, man turns to a more rational, thoughtful, problem-solving approach to conflict situations. He tries to reason through the several obstacles confronting him or the alternatives to action which are available to him.

We can solve problems, resolve conflicts, and restore equilibrium much more effectively if we use our intelligence as objectively as possible without being overly swayed by emotions. Solving problems in a rational, systematic way involves at least four major steps:

1. Define the problem as accurately as possible. Unless we know clearly what our objective is, we will not be able to identify and move toward a solution.
2. Assemble all the available information and establish the possible alternatives or solutions.
3. Analyze and evaluate each of the alternatives in order to see the major advantages and disadvantages of each.
4. Choose one of the alternatives and test it to see whether or not it does solve the problem.

If a manager, for example, needs another person in his office, he may recruit candidates through newspaper advertising, referral sources, his present employees, etc. He then interviews the candidates as objectively as possible and evaluates the available information concerning them, trying to weigh their relative chances of success. He then makes a decision and picks the candidate who he feels will do the best job. He then tests the man in actual work to satisfy himself that he did, indeed, find a solution to his problem. If the man does not succeed, the manager is again faced with the original problem and must try the process again.

Much of business is conducted in this rational, straightforward, problem-solving way. Business enterprises experience a constant stream of crises and conflicts which must be resolved. Recognizing the problem and finding the most reasonable solution will more than likely lead to more predictable and satisfactory efforts to maintain proper equilibrium in business activities. But even this rational problem-solving approach can lead to further problems. The salesman who attempts to overcome the objections of the prospect may use his best reasoning facilities in an effort to find things to say to satisfy him. The salesman may also distort the truth or misrepresent the product or say something incorrect to overcome the prospect's objection. Making untrue statements in order to solve the problem and make a sale cannot be criticized if we are thinking only in terms of resolving the conflict which is posed by lack of sales. This approach may solve the problem for the salesman and remove him from a conflict situation, but it immediately raises the question of the "rightness" or "wrongness" of his action. Such actions may temporarily solve the problem for the salesman, but they may not necessarily solve the problem for the prospect. Because man has not been entirely satisfied with the results obtained when he conducts himself solely with the aim of doing what is necessary to solve problems or get the job done, he has felt it necessary to consider kinds of activities which *ought* to be done. Whenever we consider what *ought* to be done or what our personal *obligations* are to each other, we are considering the question of *ethics.*

We Move Toward an Equilibrium
Through an Awareness of Ethics

When we face the dilemma in conflict between several possible ways of reacting to a human situation, we ask ourselves, "What should I do?" If one believes in a code of ethics and can relate it to a conflict situation in which he finds himself, then he may easily resolve his conflict and reestablish an equilibrium by doing what is the "right" thing to do. If an employee is late for work and is in a state of conflict because he does not know what is the best excuse to give his boss, one way of resolving this conflict is to do what he knows is right and answer the boss truthfully.

We have discussed briefly three general methods which man uses, either consciously, or unconsciously in making decisions which help him maintain a satisfactory equilibrium. We need to emphasize that at any one given moment an individual will probably use all these methods simultaneously. In each of us there is a constant on-going, emotional automatic mechanism which makes us lean toward maintaining or reestablishing an equilibrium at the same time that we are consciously doing our level best to engage in effective problem-solving so that we can do what is morally right. It is characteristic of man to make value judgments and to be aware of the concepts of right and wrong. It is equally true that man often does what he knows is wrong. Because of its importance in influencing human behavior, the general concept of ethics must not be ignored.

Acquiring more knowledge about human behavior can make us more free. We can minimize self-defeating ways of living and working. But freedom is not license. With more knowledge it may be easier to fool or manipulate others for purely self-gain. Brain-washing can be skillfully used to alter basic values so that soldiers betray one another in an enemy concentration camp. Intelligence can be used for good or evil; interpersonal skills can harm or help; increased personal freedom can lead to a greater life or to premature death. Our individual efforts to achieve mutual satisfaction in cooperation with others come not just from making knowledgeable choices but from making knowledgeable, *ethical* choices. Realizing that each of us is free to make such choices is both stimulating and frightening; but it is a freedom we cannot escape.

SUMMARY

An essential part of understanding human behavior is to recognize the influence of ethics. The behavioral scientist, the businessman, and family member all share a concern with not only solving problems but with how those problems *should* be solved. Our concern with the proper ethics of interpersonal relationships is closely connected with our perceived purpose in life. Finding out what life means to us and what our individual purpose is helps reduce the anxiety which may prevent us from achieving our goals.

We develop a sense of what we should be doing from the early influence of parents, the ongoing pressure of public opinion, and the teachings of organized religions. With all of these pressures, a series of conflicts develops between what we want to do and what we feel we should do. Seemingly confusing behavior is often more understandable if we can see these conflicts for what they are. We do seek a balance between opposing and conflicting pressures but also deliberately upset this balance. In resolving conflict we can use each one or all of the three methods of making decisions: the emotional, the rational, and the ethical approach.

QUESTIONS FOR DISCUSSION AND THOUGHT

1. What is the relationship between knowledge, freedom, and responsibility?
2. Why is a study of human behavior inseparable from ecology?
3. Is it possible for any person to be uninfluenced by ethics? Explain.
4. Why is faith important to man? Give examples of this importance from organizational life, the family, and society in general.
5. Are ethics absolute or relative? Or both? Relate your discussion to the concept that individual needs largely determine perception.
6. How do you explain that we occasionally make conflict for ourselves?
7. How do emotional decisions compare to rational ones? Is one better than the other? Explain.
8. Discuss the close relationship between the scientific method and the method of resolving human conflict through ethical means.

BIBLIOGRAPHY

Berelson, Bernard and Steiner, Gary A. *Human Behavior, an Inventory of Scientific Findings.* New York: Harcourt, Brace & World, Inc., 1964.

Berger, Peter L. *Invitation to Sociology: A Humanistic Perspective.* Garden City, N.Y.: Doubleday & Company, Inc., 1963.

Berkowitz, Leonard, ed. *Roots of Aggression.* New York: Atherton, 1969.

_____. *The Development of Motives and Values in the Child.* New York: Basic Books, 1964.

Brenton, Myron. *The American Male.* New York: Fawcett World Library, 1967.

Cooper, David. *The Death of the Family.* New York: Pantheon Books, 1971.

Drucker, Peter F. *The Age of Discontinuity.* New York: Harper and Row, 1969.

Ehrlich, Paul and Ehrlich, Anne. *Population Resources Environment.* San Francisco: W. H. Freeman & Company, 1970.

Helson, Harry and Bevan, William eds. *Contemporary Approaches to Psychology.* Princeton, N.J.: D. Van Nostrand Company, Inc., 1967.

Janeway, Elizabeth. *Man's World, Woman's Place: A Study in Social Mythology.* New York: William Morrow and Company, Inc., 1971.

Jourard, Sidney M. *Disclosing Man to Himself.* Princeton, N.J.: D. Van Nostrand Company, Inc., 1968.

Maier, N. R. F. *Problem Solving·and Creativity.* Belmont, Calif.: Brooks/ Cole Publishing Company, 1970.

May, Rollo. *The Meaning of Anxiety.* New York: The Ronald Press Company, 1950.

———. *Psychology and the Human Dilemma.* Princeton, N.J.: D. Van Nostrand Company, Inc., 1967.

———. *Love and Will.* New York: W. W. Norton and Company, Inc., 1969.

Mead, Margaret. *Culture and Commitment: A Study of the Generation Gap.* Garden City, N.Y.: Natural History Press, Doubleday & Company, Inc., 1970.

Riesman, David, et al. *The Lonely Crowd.* New Haven, Conn.: Yale University Press, 1950.

Ruitenbeek, Hendrik M. *The Male Myth.* New York: Dell Publishing Company, Inc., 1967.

Sanford, Fillmore H. and Wrightsman, Lawrence S. *Psychology: A Scientific Study of Man,* 3rd ed. Belmont, Calif.: Brooks/Cole Publishing Company, 1970.

Smith, Henry Clay. *Sensitivity to People.* New York: McGraw-Hill Book Company, 1966.

Toffler, Alvin. *Future Shock.* New York: Random House, 1970.